Advance Praise for
The Last President of Europe

"This fascinating, well-researched book sheds new light on the vicissitudes of Emmanuel Macron's consequential political career. Read, learn, and enjoy."

> —**George P. Shultz**, former United States secretary of state

"Bill Drozdiak offers a sharp analysis of the tumultuous events that marked Emmanuel Macron's first years in the French presidency in this eminently readable and admirably concise volume. His journalist's keen eye, deep knowledge of contemporary European affairs, and first-person interviews with President Macron and his team are used to particularly good effect in the chapters on Macron's efforts to reach out to the French public after a series of domestic policy missteps. The book highlights the daunting challenges that Macron faces in implementing his grand vision for France at home and abroad."

> —**Dr. Fiona Hill**, former senior director for Europe and
> Russia at the White House National Security Council

"Bill Drozdiak's *The Last President of Europe* is a thoughtful interpretation of the dilemmas facing France and Europe. It is also an insightful portrait of a leader who may define these issues' resolution."

> —**Henry A. Kissinger**, former United States secretary of state

"*The Last President of Europe* is the extraordinary story of the ambition of a young, audacious, inexperienced politician to transform not only his country, France, but also Europe, for the challenges of the twenty-first century and the new great power competition. In this riveting, well-informed book, William Drozdiak takes us to the heart of Emmanuel Macron's fight, through the hopes and failures, the bold vision and the disastrous mistakes. The violence of the Yellow Vests' revolt, Angela Merkel's quiet passivity, Donald Trump's rage, and Vladimir Putin's disdain set the stage for an enlightening look into one of the most original political experiences of today's Europe."

—**Sylvie Kauffmann**, columnist and editorial director, *Le Monde*

"There are not many readable, well-informed books on Europe available to Americans these days. William Drozdiak's book on French president Emmanuel Macron is both. What's unique is Drozdiak's access to Macron, who wants very much to connect with American public opinion."

—**Ronald Tiersky**, professor of political science emeritus, Amherst College

"An eye-opening account of world politics and how the globe's most consequential leaders deal with each other in private. Drozdiak explains in clear and compelling prose how and why Macron's last-ditch efforts are vital for citizens in the US and elsewhere in the world."

—**Jim Hoagland**, *Washington Post* columnist and two-time Pulitzer Prize winner

"It is fascinating to read a portrait of this young and intelligent French president as seen through American eyes. Drozdiak demonstrates a sense of objectivity and a well-documented and informed knowledge of Macron's European passion. This is a very serious and complete work, yet written in clear and readable prose. The virtue and quality of Drozdiak's book lies in his shrewd analysis and judgement of Macron's presidency and his place among today's world leaders."

—**Philippe Labro**, best-selling French author, journalist, and film director

THE LAST
PRESIDENT
OF EUROPE

THE LAST PRESIDENT *of* EUROPE

EMMANUEL MACRON'S RACE TO REVIVE
FRANCE AND SAVE THE WORLD

WILLIAM DROZDIAK

PUBLICAFFAIRS
New York

PublicAffairs
Hachette Book Group
1290 Avenue of the Americas, New York, NY 10104
www.publicaffairsbooks.com
@Public_Affairs

Printed in the United States of America

First Edition: April 2020

Published by PublicAffairs, an imprint of Perseus Books, LLC, a subsidiary of Hachette Book Group, Inc. The PublicAffairs name and logo is a trademark of the Hachette Book Group.

The Hachette Speakers Bureau provides a wide range of authors for speaking events. To find out more, go to www.hachettespeakersbureau.com or call (866) 376-6591.

The publisher is not responsible for websites (or their content) that are not owned by the publisher.

Print book interior design by Amy Quinn.

Library of Congress Cataloging-in-Publication Data

Names: Drozdiak, William, author.
Title: The last president of Europe : Emmanuel Macron's race to revive France and save the world / William Drozdiak.
Other titles: Emmanuel Macron's race to revive France and save the world
Description: First edition. | New York : PublicAffairs, 2020. | Includes bibliographical references and index.
Identifiers: LCCN 2019059454 | ISBN 9781541742567 (hardcover) | ISBN 9781541742574 (ebook)
Subjects: LCSH: Macron, Emmanuel, 1977– | France—Politics and government—2017– | France—Relations—European Union countries. | European Union countries—Relations—France. | Populism—European Union countries. | Nationalism—European Union countries.
Classification: LCC DC435 .D76 2020 | DDC 9440.84/12092 B n—dc23
LC record available at https://lccn.loc.gov/2019059454

ISBNs: 978-1-5417-4256-7 (hardcover); 978-1-5417-4257-4 (e-book)

LSC-C

10 9 8 7 6 5 4 3 2 1

For Renilde and the next generation:
Nicholas, Karen, Natalia, and Lily

Old France, weighed down with history,
prostrated by wars and revolution, endlessly
vacillating from greatness to decline, but revived,
century after century, by the genius of renewal!

—Charles de Gaulle,
The War Memoirs, 1940-46

CONTENTS

PART ONE

FRANCE

CHAPTER 1

A FAST START

The inauguration day of France's youngest leader since Napoleon was strangely subdued. There was little of the grandiose pomp and splendor that accompany the passage of power in other capitals. In his first act as commander in chief, Emmanuel Macron perched himself in the back of a camouflage military jeep as he rode up the Champs-Élysées to light a flame in honor of his country's war dead at the Tomb of the Unknown Soldier at the Arc de Triomphe. He paid a personal visit to a military hospital, where he comforted soldiers wounded in operations in Mali and Afghanistan. That rainy Sunday morning, Macron walked silently past an honor guard on a crimson carpet laid out on the gravel courtyard of the Élysée Palace. He climbed the steps to his new residence, where he was greeted stiffly by outgoing president François Hollande. Macron had served as Hollande's deputy chief of staff and economy minister before launching a campaign that would betray his mentor and demolish the country's political establishment.

The two men briefly huddled in private so that Hollande could pass along the "secrets of state," including launch codes for France's nuclear arsenal. Under the gold chandeliers in the Salle des Fêtes, about two hundred people had gathered to mark the occasion, including Macron's wife, Brigitte, her adult children, and members of the new president's staff. Laurent Fabius, the head of France's Constitutional Council, administered the oath of office and urged Macron to "calm the anger, repair the wounds, alleviate the doubts, show the road forward and embody the hopes" of all French people.[1] Fabius said that Macron fulfilled the dictum of François-René de Chateaubriand, one of France's greatest writer-philosophers: "To be a man of his country, one must be a man of his times." In brief remarks, Macron declared that "the world and Europe need a strong France with a sense of its own destiny." He promised to heal social and economic divisions in French society and restore the self-confidence of a fractured nation plagued by "doubts and fears." Noting the grim challenges that lay ahead, Macron assured his listeners "that not for a single second did I think that everything changed as if by magic" with his election. He then turned to several close aides and told them that the celebration would be short and swift. "There's no time to lose," Macron said. "The work begins tonight."[2]

Inspired by his hero Charles de Gaulle, who wrote in his memoir that "all my life I have had a certain idea of France," Macron entered office with a clear vision of what he wanted to achieve during his presidency. He had seen up close how France's sclerotic economy had deteriorated as his predecessors failed to adapt a recalcitrant nation to the rigors of global economic competition. Public debt was nearly 100 percent of the country's gross domestic product, and the jobless rate hovered around 10 percent, with six million people unemployed. Macron recognized that decades of paralysis now endangered France's leadership role alongside Germany in charting the course toward European unity. That crusade had advanced steadily under the stewardship of de Gaulle and Konrad Adenauer, Valéry Giscard d'Estaing and Helmut Schmidt, and finally François Mitterrand and Helmut

Kohl. The rocky relations between Paris and Berlin in recent years, however, had left Europe adrift, struggling to cope with the repercussions of the global financial crisis and the resurgence of big-power competition. "I knew this was the key question of our times," Macron said, describing the state of the world he faced after his election in May 2017. "Nearly thirty years after the fall of the Berlin Wall, I realized we were at a new inflection point with the rise of China, the return of an aggressive Russia, and the retreat of America from global leadership. So where is Europe? Rather than trapped between these superpowers, as a zone to be fought over by others, I believe Europe needs its own renaissance to leap beyond its past and become an autonomous power equal to others. This cannot be done by any single nation-state, but only at a European level, with France and Germany assuming special responsibility to lead the way."[3]

Macron's grand strategy for his presidency was conceived with three goals in mind: to modernize France, to relaunch the drive toward a more unified continent, and to establish Europe as a major power in a multipolar world. He believes that these ambitions are closely intertwined; progress in reforming France is a necessary prerequisite to the revival of Europe as a prominent force on the world stage. After his election, Macron needed to act quickly to convince German chancellor Angela Merkel that he could succeed where Nicolas Sarkozy and Hollande had failed. The accelerated timetable was critical: Macron realized that the extensive reforms he planned—opening up the labor market, cutting taxes, streamlining welfare programs, shrinking the size of the state, and improving education—would take time to produce tangible results. By demonstrating his commitment to transforming the domestic economy, he could make the case that France was ready to rejoin Germany in steering Europe toward greater unity and influence in the world. Macron regarded the European Union as one of history's most remarkable success stories—a story of former enemies reconciling in a spirit of enduring peace and harmony by pooling their sovereignty. In a new age of ruthless competition among major powers

like China, Russia, and the United States, a revitalized Europe was
the missing actor on the world stage. A dynamic Europe was necessary to preserve the multilateral order that had helped the continent
recover from two devastating wars and achieve an unbroken era of
peace and prosperity over the past seventy years unmatched in its
blood-soaked history.

A month after his election, Macron secured a strong majority in
the National Assembly, which gave him the powers to circumvent
protracted debate and push through his reform program by presidential decree if necessary. His movement, La République en Marche
(Republic on the Move), captured 308 of the Assembly's 577 seats in
the legislative elections. This impressive victory ushered into France's
governing institutions a new generation of fresh faces who, as Macron
described his followers, were "neither left nor right." Like Macron,
most of the new legislators were elected to political office for the first
time. Nearly three-quarters of the cabinet ministers he appointed had
never before served in government. A powerful new wave of Macron
loyalists swept away the old guard, and the electoral annihilation of
the traditional ruling parties, the Socialists and the conservative Republicans, confirmed voter disgust with the political establishment.
Their demise left no serious opposition in Parliament to oppose Macron's radical prescription for change. In those early days flush with
triumph, Macron's stunning ascendancy and the powerful majority
he secured in Parliament created such momentum that it seemed like
France might undergo a metamorphosis that few experts could have
imagined. "Macron's election is like Hiroshima year zero," said Laurent Bigorgne, director of the Institut Montaigne, a Paris-based think
tank, who assisted Macron in launching his political revolution. "A
nuclear bomb has fallen on French politics and we're still standing in
the rubble."[4]

Macron's honeymoon phase lasted for several months. A new
sense of pride and wonder permeated the streets of Paris, replacing the
morose cynicism that had prevailed during the years when the nation
seemed stuck in decline. The stock market jumped by 15 percent,

economic growth picked up, jobs became available for young people, and the housing market soared. The French public enjoyed the international attention lavished on their youthful new president, who displayed some of the charm, energy, and charisma that John Kennedy brought to the White House after the somnolent Eisenhower years. His compatriots and the media were fascinated to learn that Macron's hectic schedule reflected his restless nature. Staff members became accustomed to getting 3:00 a.m. messages from him on WhatsApp or Telegram. Macron would rise early after four or five hours of sleep, setting aside ninety minutes for private reading before his first meeting at 9:00 a.m. He would stay fit by jogging three times a week, playing tennis, boxing, and exercising with his bodyguards. His wife, Brigitte, supervised his diet, banning all junk food and ensuring that he consumed copious amounts of fruit and vegetables. But Macron still found time to savor the pleasures of his native land. He admitted that he enjoyed drinking wine at both lunch and dinner, provoking expressions of disapproval from the medical establishment but great satisfaction among the nation's vintners.

During the campaign, Macron took pains to explain in great detail his vision for an invigorated French society that would empower individuals and curtail much of the population's dependence on government handouts. He wanted to unleash the imagination of the country's entrepreneurial class and encourage young people to embrace the digital age by taking advantage of France's vaunted skills in mathematics. Above all, he extolled the vision of a "new France" in which citizens would take greater control of their own destiny and fulfill personal ambitions through a more dynamic private sector liberated from cumbersome regulations, which were enforced by a bloated government sector that accounted for one out of every five jobs. Macron vowed to shrink the role of the French state, which controlled 56 percent of the economy, higher than any country in Europe, and slash public payrolls by more than one hundred thousand workers. He published a book spelling out his plans to transform society with the portentous title *Revolution*. It was important, he emphasized, for French voters to comprehend the scope of the dramatic changes in store for them. He insisted that his policies bear the stamp of democratic legitimacy; he did not want to be forced to renege on promises, as his predecessors had done. By the end of his five-year term in office, Macron hoped that his expedited reforms would achieve nothing less than a "Copernican revolution" in the relationship between the French state and its citizens.

Macron believes that in order to get the French economy moving again, he needs to convince foreign investors that his government is friendly toward business. One of his first acts as president was to cut corporate tax rates and reduce levies on capital gains. He also abolished the "solidarity tax on large fortunes," otherwise known as the wealth tax; introduced in 1981 by the Socialist government, this tax was levied on all those who held more than $1.5 million in assets. Critics said that the wealth tax caused the loss of billions of dollars in revenue because it motivated rich people to shelter their assets abroad. Macron's decision to eliminate the wealth tax and replace it with a real estate tax was welcomed by foreign companies, which would soon reconsider their previous reluctance to commit to long-term investments in France. Macron received them with open arms. He invited an international group of business executives to a lavish dinner at the Versailles Palace and told them that his government would adopt a business-friendly attitude to encourage expansion of the private sector, spur growth, and create jobs. "France is back!" Macron roared to loud applause. Soon Microsoft, IBM, Facebook, Apple, and other titans of technology and industry pledged to enlarge their corporate presence in France.

Some of Macron's advisers worried about the political impact of his tax cuts, especially the elimination of the wealth tax. As they feared, with his probusiness attitude and background as an investment banker with Rothschild, he was quickly labeled "the president of the rich." Jean Pisani-Ferry, who served as the architect of Macron's economic program during the campaign, proposed coupling the tax cuts for the wealthy with other measures to assist the middle and lower classes. Macron worried that too many tax cuts and subsidies would blow a hole in France's deficit and break the budget rules of the European Union (EU), thereby undermining the confidence of Germany and other European partners in his reform program. Pisani-Ferry argued that Macron needed to do more to help the downtrodden or he would eventually lose public support for his reform program. "I explained that he would be perceived as catering only to the wealthy," Pisani-Ferry said. "It would appear to the public as if he was indifferent to those who are struggling and that would badly damage his image."[5] Pisani-Ferry's warning proved prescient.

Over the summer of 2017, Macron turned his attention to the centerpiece of his reform plans: France's antiquated labor laws. He and his labor minister, Muriel Pénicaud, launched negotiations to overhaul the nation's labyrinthine labor code, contained in three thousand pages of arcane rules and regulations dating back to the Napoleonic era. France's rigid labor markets made it practically impossible to lay off workers or even fire them for cause. As a result of employers' reluctance to hire people in this environment, many young people were forced to work under short-term contracts that failed to give them much traction in their careers. Pénicaud, who had worked as an executive vice president in human resources at Dassault Systèmes (aircraft systems) and with the Danone food giant, was well acquainted with the difficulties of getting union bosses and business leaders around a table to negotiate a deal. She and Macron abandoned the old format, which almost guaranteed a stalemate, and decided to make a great spectacle of individually consulting labor leaders of every stripe, from those representing white-collar employees to the heads of factory workers' unions. The televised footage of every union boss arriving at and then leaving the Élysée Palace demonstrated that the government was making enormous efforts to consult at every level before moving ahead with its reform program.

This maneuver enabled Macron to use divide-and-conquer tactics against the union bosses, preventing them from forming a united front in opposition to his reforms. Small companies were allowed to negotiate contracts directly with their workers rather than with unions, while a cap was imposed on damages for wrongful dismissal. The government also approved a $17 billion job-training program for young people under twenty-five years old, nearly one-quarter of whom were unemployed. During his time as economy minister, Macron had seen how France's rigid labor code cosseted existing workers, who enjoyed guaranteed paychecks, excellent benefits, and a mandatory thirty-five-hour workweek. The code's glaring weakness was its failure to help the young and long-term unemployed find jobs. Public support for labor reforms began to rise with the spread of Macron's central message that the need to expand the workforce was a top priority. France was the only large European country not to have resolved the problem of mass unemployment in the past three decades. While France's largest left-wing workers' union, the General Confederation of Labor, expressed outrage and staged strikes against Macron's labor reforms, other union leaders took note of public opinion and declined to follow its example.

Emboldened by his early success, Macron felt confident enough to challenge one of France's most sacred cows: the SNCF (Société nationale des chemins de fer français) railway system, the country's biggest single employer, with 150,000 workers. France's high-speed rail network is widely admired—it has cut travel time between Paris and Bordeaux to two hours—but its cumulative debt of more than $60 billion had become a colossal burden on the state. Nobody had dared to confront the train unions since 1995, when then–prime minister Alain Juppé was forced to scrap his reform plans and leave office after a three-week railway strike brought the country to its knees. Macron sensed that public opinion was changing, however, because of growing dismay over the generous treatment accorded to railway workers. French train drivers can retire as early as age fifty-two, ten years before everybody else, a privilege dating back to the days when they had to shovel coal into steam engines. They and their families also enjoy free train tickets, free health care, and subsidized housing. But with the rail system losing more than $10 billion a year and the

European Union poised to allow rival operators to gain access to the market in 2020, Macron gambled that he could win a showdown with the country's powerful rail unions early in his tenure.

Macron told the unions that existing workers could retain their benefits but new employees would be compelled to accept less generous terms. He gave them two months to negotiate a final deal with the government or else he would impose his reforms by executive decree. The union leaders were incensed and vowed to carry out rolling strikes until he backed down. Other politicians sympathized with the rail workers: Olivier Faure, leader of the Socialist Party, said that Macron's demand was like inviting people to negotiate "with a revolver at their temple."[6] The confrontation became the biggest test of Macron's first year as president. Rail workers carried out strikes every three days, disrupting the lives of millions of travelers for several months. But without the strong public sympathy they had received in the past, the strikes slowly petered out. Macron won a test of wills by patiently explaining to the French public why his demands were perfectly reasonable. Opinion polls showed that more than two-thirds of French voters supported his tough stance. Macron's triumph over the railway unions surprised even his most ardent supporters, who, like many politicians and pundits, believed that challenging the powerful unions was akin to a death wish. Alain Minc, a prominent business consultant who has known Macron for two decades, was amazed that the young president could win his bold gamble and speculated that Macron succeeded in getting the rail unions to back down through divine intervention. "I'm convinced that you must have some kind of a special contract with God," Minc told him. "As long as it's a perpetual contract with Him, that's fine with me," Macron replied.[7]

But Macron's extraordinary run of good luck would not last long. Pisani-Ferry's warning about the perception that he was too solicitous of the wealthy class came back to haunt him through several blunders that reflected his lack of political sensitivity. He hosted a lavish fortieth birthday party for himself at the magisterial Château de Chambord in the Loire Valley, prompting comparisons with Louis

XVI for behaving like a profligate monarch. The media mocked him for installing a swimming pool at the presidential summer retreat at Fort de Brégançon, on the Côte d'Azur in the south of France, and for paying a makeup artist as much as 26,000 euros for three months' work. He and Brigitte were chastised for purchasing an elaborate porcelain dinner service for the Élysée Palace at a cost to taxpayers that some estimates put as high as 500,000 euros. He was televised giving a public scolding to a teenager who had the audacity to address him as "Manu" instead of "Monsieur le Président." He was shown on newscasts chiding an unemployed gardener for complaining about lack of work, urging him to accept personal responsibility for his plight and not seek help from the state. All he had to do, Macron told him, was "cross the street" and he would find a job. He provoked an uproar from leftist opponents when he described those who opposed his labor reforms as "slackers." After his personal bodyguard was forced to resign for beating up a protester on the streets, Macron was accused for months of orchestrating a cover-up. The cumulative effect of these fiascoes drove down his approval ratings as the public expressed dismay over his arrogance.

At the outset of his presidency, Macron tried to project a more aloof image as a leader who hovered above the fray. He acquired the nickname of "Jupiter," the king of the gods in Roman mythology. Macron was convinced that the French people yearned to recapture the glory of the monarchy. He had seen how Hollande's presidency failed in part because he tried to portray himself as "Monsieur Normal," a common man of the people. While serving as Hollande's economy minister, Macron gave an interview explaining why he believed that the French Revolution—which culminated in the beheading of the royals and the Reign of Terror—had "dug an emotional, imaginary and collective void" in the minds of the people. He claimed that democracy had not filled that void, except during the rule of Napoleon and de Gaulle, because the French people "never really wanted the king to die."[8] Macron's monarchist affectations, however, proved unconvincing. As president, he turned out to be an inveterate micromanager who insisted on controlling all policy details from the Élysée Palace. He could never master the philosopher-king role played so effectively by François Mitterrand. Hubert Védrine, who served as Mitterrand's chief of staff and later as foreign minister, told me that he once advised Macron to emulate Mitterrand's methods in coping with controversies. He urged Macron to disappear from public view for a few days, as Mitterrand would occasionally do, in order to impress upon the nation that he was too busy "thinking great thoughts" about the state of the world to be troubled by the daily grind of politics. Macron complained that Mitterrand's vanishing act was now impossible with the omnipresence of social media, podcasts, and cable news networks.[9]

Despite his declining approval ratings, Macron was determined to accelerate the reform process. He disregarded the advice of those who warned him that he risked alienating the public with his bewildering pace of change. He and his staff stuck to their game plan of front-loading reforms in the first two years of his presidency so that he might reap political dividends by the end of his five-year tenure. "It was our year of living dangerously," Ismaël Emelien, Macron's top political adviser during the first two years of his presidency, told me. "We knew we had to move quickly right after the election or risk losing momentum in ways that would paralyze his presidency, as happened to others before him."[10]

Macron followed up his success on the labor front by enacting new measures to improve health care and education, two sectors long neglected by his predecessors as too politically volatile to touch. France's health-care system is considered the best in the world, according to the World Health Organization, but it has been plagued by rising costs, the burdens of an aging population, and the closure of many clinics in rural regions. As the son of doctors, Macron had promised during the campaign that he would preserve the high quality of French health care and ensure that it reached the entire population. "In France, we treat well, but we are not necessarily healthier than our neighbors because we do prevention poorly," Macron told the nation as he unveiled his plans to revamp medical care. "The health system does not suffer from underfunding but from an organizational problem."[11] Macron promised to dispatch four hundred doctors to rural areas that were not well served with medical clinics and to create four thousand new positions for medical assistants to help doctors carry out their tasks. To expand the health-care network, he vowed to overhaul medical training and abolish limits on the number of students allowed to study medicine, which he said would bring as many as twenty-five thousand more doctors into the health-care system.

Education reform was another key pillar of Macron's campaign to revitalize France and shake up its ossified society. He strongly believes that education is the best pathway toward a more just and equitable society. He personally flourished as a precocious child from the northern provinces who went to France's most elite schools, notably Sciences Po (Institut d'études politiques de Paris) and the National School of Administration (École national d'administration), which nurture the nation's top civil servants. Macron's two principal mentors, the former Socialist prime minister Michel Rocard and the philosopher Paul Ricoeur, emphasized the importance of access to high-quality education for all sectors of society if France hoped to fulfill its hallowed motto of "Liberty, Equality, and Fraternity." Today France ranks at the bottom of major developed countries in social mobility and in helping impoverished pupils escape economic deprivation, according to a global education study by the Paris-based Organization for Economic Cooperation and Development (OECD). Even though France spends more money (about $60 billion a year) on education than on any other sector, including defense, Macron was shocked to discover his country's low ranking. He was also troubled to learn that many employers complained about graduates leaving French schools poorly trained in the skills needed to thrive in the twenty-first century.

Macron exploited his powerful majority in the National Assembly to ram through a comprehensive series of education reforms at all levels. Classroom sizes were cut in half for thousands of elementary schools in underprivileged areas, creating job openings for up to ten thousand new teachers over three years. The government decreed that school would be compulsory from the age of three instead of six. France's famed *baccalauréat*, the school-leaving exam introduced by Napoleon in 1808, was dramatically revised. Universities were compelled to become more selective in their admissions process and to offer more opportunities to study computer science and coding to match the needs of the digital world. "From kindergarten to university, we are changing everything," Macron said in a French television interview.[12] As with his other reform efforts, Macron encountered resistance from unions, which protested that such change would undermine the French tradition of teaching every citizen the same course of study. Nevertheless, arguing that the educational system no longer met the needs of the twenty-first century, Macron proceeded with the most far-reaching overhaul ever attempted since French schools became free and obligatory in the nineteenth century.

Like his political mentor Rocard, Macron sees education reform as one of the most effective anti-poverty programs that government can offer. During the twilight of his political career, Rocard spent much of his fifteen years as a member of the European Parliament exploring ways to open up schools and universities to people of all ages so that they would not feel locked into a single career for their entire life. He was an advocate of the *deuxième gauche* (second left) model of social democracy, which espoused progressive yet pragmatic policies that could be supported across the political spectrum. This hybrid approach, combining the dynamism of free market capitalism with the socialist ideals of helping the poor and downtrodden, later became known as the "Third Way" during the era of British prime minister Tony Blair and US president Bill Clinton. Macron was impressed with Rocard's efforts to develop policies that transcended ideological labels, and he would apply that approach when he conceived his La République en Marche movement and his plan for governing. Even though Macron started in politics working for a Socialist government, he did not hesitate to reach out to the rival conservative camp to recruit two key allies, Prime Minister Édouard Philippe and Finance Minister Bruno Le Maire. Those instincts to defy political convention were cultivated during the two years Macron spent as research assistant for the philosopher Ricoeur, who taught him the power of the individual and the need to discourage dependence on the state. Macron instilled those goals of self-reliance at the heart of his reformist program to curtail the size of the sprawling French state.

Macron became frustrated that he was not getting sufficient credit for far-reaching changes in French society, even if the economic benefits were slow to materialize. "You are committing violence with your policy. It's you who is going after the poor to give to the rich!" thundered François Ruffin, a firebrand of the leftist France Unbowed Party and one of Macron's fiercest critics. In television interviews, Macron found himself on the defensive, trying to explain the logic behind his tax cuts. "I don't believe in this French jealousy which says, 'There are rich people; let's tax them and we will all feel better,'" Macron said. He pointed out that people with large fortunes never paid the wealth tax because they simply fled the country and took up residence in neighboring Belgium or Switzerland. He insisted that his goal was not to help the rich, but only to encourage those who created wealth. "If we want to share the pie, we have to make sure that there is a pie to share," he said. Macron's offhand comments continued to land him in hot water. He declared on French television that while "we will protect those who are fragile," it would be counterproductive "to throw stones at the first in the rope line, because then it's the whole line that collapses."[13]

By the end of his first year in office, Macron had concluded that he needed to revamp his image and show more empathy for those left behind by the forces of globalization. He unveiled an anti-poverty program that would seek to reduce inequality and respond to those critics who claimed he was insensitive to the plight of the underprivileged. He had managed to carry out an impressive array of reforms that transformed France's labor markets, put the railway network on a path toward solvency, lightened tax burdens, and improved the educational system. Yet he was hurt and baffled by the constant personal attacks and accusations that he was an elitist "president of the rich" and was not helping the 8.8 million French people—about 14 percent of the population—who were living in poverty. His glacial demeanor and lack of warmth on public outings did not endear him to the French people. Although he could be charming and witty in private, Macron at times appeared stiff and ill at ease when pressing the flesh and wading through crowds. He seemed unaware of the growing polarization between the rural and urban areas of France, despite a grassroots army of 250,000 militant supporters who were supposed to help him stay attuned to the public mood.

The vitriolic hostility behind much of the criticism shocked him, even though he knew that politics was becoming a blood sport in many Western democracies. He felt that the true purpose of his reform programs was either misunderstood or distorted beyond recognition by his political opponents. By October 2018, he had retreated from the public eye, and for the first time in his presidency he became disconsolate, wondering if his presidency might eventually go down in flames. The intense workload and lack of sleep started to take their toll. His top aides expressed anxiety about his frazzled appearance and forced him to retreat to the Normandy coast for four days of rest and recuperation to restore his health and energy ahead of a hectic autumn schedule of arduous international travel, multiple summit conferences, and the centennial commemoration of the World War I armistice, when he would play host to more than fifty heads of government.

Macron believes that creating jobs by teaching proper skills through better education should serve as the foundation of his government's anti-poverty program. He saw during his time as economy minister that throwing money at the problem of endemic poverty was wasteful and ineffective. "We are paying crazy amounts of cash to people on welfare who continue to remain poor," he told his team of advisers. "People who are born poor in France tend to stay poor. We have to do something that will enable people to get out of this poverty trap."[14] Neither the right nor the left seemed to know how to help people escape poverty. He expressed particular exasperation with the tired bromides of the Socialist Party, for which he once served, saying that billions of euros spent on social welfare programs had wasted taxpayer money and failed to help successive generations to exit poverty and find productive employment. "I believe in initiatives that create jobs, because if there are no jobs there is no chance of solving the problem of poverty," Macron said in launching a $10 billion program focused mainly on training young people. "If there is no production, there is no chance of redistribution, or else it is done at the expense of the few who produce."[15]

Macron feels that to encourage greater social mobility he needs to crack open a static French society and unleash innovative energies. Harnessing the synergies of those reforms, he believes, can generate powerful momentum to break out of an intergenerational poverty trap. Young people and minorities continue to suffer as primary victims of a "blocked society" that the sociologist Michel Crozier identified four decades ago as the root cause of France's social crisis. They are consistently excluded in favor of those who are coddled and protected within the system by lifetime job guarantees. Raising taxes in the most heavily taxed nation in Europe will not work, Macron believes. What is needed is a revolution in the way French society is structured. "Let's not kid ourselves, we are seeing increasing inequality," Macron said in his 2018 State of the Nation Address to Parliament. "But what we have is really inequality of destiny, according to where you were born, how you were raised. This is what obsesses me. We need to attack the deep roots of inequality of destiny."[16]

Pierre-André Imbert, Macron's social policy adviser, told me that the economic and social transformation envisioned during the president's first term would cost as much as 50 billion euros over those five years. "It sounds like a lot of money, but you have to realize we are talking about investments in human capital through education and training that will create greater wealth, cut welfare costs for the state, and help emancipate the poor," Imbert said. "Over one million youths will be taught the kind of skills they will need for the twenty-first century. Already 80 percent of our program has been passed by Parliament. There is no alternative if we want to prepare the next generation to compete in the global economy."[17]

Macron believes that his accelerated timetable to shake up French society from top to bottom is the only way to deal with the challenge of growing inequality, which, in his view, accounts for the rise of populist nationalism that is threatening Western democracy. "This is the heart of the struggle that I am waging," Macron said. "Democracy is going through a profound crisis that is almost anthropological in nature. We need to look toward new frontiers to overcome the doubts that are plaguing our society, which have become all the more visible because of the internet and social media platforms. There is also a crisis of efficiency, as many people, especially the marginal and deprived members of our community, think that democracy no longer provides solutions to their problems. This makes politicians look powerless. So how do we revitalize democracy? Not by turning to the state, but by channeling the energies of the private sector."[18]

Macron claimed that he would be able to pay for his massive reform programs by curtailing the size of government and invigorating the private sector. But the pace of his reforms proved unsustainable and forced him to scale back his ambitions. He vowed to reduce the size of Parliament by one-third and eliminate as many as 120,000 positions in the public sector. But later, faced with the need to expand the teaching and medical workforces and police forces, he was able to reduce the number of public-sector jobs only by fifteen thousand. He promised to privatize government holdings worth as much as $100 billion, including the three Paris airports, the state energy utility ENGIE, and the lucrative gaming business Française des Jeux. But public protests caused him to postpone those plans. Nonetheless, Macron insisted that France needed to shrink its dependence on the state sector and transform itself into "a start-up nation," one that would embrace the disruption of dying industries and could inspire younger generations to become more entrepreneurial. In speech after speech during his first two years in office, Macron emphasized that the time had come for his compatriots to stop looking to the nanny state as their caretaker and instead accept greater personal liberty and responsibility for their fate.

Before he decided to run for the presidency, Macron considered launching his own education technology company with two colleagues who later helped him create his political movement, Julien Denormandie and Ismaël Emelien. The funding for the project was going to come from Xavier Niel, the billionaire French investor who earned a fortune in online porn sites and internet services. Niel later went on to create Station F, the world's largest start-up incubator, in a vast rail freight station in Paris that would soon play host to three thousand nascent entrepreneurs. At the inauguration ceremony of Niel's brain factory in June 2017, Macron acknowledged that he had once promised his wife that he would abandon politics in order to set up his own company with Niel's help. But Macron was persuaded in 2014 to become Hollande's economy minister, which set the stage for his decision to start his own political movement and pursue the presidency. "I basically pivoted the business model," he told a cheering throng of entrepreneurs clustered around him.

Macron vowed to inject massive public investments into building out his vision of a futuristic France. His government pledged to spend $23 billion on promoting ecological transition toward renewable energies so that France could reduce its dependence on nuclear power. He also earmarked another $17 billion for vocational training for unemployed youth, $15 billion for encouraging innovation in the industrial and manufacturing sectors, and $10 billion to create a digital state in order to have a paperless government by 2022. Macron recognized the uphill struggle he faced in convincing his reluctant compatriots to embrace change and disruption on such an enormous scale. During a visit to Denmark, he was astounded to learn that Scandinavian nations preserved their social welfare commitments

while encouraging the rapid growth of new industries that compelled one in four Danes to change jobs every year. In noting that "in
France, there is an obstinate refusal to accept this scale of change," he
used the harsh word *refractaire* to describe the stubborn nature of the
French, generating an angry uproar.

Macron believes that France has no choice but to prepare for the
momentous impact of artificial intelligence and other transforma-
tive technologies that loom on the horizon. "Europe must develop
its own model for artificial intelligence," he said. "America is driven
by the private sector, with some help from government in military
research. China has an enormous home market with projects shaped
and guided by the central government. We need to find a different
path. We have special assets: good people, good education, and good
aspirations. We have some of the best schools and laboratories in the
world for technology and innovation." He is pleased that his reform
programs have already convinced some of the sixty thousand young
French expatriates to return home from London and the leading
technology companies in Silicon Valley to seek new opportunities
in France and help him develop a modern nation. "We have a lot of
talent in the students that we nurtured in our schools before they
decided to go abroad," Macron said. "The brain drain is now being
reversed. It's great to see so many young French people coming back
home to participate in developing these new technologies."[19]

France as a start-up nation still has a long way to go. Despite
Macron's efforts to attract talented scientists from all corners of the
world to live and work in France, cultural resistance in much of Europe to the entrepreneurial way of life that thrives in Silicon Valley
still poses big obstacles to realizing Macron's vision. According to
Kima Ventures, which, as Niel's venture capital arm, manages more
than five hundred investments in start-up companies, none of the fifteen largest European "unicorns" valued at more than $2 billion have
originated in France. But that has not prevented foreign companies
from making significant new investments in France, largely because
they are impressed by the quality of talented French graduates, who

are well trained in mathematics and engineering. Since the first wave of Macron's reforms, more than $12 billion has poured in from US companies eager to capitalize on the probusiness orientation of the government, including a $2.4 billion research and development center established by Disney. At the "Viva Technology" trade fair on the outskirts of Paris, chief executives from all over the world gushed over the positive change in attitude they had witnessed just a few months into Macron's presidency. "France is a country that is at the forefront of defining what this new era of technology will mean to our society globally," Microsoft's chief executive Satya Nadella observed.

The breathtaking speed and scope of Macron's reform program may have blinded him and his allies to the fierce resentments that were brewing beyond the glamorous confines of Paris. On occasional forays into the rural outposts of *la France profonde*, which felt so neglected by the state, Macron was repeatedly challenged, insulted, and even threatened. Many of those citizens complained that they felt abandoned. Macron later would regret what he lamented as his insensitive lack of judgment in failing to recognize the depth of their bitterness.

Dominique de Villepin, a former French prime minister and a close ally of the former conservative president Jacques Chirac, emphasized the perils of underestimating the temperamental nature of the French people. In his own political career, he had personally endured their fervid penchant for turning on those who wielded too much power and influence over their lives. On a brisk autumn afternoon, I went to see de Villepin in his opulent townhouse, decorated with avant-garde paintings, sculptures, and African masks. At the time, Macron was at the pinnacle of his powers and enjoying what seemed like an unassailable presidency. He faced no conceivable challenges from a compliant Parliament and a prostrate political opposition.

But de Villepin sensed that something was not right. "Macron is making a big mistake by linking himself so closely to the reform process," de Villepin said. "Sooner or later, a lot of disgruntled French citizens will take to the streets to protest against all these changes that are confusing them and disrupting their lives. And Macron will be the main target because there is nothing standing between him and the wrath of the people."[20] De Villepin's warning turned out to be prophetic. Within weeks, small protests against a token increase in fuel taxes would swell into a ferocious insurrection aimed directly at Macron and his presidency. The "Yellow Vest" rebellion would spread from a few ragtag protesters gathered at traffic roundabouts and spill out into the streets of cities and towns across France. What began as the charmed presidency of a youthful and energetic leader determined to shake up his country would suddenly be threatened by a violent human hurricane that would bring Macron and his entire government to the brink of an existential crisis.

CHAPTER 2

LA RÉSISTANCE

When Priscillia Ludosky posted an internet petition in May 2018 calling for a reduction in gasoline prices, she had no idea that it might spark the nation's gravest political turmoil in five decades. She lived in Savigny-le-Temple, a quiet suburb about twenty miles outside Paris, and the expense of commuting into the capital, with gasoline costing more than six dollars a gallon, had become intolerable to her. Feeling compelled to quit her bank job, Ludosky decided to start an online cosmetics business. When the French government announced that fuel taxes would have to rise to help curtail carbon emissions, her complaint began to resonate with other frustrated motorists. By October, when Éric Drouet, a truck driver who lived nearby, circulated her petition, newspapers began to cover the story, and the gas tax protest soon attracted hundreds of thousands of endorsements. Then Jacline Mouraud, a hypnotherapist in Brittany, released her own video tirade on YouTube and Facebook, accusing President Macron of persecuting drivers since the day he took office.

Her angry rant went viral and was viewed by more than six million people.[1]

The populist explosion inspired by their initiatives would soon evolve into a mortal threat to Macron's presidency. When Drouet proposed a nationwide blockade of roads to demand lower gas prices, the message spread like wildfire across social media networks. More than one million people signed the petition, which also encouraged them to join the protest. Those who supported the grassroots movement against higher fuel taxes were told to wear the fluorescent yellow vests, or *gilets jaunes*, that all French drivers are required to carry in their cars in case of emergencies. On the appointed day, more than three hundred thousand "Yellow Vest" supporters turned out across the country, many of them clustered at the ubiquitous traffic roundabouts that surround France's villages and towns. There they could command the attention of drivers passing through the strategic checkpoints, where protesters solicited donations and other gestures of support before the cars were allowed to pass. Opinion polls showed that more than 70 percent of the French people sympathized with their cause. Many motorists placed their yellow vests on their dashboard to show their support for the farmers, small-business owners, nurses, contractors, and craftspeople who claimed that their tax burdens had become unbearable. Soon the roundabouts (France possesses thirty thousand traffic circles, half the entire world's total) became communal gathering places, fulfilling the social role once served by the town squares now largely deserted with the rise of malls and megastores.

The rise in the gasoline tax, though only a matter of pennies, was, to paraphrase a French proverb, the drop of water that caused the vase of public discontent to overflow. Ever since major autoroutes and high-speed train lines bypassed rural areas in favor of connecting urban centers, the provincial areas once celebrated as *la France profonde* for their quaint stone villages and picturesque tree-lined roads have suffered drastic cuts in services and local budgets. As a result, many French people in the countryside rely almost exclusively on their automobiles to commute from their homes to their jobs, to do their shopping, to visit hospital and doctor offices, or to attend schools. Opinion surveys show that about one-third of French people are "very dependent" on a car in their daily lives and another one-third are "somewhat dependent," making the high price of gas a critical issue for a majority of French people, particularly those living in rural areas. Jérôme Fourquet, head of polling for IFOP (Institut français d'opinion publique), a leading French opinion research firm, said, "The price of fuel now is as politically and sociologically sensitive as the price of wheat was in the days of the ancient regime," referring to the eighteenth-century bread riots that fomented the French Revolution.[2]

As the Yellow Vest movement swelled in size, the motives behind the populist rebellion mutated beyond the fuel tax increase to target other inequities in French society that divide rich and poor, as well as rural and urban communities. Not only are those living outside of cities compelled to drive longer distances and spend more on gasoline, while urban dwellers enjoy subsidized public transport, but they also receive less government support than urban dwellers, even though they are forced to pay the same high level of income and payroll taxes. France is one of the most highly taxed states in Europe because of hefty payroll levies that pay for the country's generous health-care, education, and pension programs. But for those earning an average income of 1,700 euros (about $2,000) per month, it has become harder to make ends meet with the rising cost of basic necessities like food, shelter, and transport. Over the past fifteen years, the tax burden on French citizens has grown by 25 billion euros ($28 billion) a year, with a disproportionate share borne by the working poor. By the time of the Yellow Vest movement, the steady erosion of purchasing power for lower-middle-class families over the past decade had evolved, almost unnoticed by the government, into a genuine social emergency. Although many protesters said that they approved of the government's ambition to do something about climate change, they objected to carrying so much of the fiscal burden, particularly when cosmopolitan elites were spared onerous taxes for traveling in planes, which pollute more than cars do. "Macron thinks about the end of the world, while we worry about the end of the month," became a popular rallying cry among the demonstrators.

While the mood of the protesters in the French countryside remained mostly peaceful, the atmosphere in the capital and other large cities quickly turned ugly. Like their revolutionary forebears, more than one thousand demonstrators at one point tried to breach the gates of the Élysée Palace, shouting "Macron resign!" as police forces used tear gas and water cannons to drive them away from the presidential residence. Clouds of smoke enveloped the elegant boulevard of the Champs-Élysées, where militants threw paving stones and shattered store windows. Many of the demonstrators disavowed any connection to the violent protesters, identified by police as hard-core *casseurs* (vandals) who belonged to Black Bloc, an extremist group that seemed intent on damaging and robbing properties in the most affluent streets of Paris. After the protests continued on successive Saturdays, the government grew alarmed at the escalating intensity of the violence as demonstrators began burning cars and attacking riot police in the heart of Paris. Scenes of mayhem, pillaging, and wanton destruction spread to the capital's most famous settings, including the Tuileries and the Opéra. Masked protesters even trashed the Arc de Triomphe, spraying the monument with graffiti that read YELLOW VESTS WILL TRIUMPH and ripping apart its statuary, leaving Napoleon's marble head lying in the stairwell.

By the third Saturday, with shopkeepers complaining that their livelihoods were being endangered and the riots showing no signs of dissipating, it was clear that what had rapidly become the worst crisis of Macron's presidency was threatening to spin out of control. Even though the number of protesters declined to eighty thousand nationwide, their anger and hostility seemed to be growing. Worse, public support for the anti-Macron protests was holding firm at 70 percent. The government announced that it might need to impose a state of emergency to prevent a recurrence of the worst vandalism seen in

France for decades. Macron rushed back from Argentina, where he had been attending the G-20 summit conference, seven thousand miles away from the insurrection taking place at home. Before leaving Buenos Aires, he expressed shock and outrage at the destructive turn the protests had taken. "What happened today in Paris has nothing to do with the peaceful expression of legitimate anger," Macron declared. "Nothing justifies attacking the security forces, vandalizing businesses, either private or public ones, or that passers-by or journalists are threatened, or the Arc de Triomphe defaced."[3]

As soon as he arrived back in Paris, Macron headed straight to the Avenue Champs-Élysées to see for himself what had transpired. A phalanx of security guards surrounded him as an angry crowd gathered to jeer his arrival with catcalls, whistles, and boos. "He could not believe what had happened," a presidential aide told me. "It was nothing short of traumatic for him because he could not comprehend the degree of hatred he was seeing in the streets." The area resembled a veritable war zone, with broken glass littering the streets that extend from the Arc de Triomphe, along with dozens of empty tear gas canisters, smashed ATMs, and the burned-out carcasses of several automobiles. Upon returning to the Élysée Palace, Macron summoned his top ministers for an emergency security meeting. His chief of staff, Alexis Kohler, insisted that the government should not make any concessions to the protesters. Kohler warned that if he did so, the president could suffer the same kind of humiliation and loss of authority that had undermined his predecessors, who wilted from the heat of street protests. Kohler also believed that the Yellow Vests would lose credibility as the public grew disenchanted with the chaos they caused. But Interior Minister Christophe Castaner warned that the police forces were already exhausted and stretched too thin as they struggled in vain to prevent the capital's wealthiest neighborhoods and renowned landmarks from becoming ritual battlegrounds every Saturday. He argued that if the protests extended into the year-end holidays, they could paralyze the country. François Bayrou, the leader of the moderate Democrats, who supported Macron, told the president that he would not win a showdown because "you cannot govern against the people." Finance Minister Bruno Le Maire insisted that unless calm was restored soon, the widespread property damage and loss of investor confidence could prove ruinous for the French economy and sabotage Macron's reform efforts.[4]

What complicated the government's efforts to defuse the protests was the amorphous and leaderless nature of a populist rebellion organized through social media networks. France has a long history of strikes and social upheaval, including the Jacquerie peasant revolt of 1358, the anti-monarchist revolution of 1789, the Poujadist shopkeeper rebellion in the 1950s, and the May 1968 protests led by students and labor unions that all but shut down the country. In each of those cases, rebel leaders eventually emerged who proved capable of striking a deal with the authorities. But the Yellow Vest movement seemed to revel in an anarchic style that defied ideological labels and rejected anybody who tried to speak on its behalf. When Prime Minister Édouard Philippe sought to meet with eight prominent Yellow Vest supporters, the negotiations foundered when several were disavowed by the movement and others refused to attend after receiving threats. Only two representatives bothered to show up, but since they were not empowered to speak for the movement, the meeting was futile. None of Macron's political opponents, from Marine Le Pen on the far right to Jean-Luc Mélenchon on the far left, managed to capture the allegiance of the Yellow Vest supporters. Like Macron's own "radical centrist" movement that destroyed the traditional ruling parties, the Yellow Vests professed to despise the entire political establishment. "This is the first time we're seeing a mobilization that's coming from social networks, and not led by political parties or the unions," observed Jean-Yves Camus, a political scientist who heads the Observatory on Political Radicalism. "This is really a populist-type movement, and it's an extremely strong protest against elite France. It's a protest against tax policy that's considered confiscatory. And there's been an undeniable drop in the buying power not just of workers, but of the middle class."[5]

On Tuesday, December 4, with a fourth consecutive Saturday of protests looming, Macron's prime minister, Édouard Philippe, shifted course and agreed to offer new concessions. Earlier, the government had offered to spend 500 million euros (about $570 million) on increased subsidies for the purchase of fuel-efficient cars and home heating systems that emitted less pollution. But those measures were ridiculed by many demonstrators who claimed that they simply could not afford these purchases, even if subsidized. This time Philippe, a slender, bearded man with a calm and deliberate style, appeared genuinely contrite and effectively acknowledged that the government had committed several policy blunders. These included a reduction in speed limits for rural areas and an expansion of radar detection points that infuriated French motorists, who had to pay large fines when caught in speed traps. The reduction in speed limits was a measure that also appalled Macron. He was well aware of the risks of backtracking on policies, which he had frequently criticized other presidents for doing. But he also reminded Philippe that as a former Gaullist, he should have remembered the advice of de Gaulle's successor, Georges Pompidou, who said the first rule of governing was "n'emmerdez pas les Français" (don't mess with the French people).

Philippe announced that the hated fuel tax increases that ignited the protests would be suspended for six months. Later, the tax hikes were canceled entirely. He also promised to raise the minimum wage and delay increases in electricity rates to boost the purchasing power of working-class families. "No tax is worth putting in danger the unity of the nation," the prime minister said in a conciliatory statement. "The French who donned the yellow vests love their country. If the events of recent days show anything, it is that the French want their taxes to go down." He admitted that his government had neglected to address the basic grievances and financial difficulties of the lower classes, whose anger went well beyond the impact of fuel tax increases: they were growing increasingly frustrated with not being able to pay their bills. "This anger is widespread and has been simmering for a long time, and it's often remained silent out of modesty or pride," Philippe said. "It's the anger of a France that works hard, and has trouble making ends meet. You would have to be deaf or blind not to see or hear it."[6]

That same day, while his prime minister addressed the nation, Macron decided to travel to Le Puy-en-Velay, a small town in the Auvergne region of south-central France. On the previous Saturday, protesters had set the prefecture on fire, and Macron wanted to show his support for the mayor and other civil servants who felt terrorized by the violent turn in the Yellow Vest demonstrations. At a roundabout on the road into town from the local airport, protesters had erected a scaffold with an effigy of Macron and a sign that read: SENDING YOU TO THE GUILLOTINE IS OUR MISSION. At the prefecture, the mayor showed Macron how some two hundred militants had breached the gates, broken down doors, and shattered windows before setting it on fire. As flames engulfed the building, the protesters had blocked firefighters from entering as they shouted to those still inside: "We're going to barbecue all of you like chickens!" The mayor and other civil servants managed to escape through a rear door, but not before more than thirty people suffered injuries. As word spread about Macron's visit, dozens of Yellow Vest supporters gathered outside the blackened building. They shouted, "President of the rich!" and "Resign, you asshole!" as Macron left the building. Macron likes to mingle and wanted to engage the militants in impromptu debate, but his security guards feared that things might get out of control and pushed him inside his limousine as the menacing crowd approached. Several protesters jumped in front of his car, shouting obscenities and chanting, "We hate you!" As loud boos rang out, Macron opened his window and tried to speak with a woman, but she spit at him and screamed, "You bastard! I hope you crash and die on your way out of here!"[7]

Macron returned to Paris dazed and baffled. It was clear that the Yellow Vest movement was now focusing its vengeful wrath on Macron personally, not just on high taxes. As the Saturday protests continued, demonstrators frequently portrayed Macron as an aloof monarch who was as insensitive as Louis XVI to the suffering of the masses, often tinging that caricature with bloody revolutionary symbols. Mock guillotines and effigies of Macron carried aloft by crowds depicted him with knife wounds, in chains, covered in blood, or with a noose dangling around his neck. Facebook and Twitter carried images of fake arrest warrants issued against Macron on grounds of "high treason." His wife, Brigitte, who has always been one of Macron's most intimate and astute advisers, sought to console her husband and urged him not to take such personal attacks too seriously. Macron has always praised her steely resolve, which he believes was forged during the difficult years when their romance was blossoming in spite of staunch opposition from their families and friends. Brigitte was reminded of the vulgar attacks she had experienced more than two decades earlier when rumors circulated about their love affair, which scandalized their hometown of Amiens in northern France because, at the time, she was a drama teacher twenty-four years older than the adolescent Emmanuel. She learned then how viciously people could behave; in conversations with her staff members, she recalled the obscene letters that were often stuffed in her mailbox and the neighbors who spat on the windows of her family's chocolate shop while shouting insults at their employees.[8]

Brigitte served as Macron's personal rock of stability during those turbulent early days of the Yellow Vest protests. She is one of two women who have played dominant and formative roles in his life. The other is his maternal grandmother, Germaine Noguès, known as Manette, who inculcated in him a strong work ethic and a deep affection for music and literature during their time together at her home in the Pyrenees. Even when Macron's parents and many residents in Amiens were mortified by his affair with Brigitte, Manette bestowed her approval on the relationship, which for Macron was decisive. Brigitte Auzière became the love of his life. He pursued her assiduously even after his parents sent him away to school in Paris, hoping he would get over his adolescent crush. While other students partied on weekends, he would hop aboard a train to travel back to Amiens to see her. Eventually, Brigitte left her banker husband, with whom she had three children, and married Macron in 2007. When he entered politics, she traveled with him as much as possible and became a distinct asset during the campaign. She advised him on education and cultural issues, helped him select his ministers, and attracted legions of female voters who were delighted to see a mature woman at the side of a young male politician. It was a refreshing contrast to the usual French custom of older men running for office who consorted with much younger mistresses. Not only did she help Macron enlist women voters in his movement, but once in office she became more popular than her husband, each year receiving hundreds of letters delivered to the Élysée Palace addressed to "Madame la Présidente."

Brigitte had warned Macron early on that he was developing a reputation for arrogance among rural French men and women that would be hard to shake. During an eight-day tour of World War I battlefields ahead of the centennial anniversary marking the armistice that ended one of history's most hideous wars, Macron confronted many resentful citizens across France, who complained that he was too remote from their everyday lives and did not seem to care or understand the true nature of their hardships. They, like him, were frustrated that the fruits of his reform efforts were so slow in coming. Even Macron's wealthiest supporters accused him of being tone-deaf to the problems of the working poor. François Pinault, whose business empire includes the Gucci fashion house, told the newspaper *Le Monde* that "Macron doesn't understand the little people. I'm afraid he's leading France toward a system that leaves the least favored behind."[9] Matthieu Pigasse, a prominent financier who heads the Lazard investment bank in France, told the business newspaper *Les Echos* that Macron needed to show more empathy for the lower classes. "He lacks an essential social dimension and a policy to fight against inequalities in all forms. Where are the plans for the suburbs, the fight against poverty and extra efforts for higher education?" he asked.[10] On the eve of the first Yellow Vest demonstrations, Macron acknowledged during an interview with French television that perhaps he had not shown enough sensitivity to the suffering of those left behind by the forces of globalization. "I hear their anger," Macron said. "I have failed to reconcile the French people with their leaders."[11]

The crescendo of violence in the recurring Saturday protests and the hostile treatment he received in Le Puy-en-Velay convinced some advisers that it was time for Macron to retreat from the public eye in an effort to defuse the demonstrations. "The president needs to protect himself," said Pierre Person, a member of Parliament and close ally. "He should regain the high ground by pulling back and speaking less in public."[12] Interior Minister Christophe Castaner, one of Macron's most loyal lieutenants and a former head of his party, urged Macron to cease all public appearances because he feared that security forces might not be able to protect him from bodily harm. "We need to calm things down, even if it may seem like appeasement," Castaner said. But other advisers argued against a bunker mentality and claimed that even a temporary retreat by the president would be tantamount to surrendering to pressure from the streets, which Macron vowed he would never do. "We do not want to live through a five-year presidential term in an atomic bomb shelter," declared Sylvain Fort, Macron's chief of communications.[13]

Macron settled the debate by deciding to curtail his appearances for several weeks—until the new year—in order to remove himself as the primary focus of outrage. He also wanted to ease pressures on his overworked security teams, who were genuinely alarmed about his safety. By tradition in France, a prime minister is supposed to serve as a political shield for the president, but Macron's nature as a micromanager, working up to twenty hours a day, had propelled him to the front lines of the Yellow Vest crisis and made him the principal scapegoat for unpopular government policies. It was decided that in the future Philippe, as prime minister, would play a more customary role as presidential surrogate to deflect some of the heat.

Meantime, the weekly scenes of chaos and disorder were spreading discontent and grumbling in the ranks of the armed forces. Some of Macron's advisers even feared a possible putsch. Castaner was so

concerned about the morale of the police and the army, amid reports
that members were being actively recruited to join the Yellow Vest
protest movement, that he procured special funding to offer them
bonus payments to secure their loyalty. A dozen retired generals and
admirals, along with some other officers of lower rank, signed an
open letter that was published on a right-wing website; it denounced
Macron for violating his constitutional duties and demanded that he
be held to account by legal authorities. Even though the officers were
not on active duty, the letter was a serious affront to the president and
his role as commander in chief of the country's armed forces.

Macron withdrew into the solitude of the Élysée Palace, spending his days holding interminable staff meetings or using the two
iPhones he carried to consult with friends and political allies on the
outside. He remained more active than ever on Telegram, his favorite mode of communication via encrypted text messages. Friends on
the receiving end of his messages noticed that he often sent them
between two and three o'clock in the morning. He and his wife abandoned favorite pastimes like going to the cinema and enjoying an
impromptu dinner at a discreet back table in the Montparnasse bras-
serie La Rotonde, and Brigitte gave up her excursions to buy fresh
loaves of bread at local bakeries. A French ambassador who stopped
by to visit him was struck by Macron's depressed frame of mind; he
had lost weight and looked exhausted and disheveled. "He was like
a boxer who had been completely knocked out," said the diplomat.
"Here was somebody who had succeeded at everything in life, and
now he saw that his presidency might be falling apart and there was
nothing he could do about it."[14]

Weeks later, during one of our interviews after the immediate
challenge to his authority had waned, Macron still seemed stunned by
the intense animosity directed at him at the peak of the Yellow Vest
protests. When I asked what had surprised him the most during his
first two years in power, he leaned back and pondered the question
for about ten seconds. "I would say the hatred that I have witnessed
in politics. The acceleration of violence in our society and the world at

large is much worse than I expected," Macron said, fidgeting on a sofa and sipping espresso in the Salon d'Orée of the Élysée Palace as sunshine streamed through the windows on an unusually warm February afternoon. "That and the disconnect between the elites and the people that led to such a situation." Macron believes that the poisoning of political discourse in many democracies is a direct result of growing inequalities between rich and poor, as well as the social gulf separating rural and urban communities in France, the United States, and other Western nations. "For many years, the political elite did not address the real underlying problems of our society, while the economic elite became very selfish," he told me. "The violence we are seeing on a regular basis is symptomatic of a profound malaise in our society." Macron feels that the polarization and intolerance in Western politics these days is not just the result of the anger and coarse rhetoric raging on social networks, but something deeper that suggests a profound moral crisis. "You can oppose my political views and argue in favor of something else, okay, that's fine. But to take politics to such an extreme level, including death threats of the worst kind, is abnormal and dangerous," Macron said.[15]

During those bleak December days while he was holed up in the Élysée, Macron pondered his exit strategy even as the Yellow Vest protests showed no signs of abating. He still could not comprehend the rationale behind the protest movement. His early reforms of the labor laws, the education system, and the tax codes had sailed through without significant opposition. He had even managed to defeat the once-invincible railway workers. But the Yellow Vest movement defied conventional political analysis, and neither Élysée officials nor French media pundits had predicted the ferocity of the protests. He summoned veteran political counselors, seeking alternative advice to the hard-line positions espoused by his youthful staff members. The elders insisted that Macron needed to offer significant concessions and open up state coffers even if it meant bowing to some of the Yellow Vest demands and backpedaling on his promise not to give in. The only path available, in their view, was for Macron to spend

his way out of trouble. Macron reluctantly accepted their advice after concluding that the country was facing an economic and social
emergency.

On the evening of December 10, Macron went on television to
speak for the first time about the Yellow Vest protests. In a somber
thirteen-minute speech that was watched by more than twenty-three
million people, a chastened Macron sat at a gilded ornate desk and
announced that his government would rescind taxes on poor retirees,
raise the minimum wage by 100 euros a month without any cost to
employers, and abolish taxes on year-end bonuses. The entire package
would cost an estimated 17 billion euros and blow a huge hole in the
budget, but he had decided that it was a necessary price to pay for sal-
vaging his presidency. Macron's ashen and haggard appearance during
his speech conveyed a tone of desperation. He vowed to press ahead
with his reform agenda and refused to reinstate France's contentious
wealth tax, saying that "going backward would weaken us." Most important, his demeanor had changed dramatically. Gone was the regal
arrogance that so annoyed his many critics, as well as the Jupiterian
pretensions that he could govern most effectively from the top down.
He sounded apologetic and acknowledged that he had committed
mistakes during the first two years of his presidency. "I know I have
hurt some of you with my words," Macron said. "I accept my share of
responsibility. I may have given you the feeling that I didn't care, that
I had other priorities." He promised to bridge the gulf between Paris
and rural France by working more closely with mayors and union
leaders in order to understand the needs of local communities, which
had for too long been neglected by the national government.[16]

Macron's concessions did not halt the protests, but his willingness to address key grievances of the Yellow Vest movement would
gradually turn the tide of public opinion back in his favor. The scenes
of wanton violence being committed every Saturday by a hard-core
group of *casseurs* began to exasperate not just Parisian shopkeepers but much of the French nation. By offering tangible benefits to
the needy while not abandoning his reform program, Macron did

not suffer from the perception of political weakness he once feared, but instead proved to voters that he was ready to govern responsibly by making justifiable course corrections. After his approval ratings had plummeted to lows close to 20 percent, they steadily began to climb upward; within six months, he had returned to the levels of popularity that he enjoyed before the Yellow Vest protests began. In retrospect, his television speech would be seen as a crucial turning point—a moment when he managed to shed his imperious image and regain his political balance to prepare himself for further challenges at home and abroad.

Macron already appeared much more confident when he gave his traditional New Year's address to the nation three weeks later. This time he stood during his entire speech and, in contrast with his earlier televised appearance, looked calm and self-assured. "We have lived through great rifts and a rising anger which dates from far back," Macron said. "I've seen and heard unthinkable, unacceptable things." He condemned the extremist rhetoric and violence of some of the protests as "quite simply the negation of France" and chastised "those who pretend to speak in the name of the people when in fact they are merely speaking for a hateful mob that goes after elected officials, the police, journalists, Jews, foreigners and homosexuals." Calling on the French people to rally behind the need to restore order, he urged them to be patient as the country awaited results from his economic reforms. Macron also said that the French people should appreciate the fact that their social benefits, including nearly free education, excellent infrastructure, and high-quality universal medical care, were some of the best in the world. France spends 32 percent of its gross domestic product on social welfare, the highest proportion in the world. "Let's stop thinking ill of ourselves or believe that France is a country where solidarity doesn't exist," Macron urged as he pleaded with his fellow citizens to set aside their penchant to bicker and complain about their daily lives.[17]

The protests badly damaged Macron's image in Europe as a progressive champion leading the fight against populism and nationalism. His election had been applauded across much of the continent as a welcome rebuke to the xenophobic and antidemocratic forces that continue to threaten the stability of the European Union. He was even hailed by some as a messiah who would rescue Europe from a possible return to the dark and dangerous years between the two world wars. But the turmoil that erupted in the streets of France undermined his authority and hurt his efforts not just to modernize France but to revive momentum for a more integrated Europe. Macron's slow reaction to the crisis, he admitted later, reflected his abiding conviction that the fuel tax was a sensible way to encourage "an ecological transition" away from carbon fuels that pollute the atmosphere and to push motorists into buying electric cars.

The Yellow Vest protests reflected a troubling malaise in French society that had been festering for many years. The anger and frustration showed the depth of resentment in the rural areas that had not thrived in recent years. The growing divide between rich and poor—the richest 20 percent of French people, according to the World Bank, now earn nearly five times as much as the bottom 20 percent—makes a mockery of French pretensions of "liberty, equality and fraternity." That yawning divide, in turn, heightens the working poor's disillusionment with Macron, who took office on a cloud of euphoria amid hopes for a resurgence in economic growth that would lift up the entire nation. "The system is in crisis," said French political scientist Dominique Reynié. "It's the provinces against Paris, the proud and contemptuous capital. Paris has never been so dissimilar from the rest of France. The fracture is very, very sharp."[18]

A major study of the Yellow Vest movement published in March 2019 by the Institut Montaigne found that an overwhelming number of its ten thousand respondents cited economic vulnerability because of declining purchasing power as their main motivation for joining the protests. The gender divide was fairly even: 53 percent of those who identified as Yellow Vest protesters were men and 47 percent were women. The significant presence in the movement of single women with children reflected their precarious economic situation. Sixty-five percent of the respondents said that they had difficulty making ends meet, and 55 percent said that their financial situation had worsened over the past year. Half of them reported serious difficulty in paying their transportation costs. Geographically, the study found the highest concentration of Yellow Vest protesters in the "diagonal void"—a vast area extending from the Ardennes in the northeast to the Pyrenees in the southwest that has been described as "in-between France" because it suffers from depopulation and remoteness from public services.[19]

Other analysts believe that Macron's failure to comprehend the growing despair across rural France resulted from a misinterpretation of his election victory as a sweeping mandate for the kind of far-reaching reforms carried out in recent decades by Germany and Britain. He won only 24 percent in the first round of the 2017 presidential election. His final score of 66 percent in the second round was largely attributed to dismay among many voters with his far-right opponent Marine Le Pen, not to any particular enthusiasm for Macron himself. The irony is that within two years of rising to power by sweeping aside the traditional political parties, Macron found his presidency imperiled by the same kind of anti-establishment hostility.

The Yellow Vest protest is often compared to other populist rebellions in Western democracies, such as those that led to Britain's vote to leave the European Union, the 2016 American presidential election of Donald Trump, and the rise to prominence of right-wing governments in Poland, Hungary, and Italy. French geographer Christophe Guilluy, who has studied the demographics of "left behinds" in Britain, Italy, the United States, and France, concludes that the sociology of these populist uprisings is remarkably similar. In each case, he has observed the gravitation of power and affluence to the cities in a process he calls *métropolisation*, which he believes is the domestic corollary of globalization. In France, cities like Paris, Lyon, and Toulouse have attracted most of the jobs and wealth; not surprisingly, those urban centers voted overwhelmingly in favor of Macron. In Britain, London and Manchester have thrived in the past decade, as have San Francisco and New York in the United States.

This economic model, Guilluy says, polarizes not just employment but also the territorial map. It can have pernicious political effects, pushing depressed rural and post-industrial areas to embrace extremist causes. As a result, British voters outside the wealth centers of London and Manchester became the principal foundation of support for Brexit. The economically depressed areas of the Midwest and the South turned to Donald Trump in the 2016 presidential election. And in France, the Yellow Vest movement took root in the working-class exurbs and deserted rural areas of France. "Geography is the common point of the gilets jaunes, Brexit and Trump, and the populist wave," Guilluy says, whose book *La France péripherique* (Peripheral France) is often cited as one of the rare works that foreshadowed the rise of the Yellow Vest protesters. He claims that many of these people, left behind by globalization and shunted aside by the new urban economic model, are struggling to preserve their social and cultural capital, as well as their individual identity. "What is very important with the crisis of the gilets jaunes is obviously the yellow vest itself; it says, 'look at me, I exist,'" Guilluy observes.[20]

Nonetheless, apart from a shared disdain for globalization, there are significant differences among the populist movements that have disrupted Western democracies. The Yellow Vests are not connected to any party, and they have neither an official policy platform nor a leadership hierarchy. They are militantly apolitical, and unlike other populist movements in Europe and the United States, they have not focused on race and immigration issues. The movement is largely a social and economic uprising by the working poor, who manifest their rage by smashing the boutiques near the Champs-Élysées, luxury establishments that they never see in their own communities. Many Yellow Vest protesters explained that they continued turning out for demonstrations every Saturday for several months because they felt driven by profound despair about economic injustice and deep cynicism toward the Parisian elite governing class, which they said had failed for decades to address the social fractures within the French nation.[21]

As the Saturday protests in France proceeded through the winter months, the crowds dwindled and a hardened core of ultra-left and extreme-right agitators assumed a more prominent role. The actions carried out in the name of the Yellow Vest movement seemed increasingly suffused by the hatred that Macron found so shocking and intolerable during his first years as president. Dozens of his political supporters became frontline proxies for Yellow Vest fury toward the president. The home of Richard Ferrand, a Macron ally and the speaker of the National Assembly, was set on fire in Brittany. The residences of up to fifty members of Parliament who backed Macron were also attacked, defaced, and damaged. Hervé Berville, a black member of the National Assembly who belongs to Macron's political alliance, received death threats, including one that lamented the fact that the Rwanda-born politician had "unfortunately escaped the machetes" during the 1994 genocide that ravaged his native land. Historians noted that never in the history of France's Fifth Republic had social movements generated such hatred and violence. Meanwhile, the attacks against political representatives only became more brazen. A group of protesters dressed in black commandeered a forklift and broke through the doors of a ministry building in the rue de Grenelle, forcing the government spokesman Benjamin Griveaux to flee as they shattered his windows. "It wasn't me who was attacked, it was the republic, the house of France," a shaken-looking Griveaux told French television. Macron himself responded on Twitter: "Once again, the republic was attacked with extreme violence—its guardians, its representatives, its symbols."

The protests also began to assume anti-Semitic overtones. Castaner, the interior minister, warned that anti-Semitism was "spreading like poison" across the country. He noted that after falling for two years in a row, anti-Semitic acts in France surged by

74 percent in 2018. Walls in the capital bore the graffiti slogan MA-
CRON THE JEWS' WHORE. The word JUDEN was scrawled across a bagel
shop in Paris, and swastikas were painted on street art that portrayed
Simone Veil, a revered former minister and Auschwitz survivor. In
February 2019, eighty graves in a Jewish cemetery in eastern France
were sprayed with swastikas. That same week, Alain Finkielkraut, a
French philosopher of Polish origin, who was one of the few intellectuals to support the Yellow Vest movement, was attacked as he was
getting out of a taxi near his Left Bank residence by a group of Yellow
Vest marchers, who were caught on video screaming at him, "Dirty
Zionist shit" and "Go back to Tel Aviv."[22] The philosopher Bernard-
Henri Lévy saw the violent evolution of the movement as an ominous
portent for France and Europe. He compared the anti-Semitic acts
linked to Yellow Vest protests to the riots of February 1934, when
several right-wing extremist movements, led by the Action Française
of Charles Maurras, marched on the Chamber of Deputies. Then, the
French authorities, fearing a fascist coup attempt, responded with brutal force; the ensuing street battles left sixteen people dead and thousands wounded. For Lévy, the 1934 assault on the Chamber and the
Yellow Vest attempts to attack government buildings and the Élysée
Palace seemed eerily similar, projecting a violent brand of political
extremism that he warned "could give birth to monsters."[23]

Macron believed that the degradation of the Yellow Vest movement into wanton acts of hatred would appall an ever-growing majority of French citizens and soon turn them against the disruptive
protests. Just before paying a visit to the desecrated Jewish cemetery,
Macron, who believed that the new climate of fear and hate across
France and much of Europe was cause for serious alarm, declared that
such displays of anti-Semitic violence were "the antithesis of all that
is France." Despite Macron's claim, anti-Semitism has deep roots in
French history, extending back through Vichy France to the Dreyfus
Affair. But the shocking degree of intolerance and hatred witnessed
across France since the birth of the Yellow Vest movement awakened
many people to the risk that their society could break apart if such

toxic attitudes were allowed to fester too long. Even Marine Le Pen, who has tried to distance her party from its xenophobic reputation while still exploiting themes of identity politics, laid flowers to honor the victims of anti-Semitism. In a rare show of political harmony, leaders across the ideological spectrum joined a march of twenty thousand people in the capital against the upsurge in anti-Semitism afflicting France.

Macron sensed a political opening that presented him with a new opportunity to respond to his critics and launch a dialogue of reconciliation across the nation. He decided to go back on the campaign trail and try to emulate the success he had enjoyed as a political upstart who slayed the traditional ruling parties. This time he would display a new sense of humility, as well as patience and understanding, in dealing with his compatriots. He would seek to win back their trust and support through a unique initiative to help him comprehend the grievances of the French people and formulate policies that would respond to their needs.

In an open letter to his fellow citizens published in January 2019, Macron announced that he would seek "a new contract for the nation" designed to "transform anger into solutions" through months of nationwide public consultations across the country. The discussions would focus on four central themes: taxation, the state and public administration, ecological issues, and citizenship and democracy. "No questions are banned," Macron wrote. "We won't agree on everything, that's normal, that's democracy. But at least we'll show that we are a people who are not afraid to speak, to exchange views and debate. And perhaps we'll discover that we might even agree, despite our different persuasions, more often than we think."[24] Mayors were encouraged to solicit the views of their constituents by asking them to detail their complaints and outline policy suggestions in hundreds of "grievance books" laid out in administrative offices that would help shape a Grand National Debate. The idea of "grievance books," or *cahiers de doléances*, dates back to the early days of the French Revolution, when Louis XVI ordered his subjects to compile their complaints in official catalogs. But that initiative backfired on Louis: rather than defuse popular anger, it escalated the insurrection against his monarchy.

Macron gambled that he would succeed where Louis XVI had failed. In his 2,300-word letter to the nation, Macron acknowledged that tax cuts, favored by so many Yellow Vest protesters, would be a major priority. He challenged his fellow citizens to be responsible and think through the consequences of their suggestions. "What taxes should we cut?" Macron asked. "How can we make our fiscal system more just and more efficient?" He warned them that any tax cuts would require reductions in public spending, which would mean sacrificing some public services that might be obsolete or too expensive. At first skeptical, the French soon warmed to the project and turned out in massive numbers to write down their thoughts and engage in animated discussions in town halls across the country. Macron's extraordinary initiative to engage in direct consultations with his fellow citizens about how they wished to be governed helped to restore relative calm across much of the nation. The Grand National Debate also extricated Macron from his gloomy isolation inside the Élysée Palace and put him back in touch with the people in a way that would energize him for act two of his presidency.

CHAPTER 3

THE GREAT CONVOCATION

The sleepy Normandy village of Grand-Bourgtheroulde had never seen anything like it. As helicopters whirred overhead, squads of gendarmes blockaded main roads and stopped traffic from entering the town. Cars were evacuated from main streets and parking was banned. Shops were shuttered and the four thousand inhabitants were advised to stay indoors. Wagonloads of police armed with tear gas and water cannons were posted around the perimeter and in the surrounding woods. The occasion was the formal launch of Emmanuel Macron's unique experiment in participatory democracy, in which France's sixty-seven million people would engage in months of spirited consultations about how they wished to be governed. For Macron, the Grand National Debate that he inaugurated on January 15, 2019, was a desperate roll of the dice.

It was Macron's first major public appearance after the hostile encounter with angry crowds in Le Puy-en-Velay in early December. His security guards were taking every precaution to ensure his safety in a region where, with over 20 percent unemployment, animosity toward the president was running high. For his part, Macron was relieved to escape several weeks of enforced isolation within the Élysée Palace. As he entered the packed gymnasium, Macron received tepid applause from six hundred mayors in attendance. He tried to ignore the jeers and catcalls from several dozen Yellow Vest protesters who managed to breach the barricades to greet him with shouts of "Macron, resign!"

Macron had cleared his schedule of foreign travel for the duration of the town hall gatherings. He devoted long hours to mastering every conceivable subject that might come up for discussion in each region, as if preparing for comprehensive oral exams. "The period we're living in poses many challenges to our country," he told the mayors. "We can turn the movement that is shaking France into an opportunity." He urged them to be forthright in expressing the grievances and anxieties felt by their constituents and said that he wanted a discussion with "no taboos." Macron brushed aside complaints that the exercise would be a waste of time or little more than an apology tour. "It's clear that people want changes in the way they are governed, and so we constantly need to ask them their opinion," he maintained. "I want to see us create a republic of constant deliberation. This debate will serve to affirm our legitimacy as elected leaders."[1]

The mayors did not pull any punches. "You've disappointed me, Mr. Macron," said Dominique Chauvel, the mayor of Saint-Valery-en-Caux, a small coastal town. "But I hope you succeed because otherwise our country is heading for disaster."[2] Jean-Paul Legendre, the president of the mayors' association, warned about the growing alienation between Paris and the rural communities, which he feared might soon break the country apart. "We have the feeling that France is living on two different levels and at two different speeds," Legendre said. "When are you going to stop grinding us down?" Another mayor, Sophie de Gibon, from Canteloup in the Calvados region, told Macron that he needed to start paying closer attention to local officials if he wanted to understand what was happening in the French hinterlands. "We are responsible people who have been elected by the voters," she said. "Allow us to do our work, show confidence in us, and listen to the mayors. It's no longer possible to think you know everything just because you went to the best schools in Paris."[3]

Macron took copious notes, jotting down observations about everything from speed limits to nuclear power and the lack of care for autistic children. He doffed his jacket, rolled up his shirtsleeves, and fielded a vast array of questions for nearly seven hours. "My goal is to listen to all of you. We have plenty of time," he told the mayors. He urged them to pepper him as well with fresh ideas and suggestions. Macron displayed extraordinary patience in his readiness to talk about local problems. He nearly exhausted his audience as the session went late into the night. The president acknowledged that stubborn persistence by those who held power was not necessarily virtuous. "I've heard you loud and clear and you will see that I can be more pragmatic in the future," he said. Macron promised that unpopular policies introduced with good intentions, like speed limits, would be corrected if they annoyed too many people. "I respect your anger, I feel your pain," Macron said, projecting a new empathy that was lacking in his early months in office. "It's clear that our country has suffered from a serious social fracture that dates back many years. I know you are looking for somebody to blame, and I am ready to fully assume that role. Nobody forced me to become president."[4]

For more than two months, Macron traversed the French countryside at a furious pace. He stopped in little-known towns to conduct town hall meetings that would sometimes finish well past midnight. He exposed himself to all kinds of verbal abuse about his policies and arrogance in office, at times causing his aides to cringe over what they saw as an exercise in abysmal humiliation. But Macron did not lose his cool. He absorbed the barrage of criticism. According to the Élysée, Macron attended fourteen debates and spent ninety-two hours engaged in these face-to-face consultations. He met with more than 2,300 mayors and other elected representatives,

1,000 young people, 400 environmental activists, and 150 community planners. Often, the audiences would greet him with glacial skepticism. But as Macron displayed his mastery of policy detail and remarkable stamina over the course of several hours, the attendees would gradually warm up and finish the discussions with prolonged standing ovations. His penchant for studious preparation enabled him to show an impressive command of even the most arcane issues, including how to improve water recycling, prevent wolves from decimating flocks of sheep, and manage the fertility of bears in the southwest Pyrenees. He knew how much it would cost the state to speed up the delivery of hearing aids, as well as the time it took to process migrant asylum requests and deal with the staggering number of different pension systems in France. His audiences seemed at times overwhelmed by his long-winded performances. One local mayor suggested that Macron's ambition was to break the speechifying records of Fidel Castro.[5]

Macron reveled in the opportunity to get back on the campaign trail. His youthful enthusiasm had captivated many voters ahead of the 2017 election and distinguished him from other presidential contenders, who seemed stale and jaded because they had been on the French political scene for so many years. The format of the town hall meetings played to Macron's strengths by allowing him to demonstrate his acute intelligence and encyclopedic knowledge of local grievances. He also managed to drive a wedge into the ranks of the Yellow Vest protesters, some of whom chose to participate in the meetings while others rejected the Grand National Debate as "the Great Blah Blah." The debates became a powerful instrument for him to skewer rival politicians, mollify the Yellow Vest protesters, and instruct French citizens about the intricate trade-offs involved in policy making.

"I know I'm walking on thin ice, but I want to transform the way we practice democracy," Macron said later. "That's what I am trying to do with this national debate, to find new ways for people to express their views and feel they can impact how they are governed.

We must once again find a collective narrative for our democracy that deals with mounting tensions in our society. We must preserve liberty for those individuals who want to expand their horizons, but also protect others who cannot fend for themselves. The challenge is to ensure that my liberty does not impinge on the liberty of others."[6]

At one town meeting, Macron told his audience that they needed to understand that the national treasury had its limits. "It's not an open bar," Macron said. "Real reforms come with obligations, because if you want something you need to pay for it." He then invited a member of the Yellow Vest rebellion to join him onstage. Macron began their discussion by emphasizing that he wanted the French people to assume greater control over their own lives because the government could not take care of everything for them. "You have to realize that, as president, I don't have a magic wand," Macron said. The activist then questioned why the French should go on paying such high taxes if the government sought to escape its responsibilities, adding that he no longer bothered to vote because he felt that his vote made no difference anyway. "If non-voters block the roundabouts because they are suddenly dissatisfied, that is anything but democratic," Macron replied. The audience showed their approval with a sustained round of applause.[7] He concluded the debate with an appeal for greater understanding of the challenges facing him and his government. "If there is one thing that characterizes our country, it is that we place everything on the head of the president," Macron said. "There may be disgruntled groups. But to consider that they are right because they are dissatisfied is to show little consideration for others. My role is to be the president of all."[8]

The Grand National Debate reversed Macron's sagging political fortunes. His popularity level started climbing as people approved his new personal commitment to bringing himself and his government closer to the people. Even his political opponents expressed grudging admiration for Macron's remarkable stamina. They praised his skills in executing a daunting logistical exercise in participatory democracy that had never before been attempted in France, or even in other Western democracies. "It worked well," said Patrick Devedjian, a former minister under conservative president Nicolas Sarkozy. "You have to admit it. He was good." Others were more qualified in their endorsement. Boris Vallaud, a National Assembly member for the shrunken Socialist Party, said that while "everyone marvels at Macron's performance, the fact that he's going over the heads of the government, the unions, and the representative institutions is weakening our democracy."[9] Some of Macron's adversaries were cynical about what they described as a political stunt to deflect attention away from the shortcomings of the government. Christian Jacob, parliamentary leader of the center-right Republicans, called it a "great masquerade."

Within the Yellow Vest movement, there were mixed feelings about Macron's initiative. About 40 percent of them, according to surveys, thought that it was a good idea and wanted to be part of the exercise, if only to see what it produced. Some of them came up with lists of their own action points and asked the government to incorporate them into new policies. Priscillia Ludosky, one of the instigators of the Yellow Vest movement, launched an online petition that cited three demands: lowering taxes, lowering salaries for elected representatives, and establishing citizen referenda that could propose or abolish legislation, change the constitution, or remove a member of government from office. More than one million people endorsed her radical populist initiative. The government said that it would consider those ideas but refused to make any commitments. Other members of the Yellow Vest movement scoffed at the Grand National Debate. Benjamin Cauchy, a spokesman for a group of Yellow Vest protesters in the south of France, scorned the nationwide conversation as nothing more than "a form of group therapy." He would later quit the movement to join a far-right party.

The months of public discussions contributed to a steady erosion of support for the Yellow Vests. Attendance at the weekly Saturday protests dropped to less than one-tenth the size of the peak crowds. "We were finally able to put the voice of the Yellow Vests into perspective with the rest of the country," said Stanislas Guerini, the head of the president's party. From Macron's viewpoint, the public discussions allowed the public to blow off steam and relieve some frustrations. They also showed that he was able to come down from the clouds, defying his Jupiterian image. Nevertheless, the violent acts and wanton destruction carried out by a hard-core group of professional vandals showed no signs of abating. Some of the worst violence occurred during the final stage of the debates. Several newspaper stands were set afire along the Champs-Élysées, fancy boutiques were looted, and the swanky restaurant Fouquet's, long known as a glamorous redoubt of the rich and famous, was trashed and pillaged. Macron was appalled and insisted that the government would make law and order its top priority in quelling the riots. The Paris police chief was fired and security reinforcements from the ranks of the armed forces streamed into the streets to prevent future outbreaks of violence. This time public opinion was overwhelmingly on Macron's side.

The high level of participation in the public debates fulfilled Macron's aspirations to bring French citizens into a national conversation that he hoped would cultivate renewed solidarity. Besides the presidential town meetings, French citizens were encouraged to organize their own communal discussions in local restaurants or in their living rooms. Mayors distributed documentation kits that included statistical data to help guide the discussions. The local organizers were asked to post summaries that could be shared on the government website. In the end, more than half a million people participated in over ten thousand meetings convened across France, over twenty-seven thousand emails and letters were sent to the presidential office, sixteen thousand books of grievances were filled out, and nearly two million suggestions were posted on an online platform set up by the government. The massive amount of data was analyzed and digitized with information technology using high-powered algorithms and other forms of artificial intelligence.

Macron reached out to some of the nation's leading writers, economists, scientists, and philosophers to solicit their views about how he could restore faith in democratic institutions. Olivier Duhamel, the president of Sciences Po and one of the country's most distinguished political analysts, said that the Grand National Debate served a unique purpose in making people think long and hard about how they wanted to be governed in a modern state. "Our democracies are more representative than participatory," Duhamel said. "They are not very deliberative, at least for the citizens who attribute power to their representatives every four or five years. So yes, calling on all citizens to express themselves, deliberate, and suggest solutions is unprecedented in France and elsewhere."[10]

Jean Pisani-Ferry, Macron's former adviser who was the architect of his original economic program, said that while the debates helped Macron regain his political equilibrium, they did nothing to address the economic inequities that had plagued France for the past three decades. Real household income in France had increased by 8 percent over the past decade despite the financial crisis. But most of those gains went to the rich, who expanded their wealth while the plight of the working poor grew worse because of regressive taxes that hurt their living standards. The profound conflict between metropolitan and rural France became aggravated by the collapse of twentieth-century ideologies like communism, socialism, and Gaullism, which left much of the population feeling abandoned and bereft of political allegiances. "These people in peripheral France feel alienated and want to reclaim their lost identities, which is what they were seeking with the Yellow Vest movement," Pisani-Ferry said. "We see the same phenomenon in the United States with people who voted for Trump, the rural Brits who opted for Brexit, and Italians who have turned their backs on Europe in favor of populist nationalists." He added that unless progress is achieved soon in restoring social mobility and a better future for the next generation, the protests could return with a vengeance.[11]

As the town hall meetings drew to a close and the data were being analyzed, Macron invited more than sixty intellectuals to the Élysée Palace to discuss his priorities in leading the country out of the crisis. On a Monday evening, just two days after some of the worst violence in the streets of Paris since the Yellow Vest movement erupted, Macron expressed his determination not to allow roving gangs of thugs to disrupt the healing conversation he had started. "I need you to help me carry this project forward," Macron told the group, which included historians, philosophers, sociologists, and climate change experts. "You have a responsibility to help me structure this national debate. Not all opinions have the same value; intellectuals should know more things because they've read more books."[12]

For nearly eight hours, Macron conducted a Socratic dialogue with the smartest minds in Europe over topics that included Algeria's revolution, the separation of church and state, psychiatry, the rise of a carbon-neutral economy, the social impact of in-vitro fertilization, and the finer distinctions between narrative and coagulated identity. Well past midnight, Macron finally broached the subject of what to do with the Yellow Vest movement. He said that the destructive riots were being fomented by what he called "the uninhibited language of violence and anger under the cover of anonymity" provided by social media. At what point, he asked, would it be necessary to suppress liberty to restore peace and order? As the discussion broke up close to 3:00 a.m., nobody could muster the energy to offer a definitive answer. "It was an impressive feat," remarked Philippe Aghion, an economist at the College of France and Harvard University. "We were all about to drop from exhaustion, and he was just getting better." Michel Wieviorka, an immigration specialist, thanked Macron for hosting the marathon discussion, noting dryly that "it would be hard to imagine this kind of gathering taking place in the White House!"[13]

As Macron's team of advisers pored over the data from the debates, they were struck by some points of national consensus but also apparent contradictions. It was unsurprising that many respondents complained that they paid too much tax, since France has the highest tax burden—46 percent of gross domestic product—of any developed nation. Prime Minister Édouard Philippe said that the government heard that message loud and clear. "We've got to lower taxes,"

Philippe said. "There is an immense fiscal exasperation." Yet many French citizens also demanded more public services and wanted Paris to surrender more decision-making powers to local authorities. They also wanted to sustain expensive programs—such as universal health care, nearly free education, and early retirement at age sixty-two— that impose a huge burden on government finances. An overwhelming majority of French people said that they regarded climate change as an urgent problem that needed to be addressed by the government, yet 58 percent said that they would not be willing to pay a carbon tax to encourage a cleaner environment. Another conclusion that emerged from the data was that many people in the French countryside felt abandoned by their government and wanted to see public officials respond more efficiently to their needs. On the volatile issue of immigrants, French citizens were almost equally divided in their views about whether the country should welcome them or adopt a tougher attitude about deporting them.

The contradictory findings of the Grand National Debate came as no surprise to Macron. As a presidential candidate in 2017, his upstart movement conducted a massive door-to-door survey of thousands of French households in what they called La Grande Marche. That polling produced similar results. The French wanted to have it all: lower taxes, better social services, and greater purchasing power. Macron promised during the campaign to act on their grievances once he became president. He vowed to stay in close and regular touch with local communities in order to tap into their thinking. But once in office, Macron became consumed with daily presidential duties and lost sight of his commitments to stay connected to regular citizens and to govern in a more responsive manner than his predecessors. As a result, the disappointment felt by those who had placed their faith in a neophyte politician who shattered the traditional ruling establishment only hardened cynicism toward Macron and his government.

The resounding success of the Grand National Debate showed that the French people were willing to give Macron a second chance.

According to a Harris poll, more than eight out of ten respondents expressed a positive view about the debates for giving citizens an opportunity to express their views on how they wanted to be governed. Yet the debates themselves were skewed by the background of the participants. Another survey, conducted by Sciences Po's research center, of the social and demographic background of those who attended the debates showed that 65 percent of participants were well educated and 75 percent were homeowners. More than two-thirds of the participants were over fifty years old, many were elderly retirees with time on their hands, and only 5 percent were under the age of twenty-five. Indeed, 70 percent of French people under the age of thirty—many of them frustrated by their inability to find long-term employment—continued to express disenchantment with Macron's leadership despite his youthful and energetic image.[14]

Macron realized that he could not afford to disappoint public expectations for dramatic reforms in the wake of the Grand National Debate. After a team of more than one hundred technical experts sifted through the accumulated data with the help of high-powered computers, Macron and his top aides meticulously prepared several initiatives to be unveiled in a nationally televised speech. Macron and his aides knew that the measures had to be sufficiently impressive to justify the enormous amount of time and effort expended in organizing the nationwide discussions. They struggled to coordinate the stupefying amount of data and innumerable suggestions and opinions that had been collected. Macron knew that the government's response to the national debate might represent the last opportunity to inflict a knockout blow against the Yellow Vest movement. A botched rollout might ignite another round of protests that could imperil Macron's presidency. The timing of the broadcast, to be carried by France's major radio and television channels, was set for 8:00 p.m. on Monday, April 15—exactly three months to the day following the launch of the Great National Debate.

It was the speech of his lifetime, and Macron agonized over every word and cadence. A respected staging director, Jérôme Revon, was brought in to orchestrate the setting. For several days, Macron consulted with top ministers in his government over the scope of the actions that he would soon announce. The proposals included a significant reduction in the number of legislators in the National Assembly to satisfy those who complained about the bloated size of the governing class. He would halt any further closures of schools and hospitals until the end of his presidential term in 2022. School classrooms would be limited to no more than twenty-four students. He would declare a further round of tax cuts to improve the purchasing power of the working poor, dole out special subsidies for widows and single mothers, and prod enterprises to dispense bonus payments up to 1,000 euros per employee to spur the economy. In a significant concession to the Yellow Vest protesters, he would review his decision to eliminate the "wealth tax" in order to determine whether the promised windfall in investments had materialized. Finally, in a bow to critics of France's ossified power structure, he would propose abolishing the National School of Administration, which had served for decades as the training ground for France's ruling elite, including Macron himself.

The twenty-six-minute address was recorded late in the afternoon. Those who witnessed the taping said that it was a powerful and compelling performance. But it would never be seen by the French public. Around 7:00 p.m., Macron was informed that Notre Dame Cathedral, the majestic 850-year-old Gothic church that many Parisians consider the soul of their capital, was in flames. Soon the devastating nature of the fire would become evident when the famous spire and the wood-timbered roof began to collapse. Twenty minutes before the president's speech was set to go on the air, the Élysée announced that it would be canceled because of the terrible tragedy afflicting the beloved landmark, which attracts thirteen million visitors a year. Initially, there were fears that the fire could have been an act of terrorism. Experts concluded, however, that it was most likely accidentally ignited by an electrical malfunction as a result of ongoing renovation efforts. But any relief over the cause did nothing to mitigate the magnitude of the loss. An entire nation and the world at large were plunged into a state of grief and anxiety over the fate of Our Lady of Paris. Once firefighters gained control of the blaze shortly before midnight, Macron was taken to the cathedral to inspect the damage. "Notre Dame is the place where we have lived all our great moments, epidemics, wars, and liberation," he said, on the brink of tears. "It is the epicenter of our lives and the point from which we measure distance from Paris. This history, it is ours and it is burning." Macron vowed that he would mobilize the nation and the world, including the best architects and engineers to be found, to rebuild the cathedral within five years—in time for the 2024 Olympics scheduled for Paris.[15]

The next evening Macron went on television to address the nation about the significance of Notre Dame and its place at the heart of French history. The cathedral had survived the wars of religion, the revolution, two world wars, and the Nazi occupation. It was also where Napoleon was crowned emperor in 1804 and where the founder of the modern French republic, Charles de Gaulle, was memorialized after his death.[16] "The fire at Notre Dame reminds us that history doesn't stop and that we always have trials to overcome," Macron said, looking solemn in a dark blue suit, seated behind his desk adorned with the flags of France and the European Union. "We are a nation of builders, and we have so much to rebuild."

The president urged the French people to show resilience in the face of the tragedy, and he drew a parallel between the cathedral fire and the political tribulations that France had endured over the past five months. "I profoundly believe that it is up to us to transform this catastrophe into an opportunity to come together and think about what we were and what we need to become, to improve ourselves," Macron said, referring to the deep political divisions that he sought to heal with the Grand National Debate. He set aside the proposals that he had planned to make public at the conclusion of the nationwide consultations conducted over the previous months. "I will get back to you as I promised in the coming days so we can collectively act together after the Great Debate, but now is not the time," the president said.[17]

Within days, the reconstruction of Notre Dame became a popular noble crusade that seemed, at least for a short while, to unify the country. Some of France's richest families, including business titans Bernard Arnault and François-Henri Pinault, stepped forward with pledges to donate hundreds of millions of euros to the project. Those acts of philanthropy soon stirred up the political and class animosities that continued to plague France. As protesters took to the streets for the twenty-third consecutive weekend of Yellow Vest demonstrations, some of them denounced the hypocrisy of elites who offered to raise large sums of money to rebuild the cathedral while allowing France's working poor to suffer. "If they are able to give tens of millions to rebuild Notre Dame, then they should stop saying that there isn't any money to address social emergencies," said Philippe Martinez, the head of CGT, France's largest union. Some marchers carried banners that read, WE ARE ALL CATHEDRALS and NOTRE DAME, BUT NOT US, as they walked from the Place de la Bastille to the Place de la République. Security forces blocked their access to the Champs-Élysées and major tourist destinations. Critics accused the billionaire moguls of soliciting tax benefits for their contributions to the Notre Dame fund, which they denied. "This is a false controversy," said Arnault, who heads the LVMH Louis Vuitton–Moët Hennessy luxury goods conglomerate. "It's quite concerning to see that in France you are criticized even when you do something that is clearly in the public interest."[18]

The immediate shock of the Notre Dame fire overshadowed the protests by the Yellow Vest movement. The magnitude of the disaster made complaints about reconstruction pledges by wealthy donors, which soon topped one billion euros, seem petty. Macron's show of deference to the tragedy in canceling his address about the Grand National Debate and his emotional late-night remarks in front of the smoldering cathedral struck the proper tone and cast him in a presidential light. For once, his political instincts were right on the mark. In contrast, the Yellow Vest movement continued to hemor-rhage supporters. Some of its founding voices would soon abandon the cause out of frustration with its rudderless lack of direction and a grudging realization that Macron's initiatives had drained the pro-tests of any purpose or meaning. "The movement has lost its essence," observed Jacline Mouraud, the hypnotherapist from Brittany whose YouTube polemic accusing Macron of ignoring the plight of rural commuters helped ignite the protests. "All that is left is the confetti on the streets."[19]

Ten days after the Notre Dame fire, Macron felt the timing was appropriate to announce the new measures he planned to take in re-sponse to the consultations held during the Grand National Debate. For the first time in his presidency, he convened a press conference and invited more than three hundred journalists to the Salle des Fêtes at the Élysée Palace. Throughout his first two years in office, he had maintained a distant and uneasy relationship with the French media. He often complained that journalists were too quick to pounce on his mistakes rather than show more tolerance and understanding for the difficulties of governing. On this occasion, he displayed a new sense of humility as he spoke for an hour about his impressions from public encounters during road trips across France. "I've learned a lot about this country," Macron explained. "This period has changed me. Our democracy has been called into question. I want the French people to know that I felt in my flesh their anger, what they were saying and expressing. We haven't always put the human at the heart of our project. I have at times conveyed the feeling of always giv-ing orders, of being unfair. One can always do better. I think I can do better, too." He vowed that during the second phase of his presi-dential term he would demonstrate "a profound reorientation of the philosophy I believe in, one that is more human, more humanist."[20] When asked about the personal vitriol directed against him during the protests, Macron acknowledged his share of the blame for mak-ing remarks that portrayed him as arrogant and uncaring about the working poor. "I certainly contributed to it," he said. "This period has changed me. It has increased the feeling of responsibility that I have. But have we gone in the wrong direction? I don't think so."

Macron then proceeded to tick off all the measures he planned to carry out in response to the protests. He emphasized that more powers would be delegated to local communities and that civil servants in Paris would be relocated to the hinterlands. "There are too many people in Paris making decisions without knowing what the situation is like on the ground," he said. "We need a profound reorganization of our government so that more decisions are taken in the regions." He promised to increase pension payments and reduce taxes for the middle classes by five billion euros, in addition to the ten billion euros in tax relief and wage benefits he had offered in December. To pay for the tax cuts, Macron said that he would crack down on tax evasion and shut loopholes that enabled large multinational corporations, especially American technology giants like Facebook, Apple, and Google, to escape paying taxes in France despite their enormous revenues. He refused to retract his decision to eliminate the wealth tax; he wanted to determine, he said, whether new investments were being generated. But he acknowledged that protesters had a point when they claimed that a "profound sense of fiscal, financial, and social injustice" pervaded the country, and especially in the provinces. Although he did not dare to revoke the sacrosanct thirty-five-hour workweek, Macron exhorted the French people to work harder and to work beyond the official retirement age of sixty-two if they wanted to enjoy greater prosperity. He compared France unfavorably in that regard with its neighbors, particularly Germany. "We need to work more," he said, briefly relapsing into a hectoring tone. "The difference in the creation of wealth is tied to the fact that we work less."[21]

Macron declared that after two years of pushing through key economic reforms, he would concentrate on issues of social justice and the environment. He vowed to do everything possible to bring greater diversity into the ranks of France's political and economic elites by improving educational opportunities for the underprivileged.

"We have a system that already shares wealth better than in most countries," he said. "The true inequalities in our society are those of origins, and not of destiny." He also stressed the importance of pushing ahead with France's "ecological transition" in response to the challenge of climate change. Even though the Yellow Vest movement was inspired by a national carbon tax that many protesters felt put an unjust burden on rural communities, Macron told French citizens that "the climate must be at the heart of the national and the European project." He announced the creation of an "ecological defense council" of 250 people to be selected by lottery. Those members would be responsible for evaluating and promoting a new national strategy. The council initiative reflected Macron's desire to recruit more outsiders into governing institutions in order to broaden citizen participation in French democracy. He also promised to streamline the bloated civil service, which employed one in five French workers, and to shrink the number of professional politicians by imposing term limits and reducing the size of Parliament by 30 percent.

Despite six months of violent protests that jeopardized his presidency and paralyzed much of the French nation, Macron insisted that he would not be deterred from his reformist agenda. He was convinced that radical change was necessary and not just a frivolous option. And in fact, after his first two years in office, Macron's reforms were finally starting to show signs of gaining traction and improving the French economy. Unemployment dropped to a ten-year low, though it remained double the rate in Germany and Macron was still not satisfied. He told me that he was determined to carry out his blueprint to modernize France, despite the risk of igniting further protests. He was elected on a mandate to institute substantial reforms in the way the country was run. If a majority of French citizens were now opposed to his program, he added, they could vote him out of office in 2022.

But the Yellow Vest protests had clearly left their mark. Even as calm was restored across France, the president swore never again to take public opinion for granted. He acknowledged that the torrential

rage and frustration directed at him were still lingering in much of
the country. "We still face profound problems linked to social injustice, to economic difficulties, and to future challenges related to
the aging of our population, the rise of a digital society and to the
ecology," Macron observed as he embarked on his summer break at
the presidential retreat at Fort de Brégançon on the Mediterranean
coast. "I think these problems create fears that are too easily exploited
and we will need to respond with determination and humility," he
said. "Above all, I know the sincere anger we experienced coming
from parts of the population is not behind us." He urged his government to remain vigilant about the public mood and to carry out
his reform program with persistence and diligence. At a final cabinet
meeting just before the August summer recess, Macron told his ministers, "You should be leaving for vacation with a sense of fear in your
belly. You know, we live in an age where we will not be spared from
anything. Just keep that in mind."[22]

Macron professes to be unconcerned about remaining in office
for a second term. He would like to stay in office to carry out the
political and economic transformation that he has already started.
But he insists that he is not wedded to politics because it was never
his first calling. He told me that he writes every day and has always
aspired to become a literary figure in the great French tradition of
Gide and Stendhal. As a teenager, he wrote a phantasmagorical novel
about South America that he has kept hidden from the public, showing it only to Brigitte and a few close friends. During a trip to Argentina for the G-20 summit as the Yellow Vest protests were erupting,
he broke away from the diplomatic gathering to meet with a group of
Argentine writers at the popular bookshop El Ateneo in Buenos Aires. He discussed with them the "infinite and inexhaustible" sources
of imagination in Latin American literature and promised to help
publish the personal diary of the Argentine author Jorge Luis Borges
in France. Then he returned to the grind of the G-20 summit, calling
his brief excursion "an enchanted break" from the drudgery of international diplomacy. "Once I will be done with all that, I will come

back to the truth," he told the writers as he bade them farewell. "But I don't know when that will be."[23]

Macron's political ambitions have always extended beyond France. He ran for the presidency convinced that he could restore his nation's grandeur only as part of a larger crusade to fortify Europe as a global power that could compete on the same level as the United States, China, and Russia. In Macron's perspective, France and Europe should inspire the rest of the world by serving as the contemporary incarnation of the Enlightenment and its ideals. Europe's emergence as a postmodernist force that cherishes peace, Macron believes, carries influence because the continent has learned painful lessons from two world wars in the past century. Europe's primary goal should be to prevent similar catastrophes from happening elsewhere in the future. In his first months in office, Macron had spelled out a bold and ambitious vision for a more integrated continent. He believed that his plan was the most effective way to defeat reactionary nationalists who threatened to blow apart the European Union. But the Yellow Vest crisis badly damaged Macron's credibility with his peers. The violent protests on the streets of Paris contributed to Angela Merkel's reluctance to support him and reinforced German prejudices that France was unreformable, if not ungovernable. Other leaders felt that Macron's vision was utopian and even dangerous. "I am not made to lead in calm weather," Macron told the French novelist Emmanuel Carrère. "I'm made for storms. If you want to take a country somewhere, you have to advance at all costs. You can't succumb, you can't fall into a routine."[24]

Macron saw the twin missions of reviving France and strengthening the EU as inextricably linked. If one failed, it could bring down the other, with potentially grievous consequences. Macron understood the stakes more clearly than any other leader, even though he was young enough to have no memories of World War II and to be unable to recall very much about the Cold War era. "I am part of a generation that has never experienced war and allows itself the luxury of forgetting the experiences of our ancestors," Macron declared in an impassioned defense of liberal democracy before the European Parliament. "I don't want to belong to a generation of sleepwalkers that ignores its own past and refuses to face up to the problems of the present. In the face of the authoritarianism which surrounds us, the answer must not be authoritarian democracy but the authority of democracy. The worst possible mistake would be to give up on our model and our identity."[25] Europe, he feared, was heading into a new kind of civil war. And its closest expression was right across France's southeastern frontier.

PART TWO

EUROPE

CHAPTER 4

THE POPULIST MENACE

A s the operatic aria *"Nessun dorma"* (None shall sleep) from Puccini's *Turandot* wafted over the heads of ten thousand people gathered in Milan's cathedral square, Italy's deputy prime minister Matteo Salvini climbed to the stage on a soggy Saturday in May along with ten other right-wing nationalist leaders from every corner of Europe. Riding high in opinion polls as Italy's powerful interior minister and its most influential politician, Salvini convened the gathering just days ahead of European Parliament elections to celebrate a populist alliance that he said would "protect European civilization" from being overrun by illegal immigrants and radical Islamists. One by one, xenophobic politicians railed against Emmanuel Macron for defending open borders and the idea of a European superstate. Under Salvini's orchestration, they endorsed his pan-European coalition behind the slogan "Towards a Common Sense Europe: Peoples Rise Up." Anti-EU nationalists such as Marine Le Pen of France and Geert Wilders of the Netherlands took turns shrilly denouncing the surrender of national sovereignty to faceless and feckless bureaucrats in Brussels.

As Salvini stepped forward to speak, the vast Piazza del Duomo resonated with chants of "Matteo! Matteo!" and "Il Capitano!" He vowed to transform the European Union and restore greater control to national capitals by liberating the continent from "the illegal occupation organized by Brussels." Quoting the British writer G. K. Chesterton, Salvini declared that "the true soldier fights not because he hates what is in front of him but because he loves what is behind him." He claimed that his international coalition of nationalists was driven by the honorable motive of building a better destiny for future generations in Europe. "There are no extremists, racists or fascists in this square," he said. "We want to remake Europe not for our sake but for our children. The real extremists are those who have governed Europe for twenty years in the name of poverty and precariousness."[1] As he clutched a rosary and invoked Europe's patron saints while gazing at a statue of the Virgin Mary atop the cathedral, the weather suddenly improved and the crowd folded up their umbrellas. "Look, we even made the rain stop," Salvini said, adding that the clearing skies were an auspicious omen for his cause.

When Macron won the French presidency by thrashing Marine Le Pen in the second round of voting in May 2017, his victory was greeted with relief in many capitals and seen as an encouraging sign of voter repugnance toward populist forces. Yet in the wake of Macron's triumph, the appeal of antidemocratic, illiberal, and anti-European policies became more visible across the continent. Austria's Freedom Party entered government as part of a center-right coalition and took control, for a while, of the Interior Ministry. Poland's Law and Justice Party solidified its grip on power by cracking down on dissent. Hungary's prime minister Viktor Orbán won reelection on an anti-immigrant platform. Germany's far-right Alternative for Germany (AfD) Party emerged as the strongest opposition force in the Bundestag. And Boris Johnson, a leading Euroskeptic and EU antagonist, succeeded Theresa May as Britain's prime minister.

Far-right parties secured a foothold in twenty-three out of twenty-eight legislatures across Europe. But perhaps no other manifestation of growing nationalism in Europe matched the remarkable ascendancy of Salvini, who became almost overnight the dominant figure in Italian politics and the most galvanizing personality among pan-European populists. *Time* magazine described him as "the most feared man in Europe."[2] Soon after becoming deputy prime minister and interior minister, he vowed to expel one hundred thousand migrants during his first term in office and declared that for illegal aliens, *"la pacchia è finita"* (the party's over).

Salvini took the once-dormant Northern League Party—which started as a separatist movement in northern Italy before adopting an anti-immigrant and anti-Europe platform—from 4 percent in national elections held in 2013 to 18 percent in the 2018 vote that catapulted him to power. A year later, his party won 34 percent of the vote in European elections and picked up an unprecedented twenty-three seats in the European Parliament. Within Italy, Salvini's soaring popularity propelled his party to become the strongest political force in the country, according to opinion polls. His rapid trajectory led many Italian commentators to predict that he would soon become prime minister, a position that would give him a place at the table of G-7 nations as the leader of a founding member of the European Union and the world's sixth-largest economy. But Salvini overplayed his hand. He tried to provoke early elections by pulling out of the government in August 2019, but the ruling Five Star Movement sealed a new coalition with the center-left Democrats, leaving Salvini's party stranded in the opposition. Nonetheless, Salvini has maintained his standing as the nation's most popular politician, and many commentators believe that it is only a matter of time before he seizes another opportunity to regain power, perhaps as prime minister of a government that espouses his xenophobic and anti-EU policies.

A former talk radio host and master communicator on social media, Salvini still hopes to use his compelling personality to bridge significant differences among Europe's far-right parties. He is seeking to consolidate a continent-wide rightist movement that will fortify external borders, send immigrants back to their native lands, restore greater sovereignty to national capitals, and bury the dream of a "United States of Europe." Orbán, who calls Salvini "my hero and my comrade in destiny," claims that all of Europe's far-right parties are aligned in their singular disdain for Macron and his vision of a liberal, democratic, and more unified Europe. "There are two camps in Europe," Orbán said after seeing Salvini in Milan for one of their regular strategy sessions. "One is headed by Macron. He is at the head of the political forces supporting immigration. On the other hand, we all want to stop illegal immigration."[3]

There had been earlier suggestions that Salvini and his allies would seek to drop out of Europe's single currency or leave the European Union altogether once they gained power, but they have abandoned these positions in order to broaden the far right's appeal. The chaos surrounding Britain's efforts to negotiate its departure from the EU has inoculated much of the continent against following London out of the Union. Now the course advocated by Salvini, Le Pen, and other right-wing leaders focuses on transforming EU institutions from within and restoring more decision-making powers to national capitals. In the aftermath of the Brexit vote, public support for the European Union has risen to record levels in many continental nations. At the same time, there is widespread discontent with the way Europe is being managed. A May 2018 survey of more than twenty-seven thousand people conducted by the European Parliament found that support for the Union had risen in twenty-six out of twenty-eight member states. More Europeans than ever—about two-thirds of those polled—said that they favored EU membership. But a larger number of respondents (42 percent) thought that Europe was heading in the wrong direction rather than in the right direction (32 percent). Among young people under the age of twenty-four, there was strong dismay with the status quo; 63 percent said that "new political parties and movements can find better solutions than existing ruling parties."[4]

Indeed, other studies have shown that young people in Europe and America are losing faith in Western democratic institutions. Some millennials are disillusioned because they are confronting an economic outlook bleaker perhaps than any other postwar generation has faced. According to research by Yascha Mounk of Harvard University and Roberto Stefan Foa of the University of Melbourne in Australia, younger generations in traditional democracies are much less likely to consider it "essential" to live in a democracy than earlier cohorts. They also seem more attracted to authoritarian values than has been true of young people at any time in the past seventy years. A larger share of them than ever before openly reject democratic institutions. Only 19 percent of young Americans and 36 percent of young Europeans believe that a military takeover of their government would be illegitimate. One-quarter of millennials think that "choosing leaders through free elections [is] unimportant." These findings may reflect disenchantment with mainstream ruling parties and the pernicious effects on young people of the worst financial crisis since the 1930s, which are still particularly acute in Southern Europe. As public attitudes have soured on democracy, voters have grown more susceptible to the siren calls of extremist or nationalist parties that they would have shunned in the past.[5]

Macron is deeply troubled by these trends. He fears that the peace and prosperity maintained throughout the Western world for three generations are in danger. Beyond young people's mounting frustration with dysfunctional or corrupt government, he thinks that they have become too complacent about democracy. More than any other leader, Macron has welcomed the challenge of pitting his vision of an open, globalist Europe against Salvini's insular brand of populist nationalism. Both men, still in their forties, represent a new generation of leaders who rose to power in two of Europe's largest nations without having ever been elected to political office. They share the conviction that Europe's past ideological conflicts between conservative capitalists and progressive socialists are now obsolete. Both have succeeded in demolishing mainstream ruling parties in their countries and now want to elevate their personal ambitions to a European level. But their political visions could not be further apart. Salvini told his crowd of supporters in Milan that Macron belongs to a group of failed elites—who include, he said, German chancellor Angela Merkel and the financier George Soros—who have "betrayed the continent in the name of banks, multinational companies and uncontrolled immigration."[6]

Macron is equally uncompromising. He insists that Europe stands in the vanguard of an epochal struggle to defend Western democratic values against the forces of intolerance, authoritarianism, nationalism, and scorn for the rule of international law. He is convinced that this political battleground will shape the destiny of Europe for at least the next generation. "You can see them rise like leprosy more or less everywhere across Europe, in countries where we thought it would be impossible to see it again, in neighboring countries," Macron said, referring to nationalists on a visit to Brittany, one of the most pro-European regions in France. "They are saying the worst things, and we're getting used to it. They are making provocations, and nobody is horrified by that. We need to fight back against those who hate Europe."[7] He relishes the fact that he has become the main target of the extremists and insists that he will not back down from the fight. "If they want to see me as their principal opponent, they are right," Macron said in response to verbal attacks from his foes. "I will not cede any ground to the nationalists and those who advocate their language of hate."[8]

The animosity between Macron and Salvini and his far-right allies, including Orbán and Le Pen, is deeply personal as well as political. They openly disdain each other and do not mask their conviction that they are engaged in a fateful struggle for Europe's hearts and minds. They also realize that their competing visions—Macron's globalism versus Salvini's nationalism—will define Europe's role on the world stage for the next generation. "Macron needs demons like Orbán and Salvini in order to stand out," said Philippe Lamberts, a prominent Green member of the European Parliament. "They are the best kind of enemies because they feed off one another. In bipolariz-ing the debate, they have marginalized those who do not belong to either side."[9] Ever since Salvini took control of the Interior Ministry as part of a populist ruling alliance with the Five Star Movement, he and Macron have clashed over how Europe should deal with waves of illegal immigrants crossing the Mediterranean Sea. Italy's previ-ous center-left governments presided over the rescue of more than six hundred thousand migrants over three years. Salvini rose to power on the promise that he would put a stop to the flow of asylum-seekers. When the *Aquarius*, a ship run by a French charity carrying 629 mi-grants, was rescued at sea shortly after Salvini took office, he refused to allow it access to Italian ports, leaving the ship stranded in limbo between Sicily and Malta.

The *Aquarius* controversy became the first major conflict be-tween Macron and Salvini. The French president denounced the ac-tion as "cynical and irresponsible" and a violation of international maritime law. His government spokesman called Italy's behavior nothing short of "nauseating." Macron declared that "if French coasts were the nearest shores for a boat in distress, it would be able to dock." That claim infuriated the Italian government, which ac-cused Macron of hypocrisy because France had refused on several occasions to accept the migrants rescued at sea, even when they were transported by a ship operated by a French charity. Italy felt particu-larly aggrieved because it had spent close to $5 billion, it claimed, in dealing with its refugee crisis, yet had received only $77 million in aid from European Union partners. Rome also complained that Ma-cron's government had adopted a more intrusive approach in policing its frontiers and had made forays into Italian territory. The stalemate in the *Aquarius* controversy was finally defused when Pedro Sán-chez, Spain's Socialist prime minister, agreed to give the migrants refuge in the port of Valencia.[10] France's refusal to take the refugees reflected Macron's own political turn toward the right on immigra-tion issues. He has tried to expand the reach of his party among conservative voters by taking a tougher stance against the influx of illegal immigrants, even at the risk of leaving himself vulnerable to criticism from those supporters who feel he has betrayed his liberal principles.

Salvini's hardball tactics in shutting down Italian ports to illegal migrants rescued at sea clearly paid political dividends. The number of immigrants coming into Italy dropped dramatically: in the first half of 2019, only 2,700 migrants entered Italy by sea, compared to 17,000 for the same period in 2018, according to Italy's Interior Ministry. The fact that Salvini's tough approach was extremely popular with much of the Italian public only encouraged him to become more aggressive in his attacks against Macron and other liberal foes in Europe. In the wake of the *Aquarius* incident, Salvini pressed his argument about Macron's two-faced attitude on illegal immigrants: if Macron wanted to prove his humanitarian decency, Salvini said, he should make good on France's unkept promises to feed and shelter some of the hundreds of thousands of immigrants who entered Europe through Italy. He disparaged the French president's attacks against him as the misguided comments of "a polite young man who drinks too much champagne. We won't take lessons from him."[11] Yet he shrugged off the notion that he was engaged in a personal vendetta. "Macron is not a problem for me," he told *Politico*. "Macron is a problem for the French people." The following month, when France faced Croatia in the 2018 World Cup soccer finals in Moscow, Salvini flew to Russia to attend the match as President Putin's special guest. He described his trip to Moscow as a "politico-sports mission" designed to wish "bad luck to France." After France won, Salvini left the stadium in a huff before the awards ceremony, according to Russian media reports.

Some political allies have urged Macron to stop personalizing the conflict with Salvini. "It is a mistake to have a Europeanist versus populist cleavage for those pushing for Europe," said Enrico Letta, a former center-left Italian prime minister who is aligned with Macron. "It is a mistake because it is absolutely necessary to split the so-called populist camp. It is a very divided camp and we help them by creating this cleavage. They are only united if they have enemies."[12] But Macron is convinced that he won a landslide victory in the French presidential runoff by emphasizing the contrast between his platform and Le Pen's nationalism. He believes that it serves his purposes to present voters with a binary choice between an open, tolerant society and the dark, demagogic world of the nationalists and that accentuating the European debate between him and Salvini helps rally support around the liberal democratic vision for the continent.

In the months after the *Aquarius* showdown, tensions between France and Italy only grew worse. Salvini and Luigi Di Maio, the Five Star Movement leader and a coalition partner, stepped up their criticism of France's continuing refusal to accept immigrants stranded on rescue ships off Italy's shores. They insisted that their government would continue to prevent asylum-seekers from reaching Italy unless France and other EU partners offered firm assurances that they would take their fair allocation. After several months of negotiations, France, Germany, and twelve other EU countries agreed to a "solidarity mechanism" by which they promised to offer shelter to asylum-seekers rescued at sea. Salvini, who had staked much of his credibility on halting immigrant flows into Italy, welcomed the deal by tweeting, "Job done, mission accomplished."[13] But he continued to provoke Macron with his frequent critical broadsides and gloated about Macron's domestic political problems, which were caused, he said, by Macron's shortcomings as a "terrible president" and not by troubles he was having with his Italian neighbors.

Di Maio also accused France of impoverishing its former African colonies and thus indirectly contributing to the immigration crisis that Italy was facing. Macron tried to brush aside the Italian attacks, but the breaking point came when Di Maio, without notifying the French government, paid a visit to leaders of the Yellow Vest movement to show his support for their opposition to Macron. Di Maio declared that "the wind of change has crossed the Alps." He encouraged their grassroots revolt in the hope that it might cause a regime change in France similar to Italy's populist transformation.

Macron was infuriated. France's minister for European affairs, Nathalie Loiseau, declared that "playtime [was] over." Although it seemed unthinkable between two European neighbors that traditionally enjoyed a close friendship, the French government withdrew its ambassador from Rome, an action not taken by France since Mussolini declared war in 1940. "The continuing interference in French politics by members of the Italian government is unacceptable," French foreign minister Jean-Yves Le Drian said. "For several months, France has been the subject of repeated accusations, unfounded attacks and outrageous declarations that everyone knows and can recognize. This is unprecedented since the end of the war."[14]

Paolo Gentiloni, who served as Italy's previous prime minister, told me that Macron was being attacked as a convenient scapegoat for Italy's own difficulties under the awkward ruling alliance led by Salvini and Di Maio. "One of the consequences of national populism is to try and find enemies," Gentiloni said. "The only way that the populists can maintain a consensus, especially in a coalition government, is to keep finding enemies inside and outside your own country."[15] Salvini eventually sought to defuse the dispute, saying, "We do not want to fight with anyone." He offered to meet with Macron to settle their differences. But the French president ignored his appeal and instead met with Italy's head of state, Sergio Mattarella, to resolve the crisis. Both presidents concurred that the long-standing partnership between Italy and France needed to be "preserved and defended." France agreed to send its ambassador back to Rome, and Macron and Mattarella sealed the truce with the commemoration of the five-hundredth anniversary of the death of Leonardo da Vinci. The great Italian Renaissance artist spent his final years in France, and as a result, many of his paintings ended up in the Louvre Museum in Paris.

Macron later went on Italian state television to profess his affection for Italy. He sought to dismiss the conflict as nothing more than "a misunderstanding." But the sharp differences over how to deal with illegal immigrants that sparked the French-Italian crisis show no signs of disappearing. The prospect that climate change and instability in Africa and the Middle East will encourage further waves of unwanted immigrants fleeing toward Europe is likely to drive political debate on the continent for years to come. A World Bank report predicts that climate change alone will force more than 140 million people to migrate over the next three decades.[16]

The *Aquarius* case highlighted the inequities in Europe's asylum policy under the so-called Dublin Regulation, which calls for refugees to be held and processed at their point of entry into the European Union. That regulation is widely regarded as unfair and dysfunctional because it has imposed enormous burdens on Italy and Greece, which since 2015 have been compelled to accept hundreds of thousands of migrants fleeing civil wars in Syria, Libya, and Africa. Efforts to share the burden by requiring other EU member states to accept their share of refugees under a quota system have been blocked by Hungary, Poland, and other Eastern members who remain adamantly opposed to taking in immigrants, especially Muslims. Even though the tide of immigrants has greatly diminished since its apogee in 2015–2016, when more than two million asylum-seekers poured into Europe, the issue remains highly volatile and clearly influences the choices of European voters. The European Parliament elections in May 2019 resulted in significant gains for far-right parties that campaigned on the need for stronger border controls, among them the National Rally Party (formerly known as the National Front) of Marine Le Pen, which came in first in France with 23.5 percent of the vote, just ahead of Macron's political movement, which was rebranded for the election as Renew Europe.

Even though Macron's party did better than expected, the French president recognized that allowing the far right to dominate the immigration issue could lead to deterioration in public support for his pro-Europe forces. He declared that the time had come to overhaul the Schengen Agreement, a treaty that abolished passport controls and ensured free flows of people among twenty-six European states. "It's not working anymore," Macron told journalists at his first press conference in April 2019. "Responsibility comes with solidarity. This is the basis on which Schengen should be reformed, even if it means having fewer states who participate." He suggested that those states that refused to abide by the EU's migrant quota system, such as Hungary and Poland, should no longer be part of the border-free zone. But since EU treaty changes required unanimity, Macron's reform proposals seemed likely to go nowhere.

When Macron's party and the Greens did well in the European elections, the resilience of liberal pro-European forces was affirmed, but only in some respects. The results also showed enduring support for populist nationalist themes, particularly the reluctance to accept more immigrants and the need to affirm Europe's cultural identity. Even centrist pro-Europe leaders, including Macron and Merkel, have since tailored their policies and now seek to woo right-wing voters. France and Germany have adopted tougher measures against uncontrolled immigration and cracked down on Islamist activists who seek to change the secular nature of European society. Macron argues that such hardheaded pragmatism does not reflect capitulation to the nationalists but rather a political imperative to restore faith in the European Union by tacking to the demands of voters, even if doing so looks like an acceptance of populist themes.

Merkel and Macron have demonstrated a new willingness to accelerate the deportation of illegal immigrants and those foreigners whose requests for political asylum have been rejected. In his 2018 New Year's address to the French people, Macron promised that forced expulsions of illegal immigrants would be increased. Soon the number of deportations from France rose by 10 percent, to more than fifteen thousand. "We can't take in everybody," Macron declared. "There must be rules. It's indispensable that we check the identities of everyone. When someone arrives in our country who is not eligible for asylum and has no chance of getting French citizenship, we can't accept that they stay for months or years in an irregular situation that is good neither for them nor our country."[17]

On his trips to France's former colonies in Africa, Macron has delivered a similar message to dissuade young Africans from trying to enter France through illicit trafficking networks crossing the Mediterranean Sea. In a meeting with students at the University of Ouagadougou in Burkina Faso in November 2017, Macron confronted a barrage of questions about why France was reluctant to offer easier access at a time when Europe's population was shrinking and job openings were left vacant. The new French president gave a blunt response that could have come from Salvini, Le Pen, or any other populist leader. "I can't tell my middle classes who work, who pay taxes, that it's great, we're going to welcome everybody into the country," Macron said. "That's just ridiculous. Who's going to pay for that? You'll just fuel racism and xenophobia. Totally open borders do not exist, because it just does not work."[18]

Other centrist leaders in Europe have taken similarly expedient measures in order to block extremist parties from gaining power. In the Netherlands, once regarded as a bastion of sympathy for the cause of a United States of Europe, the center-right government pushed through a resolution calling for a halt to further efforts at European integration. "The Netherlands has moved to more Euroskeptic territory," said Catherine De Vries, a political scientist at Amsterdam's Free University. "We now see the EU in terms of economic and not political cooperation. We've become what the Brits used to be."[19]

Macron's own shift toward the right in cracking down on asylum-seekers and escalating the number of deportations from France drew criticism from his liberal allies, who claimed that he was betraying his own values. He told me that he had wrestled with such seeming contradictions during his first two years in office and confessed that he found it difficult to reconcile certain inconsistencies between his principles and his politics. A politician must sometimes make short-term adjustments, he had concluded, in order to achieve his long-term strategic vision, and he cited the French phrase *reculer pour mieux sauter* (taking a strategic step backward before leaping ahead). Macron rejected the view that embracing stronger immigration controls and a slower pace on European integration disavowed his liberal pro-European principles. He insisted that a successful politician must be highly pragmatic and willing to modify his political views in response to voter wishes. If some European policies are not working properly, he said, then they should be changed in order to save the project as a whole.[20]

Macron also believes that such tactics can exploit serious divisions on the right and thus weaken the appeal of populist nationalists. While Le Pen's National Rally Party in France is strongly protectionist, its German and Scandinavian partners are avowed supporters of free and open markets. Salvini wants other European states to take their fair share of immigrants who enter Europe through Italy, but his allies in Hungary and Poland want to bar any of them from entering their countries. Salvini's former coalition partner Di Maio says that he found Salvini's efforts to build an alliance with those who refuse to accept a redistribution of migrants arriving in Italy "paradoxical." Russia is an even more contentious issue among Europe's far-right parties. Poland's Law and Justice Party, backed by its right-wing partners in Denmark and Estonia, remains adamant about maintaining economic sanctions against Russia, which were imposed in the wake of Russia's 2014 annexation of Crimea. But Salvini, Le Pen, and Austria's Freedom Party want to drop the sanctions and restore lucrative trade relations with Putin's Russia.

The Russia connection has become particularly sensitive because of corruption allegations that have swirled around several of Europe's right-wing parties. The charge of taking Russian money has undermined claims by Europe's populist nationalists that they are righteous defenders of the common people against corrupt elites at the top of the traditional ruling parties. During the French presidential election campaign, Le Pen traveled to Moscow to meet with Putin and was later awarded a $12 million loan from an obscure Russian bank. In early 2019, Markus Frohnmaier, a prominent member of Germany's far-right AfD Party, was reported by German intelligence to be among a half-dozen Bundestag deputies so closely engaged through business activities and connections with the Kremlin that they were believed to be under Moscow's "absolute control." In May 2019, Heinz-Christian Strache, the leader of Austria's Freedom Party and one of Salvini's closest allies, was forced to resign as vice-chancellor after a video showed him offering government contracts to a woman posing as the niece of a Russian oligarch in return for political funding. The scandal resulted in the collapse of the center-right ruling coalition led by Sebastian Kurz, the leader of Austria's People's Party.

Shortly after the Strache controversy, Salvini was implicated in allegations that his party sought covert financing from Moscow ahead of the European elections. According to BuzzFeed, a close adviser to Salvini hatched a plan with Russian businessmen at a hotel in Moscow in October 2018 that would channel money to Italy's Northern League Party through a complicated oil deal. Under the clandestine arrangement, fuel would be sold at a discount to an Italian oil firm by a Russian company through intermediaries. The difference with the world market price, estimated at about $65 million, would be diverted to the Northern League.[21] Italian magistrates in Milan soon opened an investigation into the allegations. If proven, the scheme would breach Italian electoral law, which bans political parties from accepting foreign donations.

Salvini has denied receiving any money from Moscow for himself or his party. "I have never taken a ruble, a euro, a dollar, or a liter of vodka in funding from Russia," he said. Nonetheless, his deep admiration for Putin and his frequent visits to Moscow have attracted much speculation. Salvini has praised Putin as "one of those characters who will leave his mark on history." He also has been a tireless advocate for lifting Western nations' economic sanctions against Russia. He claims that Italian businesses are losing billions of dollars every year in potential export sales to Russia. Putin himself, during a visit to Rome in July 2019, welcomed Salvini's efforts to remove the sanctions. He also remarked that the Northern League and his United Russia Party have grown close and remain "in constant contact" after signing a cooperation pact in March 2017.

Russia's contacts in Italy and in other European countries have not been confined to the far right. Under Putin, Russia has sought to exploit Europe's political divisions by engaging with a wide range of political movements, including radical leftists, regional and linguistic separatists, and anti-establishment groups. Moscow has also made

common cause with the European business community, especially
in Germany and Italy, which strongly supports the effort to remove
sanctions and revive commercial arrangements with Russia, which
were once highly profitable. Having an even greater impact than
money have been waves of pro-Russian propaganda and "fake news"
on social media outlets, which have disrupted political discourse and
election campaigns across Europe, including recent voting for the
European Parliament. But in contrast to the Cold War era, when
Moscow supported communists and leftist movements across Western Europe, Kremlin propagandists now lavish most of their attention on populist nationalists. "There is a conspiracy of all the radical
right-wing nationalists everywhere, apparently with the help of the
Kremlin, or of oligarchs around the Kremlin, to disrupt this European Union," said Guy Verhofstadt, a former Belgian prime minister
and leading member of the European Parliament, on the eve of the
European elections.[22]

The axis of illiberalism that threatens to destabilize Europe's political order goes beyond Russia's links with Europe's populist nationalists and includes conservative political allies in the United States,
including President Trump and the alt-right movement led by Steve
Bannon, the president's former adviser. Bannon has raised funds
among ultra-conservative supporters in Europe and the United States
to establish an "Academy for the Judeo-Christian West"—a far-right
"gladiator school" housed in a thirteenth-century monastery not far
from Rome for the purpose of grooming future right-wing political
leaders across Europe. Bannon has run into resistance and wariness
about the potential consequences of his project among both local residents and the Italian Culture Ministry. Nonetheless, he hopes that
his close ties with Salvini, whom he consults regularly about how
to build a cohesive alliance among right-wing groups across Europe,
will help him surmount opposition to his right-wing finishing school.

Many of Europe's ultra-conservative leaders emphasize a shared
commitment to restoring the identity and values of "Christian Europe." In Hungary, Orbán has cited the need to defend his country's

Christian traditions as justification for blocking the entry of Muslim refugees from Syria and Libya. Other rightist parties believe that they are waging a culture war against liberal secular forces that defend gay marriage, feminism, and abortion rights. In Poland, the ruling Law and Justice Party has invoked the archconservative views of Pope John Paul II in proposing to outlaw abortion and impose restrictions on birth control pills. In Spain, the Vox Party, the first far-right group to win seats in Spain's Parliament since the Franco dictatorship, wants to roll back laws against gender-based violence. Vox is supported by CitizenGO, a Spanish political action group with American and Russian ultra-conservatives on its board that conducts online campaigns against same-sex marriage, sex education, and abortion.

Like Salvini, many far-right leaders in Europe believe that their liberal secular adversaries are engaged in a direct assault on the sacrosanct notion of the "natural family," which they define as a married man and woman, preferably with many children. Italy has one of the world's lowest birth rates, which demographers attribute to the decline of Italy's familial traditions, the rise of working women, and the lack of day-care services. For his part, Salvini has condemned "gender ideology" for disrupting the central role of the family in Italian society and causing "a crisis of empty cribs." He has cultivated close ties with the World Congress of Families, an American right-wing coalition that promotes Christian fundamentalist values around the world. Christian conservatives in America contributed at least $50 million in "dark money" to far-right campaigns in Europe over the past decade, according to an investigation by the openDemocracy media platform. The largest contributor appears to be the Billy Graham Evangelistic Association, which spent more than $20 million in Europe between 2008 and 2014, according to legal filings.[23]

Even though Salvini has left government, Macron believes that his populist demagoguery and nationalistic allies across the continent still pose a serious danger to Europe's political stability. Two months before the European elections, Macron wrote an open letter to all citizens of Europe that was published in twenty-two languages and twenty-eight newspapers across the continent. In a sweeping manifesto calling for a resurrection of the European project, he warned that the nationalist instincts that provoked the chaos surrounding Brexit should serve as a cautionary tale for the continent as well. "Never, since the Second World War, has Europe been as essential," he wrote. "Yet never has Europe been in so much danger." The French president urged the creation of a pan-European liberal alliance that would confront Salvini's right-wing coalition in a decisive battle over the preservation of "European civilization." He called for leaders to convene a new continental congress to map out the future of the European Union after Britain's departure and appealed for new policies that would strengthen Europe's external borders, set a minimum wage in every country, and establish a European Security Council, a climate bank, and an agency to prevent cyber-attacks. "Freedom, protection and progress: we need to build a European renaissance on these pillars," Macron wrote. "We can't let nationalists with no solutions exploit people's anger. We can't sleepwalk towards a diminished Europe. We can't remain in the routine of business as usual and wishful thinking."

Macron's manifesto declared that sovereignty and protection from the shocks of the modern world could be achieved only by European countries working together, not as divided and isolated nation-states. Despite Salvini's high approval ratings in Italy and the growth of right-wing parties elsewhere, Macron believes that there are encouraging signs of support for those who share his vision of an open, tolerant Europe. The strong showing by pro-European Green parties, who believe that climate change must be addressed by European states working together, was one positive indicator. Another was the ouster of the left-wing populist Syriza Party, which governed Greece for four years but lost the July 2019 election to pro-Europe center-right forces led by Kyriakos Mitsotakis, who replaced Syriza's leader Alexis Tsipras as prime minister. Meanwhile, the popularity of the European Union in Central Europe was growing despite the presence of populist nationalist movements. In Poland, for example, 90 percent of the population wanted to stay in the Union despite the anti-Brussels rhetoric of the ruling Law and Justice Party.

But populist nationalism remains a long-term fact of life even in countries where fears over untrammeled immigration have abated. In Sweden, the xenophobic Sweden Democrats won 17.5 percent of the vote in the 2018 elections, an electoral performance matched by the extreme nationalist True Finns. In Estonia, long regarded as an ardent supporter of the European Union, the Conservative People's Party jumped from 8 percent to nearly 18 percent of the vote in the March 2019 elections by running on a strongly nationalistic platform.

In some respects, Europe's populist nationalists have already triumphed. Today there is no major political party in Europe that dares to advocate open borders. Far more immigrants die at Europe's frontiers, mainly by drowning at sea, than perish along the border between the United States and Mexico, yet the public only seems to care about curbing the number who can gain entry. Immigration has become a major driving force in Western politics, and surging populations in Africa and the Middle East will continue to magnify this trend. Even left-wing parties have revised their views on accepting foreign immigrants. In Germany, the former communist Left Party, led by the Marxist politician Sahra Wagenknecht, has launched a populist movement, called Aufstehen (Get Up!), that aims to lure working-class voters with a hard-line stance against immigration.

Center-left social democrats in Sweden and Denmark have also changed course and now favor highly restrictive asylum policies. They also require those immigrants who settle in their countries to learn the local language and embrace Scandinavian values, including laws allowing gay marriage and sexual equality. Multiculturalism has been discarded as social policy in many communities. "The question of whether we have reached peak populism is not up to voters. The political elites have made the populist radical right the dominant force in political debate by adopting its issues and its frames," said

Cas Mudde, a Dutch political scientist and an expert on populist extremism in Europe. "If liberal democratic politicians want to, they can make this a turning point in European politics. But for that they don't need just the 'containment' of populism, they also need a coherent and convincing liberal democratic vision."[24]

Macron has tried to work with Angela Merkel in promoting a common long-term strategy for Europe to cope with its demographic and populist political threats. At first, they believed that the economic logic of attracting young workers and new citizens from African and Arab neighbors would convince their aging and shrinking populations to embrace immigration as a welcome tonic for Europe's demographic problems. European Commission studies show that Europe will need close to a million immigrants every year for the next forty years in order to sustain current living standards. The priority should be to lure more productive workers into Europe, not to worry about their ethnic or religious backgrounds. But these studies have been ignored because they fail to take into account the powerful resonance among voters of the populist argument about saving "Western civilization" from waves of immigrants pouring in from Muslim countries—despite its overtones of blatant racist paranoia.

France and Germany are now urging the European Union to support a massive development aid program—on the scale of the Marshall Plan—that would bolster economic growth in Africa in order to keep its young people from departing for Europe. But the French-German plan may be too little too late. Africa's population is expected to grow by over one billion people in the next thirty years while native Europeans become older and fewer in number. The EU projects that Nigeria alone, already the largest source of migrants trying to cross the sea into Italy, will have a bigger population than all of Europe by 2060. As these demographic pressures build on Europe's southern doorstep, the immigration issue will continue to afflict Europe's politics and fuel the kind of populist extremism that endangers Western democracies.

CHAPTER 5

TROUBLES ACROSS THE RHINE

On his first day in office in May 2017, as soon as he had appointed his prime minister, Édouard Philippe, to head his new government, Emmanuel Macron rushed off to Berlin. His desire to meet with Chancellor Angela Merkel as soon as he took power reflected his consummate priority: establishing a close partnership with his German counterpart. Merkel was also keen to reinforce the French-German axis that had served as the engine driving progress toward greater European unity. After an enthusiastic embrace at the entrance of the Chancellery in Berlin, Merkel welcomed Macron with a quote from a poem by the German author Hermann Hesse: "A little magic dwells in every beginning." But then, reflecting her innate skepticism about the durability of political alliances, she told Macron that "the magic lasts only when there are results."[1]

Merkel's caution was understandable. During her first twelve years as chancellor, she had been frustrated by the lack of a suitable partner in Paris. She had wanted to emulate the tradition of the postwar political marriages between Germany and France that had linked Konrad Adenauer and Charles de Gaulle, Helmut Schmidt and Valéry Giscard d'Estaing, and her former mentor Helmut Kohl and François Mitterrand, but somehow the personal connections never clicked. Neither Nicolas Sarkozy nor François Hollande, in her view, were up to the job of assuming a joint leadership role in Europe. She saw Sarkozy as too flighty and temperamental, and Hollande as too weak and indecisive. But Macron was a different character altogether. Merkel was captivated by his youthful charm and quick intelligence, leading some of her close aides to speculate that she saw in him the kind of son she never had. They noticed that she looked more sprightly than usual for Macron's visit, having taken extra care to apply more makeup than was her custom and donned a bright pink jacket. Macron also seemed to enjoy the prospect of bonding with her. Merkel was the same age as his wife, Brigitte; a close Macron adviser remarked mischievously that "he has a lot of experience and feels very comfortable with women who are twenty-four years older than him."[2]

The peaceful reconciliation between France and Germany after World War II ranks as the noblest achievement of the European Union. Every generation of French and German soldiers had been engaged in deadly combat, or preparing to do so, for over five centuries. This bloody history seemed to confirm their reputation as "hereditary enemies." But the postwar vision of building a United States of Europe transformed the destiny of two embattled neighbors. Over the past seventy years, France has provided the political leadership and Germany the economic dynamism that have driven Europe's remarkable resurrection. Since Germany's unification after the fall of the Berlin Wall three decades ago, however, that delicate balance of power has shifted. As wartime memories have faded, Germany's prosperity has made its people more conscious of their own mercantile interests and less willing to make economic sacrifices for their partners. France's failure to adapt to the rigors of globalized markets has caused its political stature to diminish relative to Germany, whose power has been magnified by an expanded population from formerly communist East Germany.

Macron was determined to reverse that trend. In their first conversation, in which they both spoke English, Macron emphasized to Merkel that they needed to move quickly to seize what he called "a historic moment for Europe" that could soon disappear. He vowed to press ahead with far-reaching domestic reforms that would transform France because he realized that his credibility with Merkel and the rest of Europe depended on it. He described his intention to revive France and to relaunch the European project as "two sides of the same coin."[3]

Four months before his election, Macron had foreshadowed his intentions by giving a speech at Berlin's renowned Humboldt University. He had warned in that address that the European single currency would collapse within ten years unless Germany abandoned its obsession with running up huge trade surpluses at the expense of its weaker neighbors. Germany had to accept that more investment at home and abroad was needed to boost growth in Europe, he believed, and it also needed to stop imposing the harsh austerity measures that had plunged much of Southern Europe into deep recession in the past decade. Macron's speech did not go over well, since many Germans interpreted his message as a demand to reach into their pockets and pay for large debts accumulated by their profligate partners in the South.

Merkel had heard many unfulfilled promises from Macron's predecessors that France would soon put its house in order, but she was willing to give Macron the benefit of the doubt. She believed, she told him, that "Germany will only do well in the long term if Europe does well, and Europe will only do well if there is a strong France." She was impressed by Macron's determination and his commitment to infusing new energy into the Franco-German partnership. Macron had won early praise and sympathy in Berlin by surrounding himself with Germanophiles. His prime minister, Édouard Philippe, had attended elementary school in Bonn, the former German capital, where his father was the principal of a French school. His finance minister, Bruno Le Maire, had become fluent in German as an exchange student and made regular appearances on German television. Macron also chose France's popular ambassador to Germany, Philippe Étienne, as his national security adviser and chief diplomatic counselor.

Macron was hoping that Merkel shared his sense of urgency about the need to get Europe moving again. If he failed, he warned, Germany might have to contend with his far-right rival Marine Le Pen as his successor, or somebody even worse. He badly needed Merkel's support, but she was hesitant, in her usual cautious way, to make any premature commitments. Nonetheless, she shared his assessment of the challenges ahead. Merkel was mortified by President Trump's behavior when they first met in the White House and he refused to shake her hand in front of photographers. Those rocky first encounters with Trump had led her to tell her compatriots that perhaps "it was time for Europe to take its destiny into its own hands." She told Macron that she was prepared to work with him to ensure that Europe changed how it was governed; otherwise, the continent "would be vulnerable from every corner of the world."

The two leaders agreed to have their governments consider a range of initiatives to protect workers from the damaging effects of globalization, boost employment for young people, manage immigration flows into Europe, launch new infrastructure investment projects, and expand cooperation in foreign and security policy. This ambitious agenda was matched by an equally challenging timetable: the two leaders and their ministers would hold a joint cabinet meeting within two months to establish a road map for their European reform package. Once he secured a strong majority in Parliament, Macron started pushing ahead with his reform agenda at home. Since Merkel and her government were doubtful, however, that Macron would be able to deliver everything within the first year of his presidency, they felt confident that his inevitable difficulties at home would diminish the pressure on Germany to adopt painful measures that might irritate its taxpayers, particularly ahead of September national elections.

On the eve of the Bastille Day ceremonies in 2017, which included Donald Trump as the guest of honor, Macron and Merkel convened a special conclave of their cabinet ministers at the Élysée Palace to review a clutch of initiatives to deepen European integration in defense, security, immigration, and the economy. They gave approval for their two countries to collaborate in developing a new generation of European fighter jets, ending decades of rivalry. Military cooperation between Europe's two major powers made sense to avoid duplication and strengthen a common industrial base now that Britain was leaving the European Union and American defense commitments were being called into question by Trump.

Macron also wanted to persuade Germany to reconsider its dogmatic views about austerity and balanced budgets and consider more innovative ways to spur growth across Europe. He told Merkel that it was time for the Eurozone—the nineteen EU countries that use the single currency—to have its own finance minister, parliament, and budget in order to correct "dysfunctions" and endow the euro with "the fate it deserves." Macron's proposal would require changes in European Union treaties; Merkel and her government were loath to undertake the laborious ratification process given the difficulties of getting twenty-eight parliaments to approve the revisions. Macron said that as France started to undertake painful reforms of its economy, Germany should expand public and private investment at home and elsewhere in Europe. France also demanded a common European tax on digital giants like Apple, Google, and Facebook. Merkel appeared slightly overwhelmed and pleaded for more time to ponder the impact of Macron's ideas, and the French president began to sense that Merkel's habitual tendency to kick the can down the road on vexing issues might become a problem.

Over the summer of 2017, as Merkel prepared for critical elections that would determine whether she served a fourth term as chancellor, Macron refined his ideas about a European "New Deal."

He informed Merkel about the evolution of his plans and prudently waited to unveil his grand vision to invigorate the European Union until the results of Germany's election were known. He believed that Europe had never fully recovered from the economic and financial crisis that began in 2008; indeed, in his view, that crisis had fueled the rise of populist nationalists even more than the refugee crisis. "We have overcome our military wars of the past, but we are still weakened by other forms of conflict that we have seen over the past ten years," Macron told me. "The North–South economic split reminds me of civil wars between Catholics and Protestants. Debtors versus creditors. No solidarity unless you pay up the last cent. As a result, we have deepened the divisions in Europe. We have fractured generations by imposing brutal recessions with deep cuts in income and causing high unemployment for young people in the South, which has accelerated the rise of populism."[4]

In his first contacts with his European peers, Macron was appalled at their lack of political imagination. They seemed paralyzed by fears about the relentless rise of populist nationalism across Europe. Instead of pushing back with bold new plans for Europe, many EU heads of government, including Merkel, believed that any further moves toward a federal Europe would antagonize voters and drive them into the arms of anti-European populists. During the German election campaign, neither Merkel's conservative Christian Democrat Union (CDU) nor the left-leaning Social Democrats dared to speak up in favor of Macron's new vision for Europe, both parties having assumed that there were no votes to be gained by doing so. They were also alarmed by the rising electoral fortunes of the Alternative for Germany (AfD) Party, whose anti-immigrant and anti-Europe message showed that even the continent's most successful and prosperous nation was no longer immune to the allure of political extremism.

The 2017 election results shocked Germany and the rest of Europe. Merkel's CDU fell to its worst showing since 1949, losing sixty-five seats in the Bundestag for a drop of 8.6 percent from the previous election. The Social Democrats were also battered at the polls, losing forty seats for a decline of 5.2 percent. The AfD Party came out of no-where to win ninety-four seats, or 12.6 percent of the total vote, mak-ing them the nation's third-largest party. The upstart far-right group had seized on public dismay with Merkel's refugee policy to capture more than one million votes from her CDU. Although Merkel would remain as chancellor and serve a fourth term, she was badly weakened and found it difficult to patch together a ruling majority. She first tried to corral the liberal Free Democrats and the environmentalist Greens into a three-party coalition, but negotiations collapsed over irreconcilable differences about Europe. Merkel was forced to turn to the Social Democrats as a reluctant partner in another "grand coali-tion." The arduous negotiations to form Germany's new government took six months and would further sap her authority.

Two days after the German election, Macron took the stage in the amphitheater of the famed Sorbonne University in Paris. He was crestfallen by Merkel's weak showing but still hoped that she would rally to his cause and make a dramatic leap forward toward a more unified Europe. He spelled out his plans to build a new architecture for a sovereign Europe that would break down national frontiers to deal more effectively with the challenges of the twenty-first century and endow Europe's five hundred million citizens with a greater voice in the world. At the core of his proposals was the need to fortify Europe's single currency and prevent a recurrence of the Greek debt crisis, which had nearly destroyed the euro. He wanted to establish a European banking union and implement an EU-wide deposit insur-ance scheme to curtail the risk of financial panics that could ruin the banks. Macron feared that another devastating financial crisis could strike Europe, perhaps triggered by weak banks in Italy or even in Germany, and that the entire European project could collapse un-less his reforms were adopted quickly. But Germany and Northern creditor countries were reluctant to abandon their dogmatic beliefs in fiscal prudence and structural reforms and rejected any proposals hinting at a "transfer union" that might hold their taxpayers respon-sible for the debts of other European partners.[5]

Macron was intrigued by how the dollar became the world's leading currency and wanted to figure out how the euro could emerge as a powerful rival to the greenback. Alexander Hamilton, the first US Treasury secretary and one of America's founding fathers, took the key decision by relieving member states of their debts, which were then assumed by the new federal government. A single deposit insurance plan was eventually established to shore up public confidence in banks, just as Macron proposed for Europe. But Hamilton also endowed the US federal government with powers of direct taxation, which was what a unified Europe would require if it hoped to sustain the single currency in the long run.[6] Macron tried to convince Merkel and other leaders to embrace Hamilton's rationale, but their reluctance to cede further sovereignty to EU institutions at a time when many voters wanted powers to be repatriated to national capitals would prevent the euro from emulating the dollar and evolving into a true continental currency.

In the Sorbonne speech laying out his blueprint for a new Europe, Macron did not just speak about ways to strengthen the euro but also addressed troubling issues like unchecked immigration. He proposed the creation of a European asylum office that would synchronize rules and applications for refugees arriving at the EU's external borders and suggested that Europe bolster the resources and powers of Frontex, the EU's border and coast guard agency. Macron's suggested measures would fall short of finding a consensus about how to distribute immigrants throughout the European Union, and both he and Merkel would bow to political pressures at home by imposing new restrictions on refugees coming into France and Germany.

The third leg of Macron's reform program called for greater integration of Europe's defense and security policy. Here he managed to achieve perhaps his greatest success in rallying Europe to take control of its destiny. The new geopolitical competition posed by China's rise as an emerging superpower, Russia's resurgence as an aggressive threat, and Trump's erratic behavior in questioning America's commitments to its allies had forced European leaders to realize that in the future they could no longer passively stand aside in the expectation that the United States would protect them from external threats. This challenge revived interest among European governments in innovative ideas for the continent's defense that would fulfill Macron's vision of "strategic autonomy." France and Germany, along with twenty-one other states, agreed to a new joint program to design, produce, and procure military equipment with funds supplied by the EU budget. The PESCO (Permanent Structured Cooperation) program is not supposed to duplicate the North Atlantic Treaty Organization but rather handle defense and security tasks that NATO and the United States might not be prepared to assume. Macron also launched the ten-nation European Intervention Initiative, which is designed to keep Britain involved in helping to defend the continent once it leaves the European Union. This program, conducted outside both the EU and NATO, will share intelligence and operational capabilities among its members so that their forces can intervene rapidly in crises on Europe's periphery.[7]

Most of Macron's grandiose plans to energize the European project lingered in limbo while Merkel struggled to put together her new government. Macron was gratified when the coalition agreement she hammered out with the Social Democrats embraced many of his ideas, with a reinvigorated Europe serving as the centerpiece of their governing platform. But Merkel's weakened stature—along with her evident fatigue after so many years in office—reinforced her reluctance to get too far ahead of her people. Her natural style of governing was to take baby steps forward, then stop and consider public reaction across the political landscape before making her next move. She had dared to announce startling initiatives on only two occasions—when she declared that Germany would abandon nuclear power after the Fukushima disaster in Japan, and when she opened her nation's doors to the flood of Syrian refugees—and both initiatives had backfired on her and caused enduring political grief. Merkel's nuclear decision wreaked havoc with Germany's energy costs as the country struggled to make a sudden transition to renewable sources like wind and solar.

Her heroic decision to welcome Syrian refugees, while laudable for its generous humanitarian motives, awakened xenophobic resentment in her country that soon led to the election of the far-right Alternative for Germany Party to the Bundestag for the first time.

Merkel's defensive approach to governing stood in sharp contrast to the style of her mentor, Helmut Kohl, who had plucked her from obscurity when she was still a young East German scientist and a newcomer to politics. Kohl brought her into his CDU-led government as a minister for women's rights and the environment. (Later, she would seize the opportunity to topple him as party leader when he became embroiled in a political funding scandal.) In 1990, to win the support of French president François Mitterrand for the unification of Germany, Kohl decided to sacrifice his country's cherished deutsche mark in favor of a single European currency. Many of the nation's leading economists opposed the idea, saying that it did not make sense to impose a uniform monetary policy in a currency zone for countries as disparate as, say, Germany and Greece. Moreover, opinion polls indicated that over 70 percent of the German people were reluctant to abandon the mark. But Kohl argued that the euro was necessary to help unify Europe and would make the difference between war and peace. In the end, Kohl's bulldozer tactics prevailed and the euro came into existence in 1999.

Kohl was deeply committed to a French-German partnership as the principal foundation of European unity. He kept a picture near his desk of a poignant scene at the main cemetery of Verdun, where he and Mitterrand clasped hands to show respect for the more than 130,000 French and German soldiers whose remains are buried there. Kohl's father fought in World War I at Verdun, which is widely regarded as one of the most blood-soaked battles in history. It lasted for three hundred days and killed, maimed, or wounded close to one million people. The protracted history of warfare between France and Germany as the root cause of Europe's instability was a profound influence on many Germans of Kohl's generation who advocated a united Europe. When I visited Kohl at his home near Ludwigshafen in 1985, he told me that there was a simple way to understand what motivated his political career. He ushered me out to his backyard and pointed westward in the distance toward France. He looked at the ground and told me: "I am convinced that the blood of German and French soldiers is mixed in this earth. We must do everything possible to make sure that war never happens between us again."

Kohl's generation was the last in Germany to be personally affected by wars between France and Germany. While contemporary German politicians remain conscious of their nation's debt to history through two world wars and the horrific crimes of the Holocaust, they also yearn to be treated as a normal country with national interests that must be protected. The incorporation of eastern Germany in 1990 also diluted the psychological impact of Germany's wartime past. Wolfgang Schäuble, who loyally served as Kohl's chief of staff and later as Merkel's finance minister before becoming president of the Bundestag, was once asked at a dinner party in Berlin if there was any significant difference in their approach to politics. "Merkel is not emotionally invested in Europe in the same way that Kohl and I were," he replied.

Like Merkel, Macron, who was still a child when the Berlin Wall fell, was also personally removed from the agonizing wars that shaped relations between France and Germany, but he did view de Gaulle and Mitterrand as role models for his presidency. His official photographic portrait showed him with a copy of the general's memoirs in the background. He liked to recall de Gaulle's words fifty years earlier when he admonished his ministers: "Never forget that for France there can be no alternative but friendship with Germany." Above all, Macron was inspired by Mitterrand's impassioned appeal to the European Parliament never to allow chauvinistic forces to take control of the continent. "Nationalism means war!" Mitterrand told the European legislators in a farewell speech in 1995. "War is not only our past. It can also be our future." Macron embraced a similar creed.

But Merkel proved to be a recalcitrant partner. Macron tried to curb his impatience during the long months she needed to negotiate her new government. When she finally signed a policy pact with the rival Social Democrats, Macron sent her a congratulatory message, telling her, "This is good news for Europe!" Merkel replied that she would do her best to fulfill her new government's promises. "I know you have waited a long time, but our coalition deal . . . is a response to France's demands," she said, suggesting that it could herald a "new dawn for Europe." Merkel added that she felt it was more important than ever for France and Germany to cooperate on reaching common solutions given the volatile geopolitical context, even if their two countries "did not always agree in the beginning."[8]

But initial discussions between their governments became mired in technical detail. There was little evidence of a fresh political impulse from Berlin to accelerate change in Europe. Olaf Scholz, the Social Democrat and Germany's new finance minister, soon proved to be as flinty as his CDU predecessor in parting with German funds to invest in Europe. As for Merkel, she retreated into a shell of caution, claiming that she needed time to protect her slim majority in the Bundestag. In fact, she was getting cold feet and shying away from Macron's demands for big-bang reforms that would inject new energy into the European project. Macron's frustrations began to boil over as he sensed that Merkel was reneging on her earlier commitments. When he was informed that he would be awarded the prestigious Charlemagne Prize—named after the "father of Europe" who, from his hometown in Aachen, Germany, managed to unify much of the continent in the early ninth century—Macron decided to use the event to make a powerful appeal to the German public.

With Merkel and other previous laureates seated behind him in the lavish Coronation Room of Aachen's town hall, Macron implored Germans to get over their obsession with budget discipline, which was inflicting serious damage on the European project. "Germany cannot have a perpetual fetish about budget and trade surpluses, because they come at the expense of others," Macron said. He pointedly told Merkel and other prominent Germans that they could no longer use France's previous reluctance to enact painful reforms as their excuse to avoid taking bold initiatives to revive Europe. "Wake up!" he declared. "France has changed!" He laid out four commandments that should guide France and Germany in driving Europe forward: "Let's not be weak, let's not be divided, let's not show fear, and let's not wait!" There could be no excuse for further procrastination: the time had come for Europe to take courageous measures to secure its own sovereignty or else capitulate in meekly accepting rules laid down by others. Macron had read Christopher Clark's history detailing how European leaders stumbled into World War I through negligence and complacency; he himself did not want to belong "to another generation of sleepwalkers." He warned that Germany's smugness could soon lead into recession. Its prolonged record of economic success would not be sustained without more investment at home and abroad.

Macron's broadside struck a sensitive nerve. Merkel was taken aback by his impassioned call for action and paid tribute to his commitment to European unity, calling him "a dynamic young politician for whom Europe is a natural choice." But she offered no sign that she would budge from her cautious approach and seemed not to share his sense of urgency. "We may come from a different political past, but we can still find common ground, and that is the magic of Europe," Merkel said. By contrast, the German media was outraged by Macron's blunt comments. Several commentators argued that Macron did not understand why Germany's aging population could not afford to lavish resources on profligate European neighbors just so they could retire early and enjoy cruises around the Mediterranean Sea. The influential *Frankfurter Allgemeine* newspaper published a letter signed by 154 economists denouncing Macron's European proposals as anathema to German interests.[9]

Macron realized that he had no alternative but to cooperate with Merkel whenever possible. But he could not hide his exasperation with her hesitancy and indecision, complaining to his aides that it was difficult to develop long-term strategies for Europe when dealing with her "two-week vision." For her part, Merkel grew disenchanted with Macron's impetuous nature, which clashed with her innate caution, and became annoyed with his habitual tardiness, a grave sin in a country that prizes punctuality. The chancellor complained about the blizzard of proposals regarding Europe's future development that Macron would shower on her even though they both realized that his plans had no chance of being approved by all the EU's twenty-eight leaders. "Certainly, we have our share of confrontations," Merkel acknowledged in an interview with the Munich daily *Süddeutsche Zeitung.* "We wrestle with each other. That's because we have differences in mentality. At certain times, we view our roles in different ways. It has always been like that. But generally, we can usually find a compromise for the benefit of Europe."[10]

The arrival in power of a populist government in Italy only deepened Macron's sense of urgency. He persuaded Merkel to convene another joint cabinet meeting between their two governments in order to meet a June 2018 deadline to approve an action plan for Europe. "I think since the Second World War there has never been a moment of such historical importance," Macron told reporters at a meeting of EU leaders in the Bulgarian capital of Sofia shortly after his Aachen speech. "It is now time for decisions. France has made proposals, France has made reforms, and France has waited. The upcoming summer is a moment of truth."[11] Bruno Le Maire, France's finance minister, was even blunter in his assessment after his disappointing first encounters with his German counterpart Scholz. "Europe is in a state of decomposition," Le Maire told French television, expressing deep frustration. "It's falling apart before our eyes."[12]

Merkel's refusal to respond to Macron's pleas for France and Germany to seize the initiative in moving Europe forward dismayed some of her compatriots. "Germany has remained silent on the question of Europe's future and indicated that its primary concern is its own money," said Joschka Fischer, a former vice-chancellor and foreign minister from the Green Party. "Squandering the opportunity offered by Macron—which will not come again—would be the height of political folly and historical blindness."[13] Even members of

Merkel's CDU Party urged her to demonstrate the kind of leadership shown by Adenauer and Kohl, who understood the historical significance of European integration for Germany. Whatever its debt to history, Germany has profited immensely from an undervalued euro that bolstered its export industries, which account for nearly half of Germany's economy (a share four times greater than in the United States). "Europe is locked in a crisis dynamic of our own making," Norbert Röttgen, the CDU chairman of the Bundestag's Foreign Relations Committee, told me. "If we Germans fail to support Macron, we will have only ourselves to blame if and when Europe starts to unravel."[14]

Merkel defended her passivity by claiming that she needed time to shore up her ruling coalition. But Macron told her that as she entered her twilight years as chancellor, she should be ready to take a courageous political gamble in favor of Europe. She was no longer running for office, he reminded her, but rather for her place in history. Yet she still hesitated. When Malta's prime minister called Macron pleading for help in offering shelter to yet another boatload of refugees crossing the Mediterranean Sea, Macron reached out to Merkel and suggested that France and Germany lead the way by taking the largest shares of refugees. She demurred, saying that she would need to discuss the matter with Austria's chancellor to find out how many refugees his country might be willing to accept before making a decision. Macron nearly exploded in exasperation over her fretful dawdling. "For God's sake, Angela!" he told her in a telephone call. "You are the chancellor of Germany, and you tell me you have to talk with Vienna before you can decide about accepting a dozen refugees?"[15]

Germany's growing prosperity, even in the wake of the 2008 financial crisis, entrenched its resistance to change. The country was very comfortable with the status quo and did not want to cede more powers to EU institutions in Brussels. German taxpayers believed that they deserved more credit for helping to fund bailouts for Ireland, Greece, Portugal, and Spain. Yet much of the $330 billion in

emergency loans that Greece received from Germany and other creditors had been used to rescue German and French banks to prevent
another financial crisis. The diversion of funds to salvage European
banks instead of helping their country infuriated Greeks, who had
been forced to endure a debilitating recession and 25 percent unemployment. Yet Merkel was unmoved. As the leader of a diverse country
where power was shared among sixteen federal states, there were structural as well as political reasons why Merkel showed little enthusiasm
for Macron's vision of a more centralized Europe. She told other European leaders that she felt that many of Macron's ideas were simply un-
realistic and overly ambitious. Dominique Moïsi, a Paris-based adviser
at the Institut Montaigne who knows Germany well, told me in 2018,
"Whatever marriage of reason might have existed between France and
Germany previously, it has now given way to estrangement."[16]

France and Germany also struggled to display a united front
against hostile trade policies coming from Washington. Trump's
threat to impose tariffs on German automobile exports to the United
States in the wake of earlier levies slapped on steel and aluminum
products sent ripples of fear through Germany, whose automobile
industry serves as the cornerstone of its economy. Macron had promised that France would demonstrate solidarity with Germany and its
other EU partners in confronting the United States in any transatlantic trade war. But when Macron learned from his ambassador in
Washington, DC, that Merkel had floated the idea of offering greater
access to European markets for American agriculture products in a
bid to defuse Trump's threat against German automobiles, he felt betrayed. France's powerful farm lobby was staunchly opposed to concessions that would allow more American food products into Europe.
Any French president who allowed that to happen would face a violent insurrection. Merkel and Macron also clashed over building the
controversial Nord Stream 2 pipeline to bring Russian natural gas
directly into Germany; cutting off weapons exports to Saudi Arabia;
and deciding whether to impose a digital tax on American technology giants such as Amazon, Apple, Facebook, and Google, a move

that Merkel feared would encourage Trump to retaliate with tariffs against German automobiles.

Despite their serious differences, Macron and Merkel felt they had no alternative but to maintain an amicable partnership. In June 2018, they gathered with their ministers for another joint cabinet meeting in Meseberg, the chancellor's rustic retreat located an hour's drive outside Berlin. Macron was coming under rising pressure at home, even from his political allies, for investing so much time and effort in trying to convince Germany to support his European reform proposals. The grand bargain that he had pursued so assiduously since coming to power seemed to be slipping away. The handshake deal he had struck with Merkel called for France to show greater discipline over its finances, shrink its bloated public sector, and make it easier to hire and fire workers. In return, Germany would back Macron's plans to integrate Europe with a Eurozone budget, an EU finance ministry, and more cohesive foreign and defense policies. Within his first year as president, Macron had managed to push through a series of unpopular measures that cut social benefits significantly and reined in France's finances, yet Germany had responded by giving him next to nothing.

At Meseberg, Merkel finally accepted the principle of a Eurozone budget and promised to create an effective banking union designed to prevent future financial crises in Europe. It was the symbolic breakthrough that Macron had been seeking since his Sorbonne speech, even if it fell far short of his own ambitious goals for Europe.[17] Yet barely ten days later, the Meseberg accord began to fall apart. At a European Union summit meeting, other leaders questioned the rationale and timing of French-German proposals for a Eurozone budget and immigration reform. With nationalist sentiment rising across Europe, several leaders spoke out against taking any steps that would antagonize voters opposed to further moves toward an integrated Europe. "The people just will not accept these ideas; just look at how they are voting," said Lars Løkke Rasmussen, Denmark's liberal prime minister, whose government depended on support from the hard-right Danish People's Party to stay in power. Other leaders argued that Macron's reform initiatives were out of sync with the public mood across Europe. Even Merkel began to inch away from the Meseberg deal, claiming that her Christian Social Union allies, who comprise the Bavarian sister party of Merkel's CDU, were outraged and might be tempted to blow up her coalition government. In his determination to stand up to populist nationalists by promoting more aggressive European policies, Macron was becoming increasingly isolated among his EU peers. He looked like a union of one.

Macron refused to retreat despite his lonely position, preferring to double down on his vision of a European renaissance. He insisted that the only way to defeat his far-right enemies who advocated xenophobic nationalism and populist extremism was to engage them in battle. Unlike other European leaders, he believed that it would be political surrender to back away from challenging them. "Don't be shy with these people," Macron told the German newsweekly *Der Spiegel*. "Look at me, the National Front got many more votes than the Alternative for Germany (AfD). Le Pen ended up with 34 percent of the vote. 34 percent! But I chose to defend Europe, an open society and all my values. And today the National Front has been significantly weakened. In the debates, you don't hear anything from them anymore because we engaged them in battle. Now is the time to be bold! The only answer to the AfD is courage and ambition."[18]

Despite his political frustrations, Macron continued to nurture a personal relationship with Merkel. At the one-hundredth anniversary of the armistice that ended World War I, he invited Merkel to sit next to him at ceremonies that were held at the Arc de Triomphe in November 2018 and attended by more than sixty world leaders, including Donald Trump and Vladimir Putin. A day earlier, she seemed genuinely moved when they traveled together to the town of Compiègne, eighty miles northeast of Paris, to commemorate the armistice in a replica of a railway carriage where Marshall Ferdinand Foch, France's supreme commander of the Western Front, signed the cease-fire agreement with Germany. As the French and German national anthems played and schoolchildren from both nations cheered, Macron and Merkel clasped hands under a gray sky in the drizzling rain to mark the solemn reconciliation of former "hereditary enemies." At one point, Merkel was so overwhelmed by emotion that she rested her head on Macron's shoulder.[19]

A week later in Berlin, Macron told German legislators that they could no longer afford to procrastinate in taking more responsibility for Europe's defense and security. "There are many powers that would like to stop us, that are trying to turn us against each other," Macron declared. He warned that a failure to start building a European army would condemn the continent to secondary status as vassals of big powers like the United States, Russia, and China. He insisted that France and Germany, as the most powerful nations in Europe, "have an obligation not to allow the world to slide into chaos."[20] For three generations, Germans had learned to suppress any big-power ambitions of their own and sought shelter under America's strategic umbrella. But Merkel had been telling her compatriots for several months that "the days when we can unconditionally rely on others are gone." She welcomed Macron's vision of a common European defense and declared that "we Europeans should take our fate into our own hands if we want to survive as a European community."[21]

Ever so slowly, public opinion in Germany started to embrace that perspective, driven in part by revulsion toward Trump. The Bundestag was still reluctant to approve every military mission, but Germany was gradually shedding its inhibitions about armed missions abroad. Berlin had contributed troops to the NATO mission in Afghanistan and sent one thousand soldiers to Mali to help French forces battle Islamist insurgents. Germany seemed nearly ready to join France in leading a new era of "strategic autonomy" for Europe in which they pledged to create a common military culture and merge their military-industrial capabilities, which account for half of Europe's entire capacity.

Nevertheless, the discussions about a new treaty proved difficult. Germany remains deeply suspicious about France's expeditionary culture; Berlin opposed French intervention in Libya in 2011, and some German politicians fear that France is merely trying to enlist partners to help keep order in its former African colonies. "Germany does not need a strong army for its understanding of sovereignty," said Bundestag president Wolfgang Schäuble. "France is a different story."[22] For their part, the French are disdainful of Germany's constant hand-wringing about sending troops abroad, due in large part to the pacifist streak that took hold after the country started and lost two world wars. Until recently, Germany had cut its defense spending so drastically that its military spending as a percentage of GDP, at little more than 1 percent, ranked among the lowest of all NATO countries. Germany no longer requires young people to serve in the armed forces, and many allied military experts believe that German soldiers no longer have much will to fight. At a National Assembly hearing in 2018, France's military chief of staff, General François Lecointre, said that in joint exercises Germans had shown a different "attitude toward combat" than French soldiers, who were appalled by the poor state of German readiness. German soldiers were not equipped with thermal underwear or bulletproof vests. They were also compelled to use broomsticks in some exercises because of a shortage of rifles and ammunition. NATO maneuvers revealed serious shortcomings because of malfunctions in many German planes and submarines caused by a lack of proper maintenance and spare parts.

On January 22, 2019, after weeks of intense negotiations, Merkel and Macron signed the Treaty of Aachen, in which France and Germany vowed to "deepen their cooperation on foreign policy, defense, external and internal security while reinforcing Europe's capacity for independent action." At the ceremony, Merkel said that she and Macron had "discussed each and every word at length." They finally approved the treaty with the understanding that they would strive to create "a common military culture that contributes to the creation of a European army." A key pledge committed the two countries to "providing aid and assistance by all means at their disposal, including armed forces, in the case of aggression against their territory." A

French-German Defense and Security Council was established as the decisive political body to guide these reciprocal engagements.

In a conversation with Macron after the treaty was signed, I asked him whether the phrase "all means" included the extension of France's nuclear deterrent to cover German territory. "I compliment you for your insight," Macron said with a wry smile. "You are quite correct to notice the importance of this phrase." Neither side wanted to highlight the nuclear implications of the treaty because of possible anxieties that could be aroused in both countries. But Macron acknowledged that France, for the first time, would incorporate German and European interests in deciding how to deploy its armed forces against outside threats. That shift in defense strategy includes its arsenal of some three hundred nuclear warheads, mainly aboard four submarines capable of carrying sixteen missiles armed with multiple warheads. In addition, France possesses about fifty Mirage 2000N and Rafale fighter jets equipped with nuclear-armed cruise missiles. The binding character of the Aachen treaty in the face of outside aggression is noteworthy in that it goes beyond the NATO treaty's Article 5, which commits a member state to take only "such action as it deems necessary" to come to the aid of an ally facing an armed attack.

Germany asked France to turn over to the European Union its seat as a permanent member of the United Nations Security Council. But Macron refused, on the grounds that the UN seat was a sovereign right assigned to France when the UN was established after World War II. France promised, however, to advocate for expansion of the Security Council so that Germany could also be given a permanent seat, which it claims to deserve because it is one of the largest contributors to the UN budget.

Merkel's successor as CDU party leader, Annegret Kramp-Karrenbauer, endorses the vision set forth by Merkel and Macron for their two countries to develop a European army. In July 2019, AKK, as she is known, was appointed defense minister and declared that she wanted to build a joint aircraft carrier with France, which would require Germany to raise its defense budget significantly. As a potential chancellor candidate once Merkel leaves, AKK believes that these steps are important because Europe needs to achieve greater control over its destiny to shape the rules of "future global coexistence" or risk being trapped by the competing strategic interests of China and the United States. If France truly wants to create a more effective European Union, AKK believes, Paris will need to sacrifice some national prerogatives, including its seat on the UN Security Council. She has also suggested that it would be helpful to consolidate the European Parliament in Brussels and abandon its regular sessions in Strasbourg—a move that France has always rejected.[23]

It is perhaps a tragic irony of history that just when France is being ruled by the most pro-European president the country has ever elected, Germany has taken a divergent path headed toward what its most famous living philosopher, Jürgen Habermas, calls "vigorous economic nationalism." During her long tenure in power, Merkel has won accolades as the conscience of the West, particularly for her moral and humanitarian gestures in support of refugees and asylum-seekers. But to Macron's regret, she has fallen woefully short of her predecessors in staking out a strategic vision for the future of Europe. Merkel may believe that she has faithfully protected the interests of the German people, but Habermas and other critics have warned that leaving Macron isolated while "pursuing a policy of delay or forbearance would be enough to gamble away a historically unrivaled opportunity."[24] For those Europeans who still aspire to transform their continent into what another German philosopher, Immanuel Kant, described in 1795 as "a state of perpetual peace," the profound space between Europe's power couple is filled with foreboding.

CHAPTER 6

EUROPE IN PIECES

When the globalization boom reached its peak two decades ago, a powerful constellation of forces seemed poised to transform Europe into a more cohesive continent. A unified European market comprising more than five hundred million consumers was close to becoming a reality as national barriers fell to allow the unfettered flow of people, capital, and merchandise. For the first time, motorists could drive from the Arctic region to the Mediterranean Sea without ever having to show their passports or stop at customs outposts. The euro, the new common currency that would abolish deutsche marks, francs, and lira, was entering into circulation and would eventually be adopted by nineteen nations. Nationalism was in full retreat, and the triumph of free market democracies over communist and fascist dictatorships was no longer questioned. With three billion people from the former Soviet Union, China, and India now part of the global economy, the European Union and its twenty-eight member nations were ideally placed to exploit the surging volume of world trade through their position as the world's most powerful commercial bloc.

Yet within a few short years the momentum toward a United States of Europe slowed and began to move in reverse. Voters in France and the Netherlands rejected plans in 2005 for a European constitution that would have charted the path toward a continental federation. People began to complain that their cultural and national identities were being submerged in the quest to achieve a borderless Europe. They preferred to celebrate the diversity of their local communities and spurned increasingly homogenous politics and lifestyles. When the global financial crisis struck Europe with full force in 2008, the European single currency nearly fell apart when Greece reached the brink of insolvency and required a financial bailout that would exceed 330 billion euros. Housing markets collapsed in Spain and Ireland, while Portugal and Italy struggled with mountainous debts and tried to avoid the same fate as Greece.

A decade later, many regions in Europe have yet to recover from the worst financial crisis since the Great Depression. The harsh austerity policies imposed by creditor nations in the North have nourished resentments and stifled economic growth among the poorer debtor countries in the South. Along the East–West axis, the former communist states in Central and Eastern Europe complain that their wealthier Western European partners have exploited them through inferior wages and a brain drain that lures their best and brightest talents into leaving home. For their part, Western states accuse their ungrateful Eastern cousins of pocketing enormous EU subsidies while turning their backs on upholding basic democratic values, including an impartial judiciary and a free press. The fragmentation of Europe has been magnified by the chaos and confusion surrounding Britain's dithering quest to leave the Union, which has paralyzed practically all other efforts to chart the continent's future.

Emmanuel Macron inherited this fractured political landscape when he was elected as France's president in 2017. As far as he was concerned, the failure by ruling parties to thwart the rise of populist nationalists was directly related to the flaws in Europe's social market economy, which no longer defended the interests of the middle class but allowed too much wealth to accumulate at the top. "The market economy has slipped backwards by becoming deeply financialized and led to the kinds of inequalities that are no longer sustainable," Macron said. "It is happening not just in France but in many other countries, which is why people have lost faith in the idea of a more united Europe. This unprecedented inequality disrupts our political order. How can we explain to our fellow citizens that this is the right way to go in Europe when they do not get their fair share? It leads people to question the very legitimacy of this economic system and our democracies."[1]

Macron has struggled to find allies who share his sense of urgency about the need to arrest Europe's decline. In trying to put Europe back on the path toward greater cohesion, he has been frustrated by the weakness of traditional ruling parties in standing up to their populist adversaries instead of displaying the bolder leadership that he believes most voters crave. "The French people, as well as other Europeans, want strong leadership, even if they may express the desire to kill their leaders," Macron said. "But we cannot continue as before in playing it safe, because then we will definitely lose control. And that would mean obliteration. We know that civilizations can disappear, as well as countries. Europe, too, can disappear."[2]

Europe's geometry of power has become more complex with the erosion of the center-right and center-left blocs that once controlled nearly all governments. The European Parliament elections in May 2019 revealed that the traditional parties of conservative Christian Democrats and progressive Social Democrats are rapidly breaking down while once-marginal parties are picking up support. The conservatives still dominate in Germany and many Eastern countries, while the progressives remain strong in Spain, Portugal, and Scandinavia. But the emergence of newly powerful liberal and Green parties, as well as right-wing populists, suggests that getting Europe to speak with one voice is going to become even more difficult in the years to come. That dismal prospect of a more fractured continent has dampened enthusiasm about taking further steps to enlarge the European Union by incorporating Serbia, Montenegro, Albania, Kosovo, and North Macedonia. Europe's political landscape is already scrambled by the weakened partnership between France and Germany, the uncertain consequences of Britain's departure, and the constant struggle to reach a consensus among the EU's member states. The continent now appears to be breaking into disparate fragments that may coalesce in the future only on a temporary basis.[3]

The centrifugal forces driving Europe apart were fully on display during the frantic negotiations to choose new leadership for the Union's most powerful institutions in the summer of 2019. Over the course of three days, more than two dozen presidents and prime ministers labored through fifty hours of intense and often emotionally heated consultations, juggling the names of various personalities on the basis of considerations like gender, nationality, regional balance, political affiliation, and, not least, commitment to European ideals. The leading candidates to become president of the European Union's executive body, the European Commission—Germany's Manfred Weber for the conservatives, Denmark's Margrethe Vestager for the liberals, and Frans Timmermans of the Netherlands for the socialists—were all rejected during the first rounds of bargaining. The list of second-tier candidates looked even more feeble, making the selection process seem like an impossible puzzle to crack. Frustrations boiled over. Once again, the constipated format revealed the agonizing difficulty of reaching important decisions by an eclectic group of nations lacking clear leadership.

When Macron stormed out of a fruitless all-night round of talks, he warned that Europe was lapsing into a dysfunctional crisis from which it might never recover. "Our credibility is profoundly stained by meetings that are too long, that yield nothing," Macron declared. "We give an image of a Europe that is not serious." He complained that it was not just geographical and party divisions that hampered the deliberations. Macron decried the "personal ambitions" and "too many hidden agendas"—an allusion to some leaders' seeking sinecures for themselves—that were undermining the quest to appoint the most highly qualified people to steer the European Union through what loom as the most difficult years in its history. For a while, it seemed that the leaders could not even agree on the proper criteria for their discussions. The entire exercise looked like it would collapse in chaos. "What was lacking around the table was the spirit and determination to defend the general European interest," Macron said. "We have seen today what doesn't work."[4]

After the talks were suspended for a day so that they could catch up on their sleep, the European leaders reconvened for a final desperate attempt to reach an agreement. Macron sought to break the stalemate by proposing Ursula von der Leyen, Germany's conservative defense minister, for the powerful post of president of the European Commission. That opened the way for a French woman and another conservative, Christine Lagarde, the outgoing director of the International Monetary Fund, to be nominated as the new head of the European Central Bank. Two progressive socialists, Josip Borrell of Spain and David Sassoli of Italy, were then put forward as the EU's foreign policy czar and president of the European Parliament, respectively. That allowed Macron's liberal group of supporters to rally behind their candidate, Belgian prime minister Charles Michel, as the new European Council president. The constellation of choices struck the right balance of gender and political affiliation, though leaders from Central and Eastern Europe grumbled that their regions were deprived of any big job. Macron left the negotiating table feeling relieved and jubilant that all the important EU posts were now filled by people who shared his commitment to a more united Europe. And not coincidentally, they all spoke fluent French. "It is an Act Two that begins for our Europe," Macron said. "A new team profoundly renewed, new faces, new energy in the service of a new agenda. It is like a breath of fresh air."[5]

Macron had insisted to his fellow leaders that the time had come to abandon their old habits of adhering to nationality or party loyalties in choosing the new stewards of Europe's institutions. If the European Union was ever going to regain credibility in the eyes of its citizens, the most highly qualified people should be chosen as its leaders. While traveling to the G-20 economic summit in Japan, Macron explained his rationale and his difficulties in persuading Merkel and other leaders to drop antiquated political customs and focus on choosing the best candidates. "We want a team that is consistent, has the best skills, and is aligned with the strategy we have implemented," Macron said, before meeting with Japan's new emperor Naruhito. "I do not care if I have a Frenchman, for example, if he thought the opposite of what we put on the table. That's not how Europe works. All too often we have found compromises on people who basically could not really do what we wanted."[6]

After von der Leyen was narrowly approved by the European Parliament in a secret ballot, she briskly laid out her agenda for Europe's future. Even though she was the first German to head the European Commission in fifty years, von der Leyen, who was born and raised in Brussels as the daughter of a high-ranking civil servant in the European Commission, insisted that she thought of herself foremost as a staunchly devout European. The mother of seven children, she had also had to juggle family and professional obligations throughout her adult life. As the first woman ever to lead the EU's highest executive body, she vowed to form a "gender-balanced commission" that would, for the first time, establish parity between male and female members. In addition, as a German Christian Democrat with strong views about social justice, she promised to establish a minimum wage across Europe and to find new ways to mitigate the economic inequalities alienating citizens and breeding political extremism. Above all, von der Leyen said, she would place immigration and climate change at the heart of her policy priorities for Europe during her five-year term, insisting that these issues could not be solved by individual states and could only be addressed at a European level. It was all music to the ears of Macron, who had been desperately searching for a political soul mate among continental leaders who might share his ambitious agenda for Europe.

In her acceptance speech before the European Parliament, von der Leyen called for a new pact on migration and asylum that would include up to ten thousand border guards deployed by 2024 to protect Europe's periphery. She endorsed Macron's call to convene a conference on the future of Europe that would give citizens a leading role in deciding how they wanted to be governed. On climate change, von der Leyen dropped a bombshell proposal for a far-reaching Green Deal that would make Europe the first carbon-neutral continent in the world by 2050. She said that bold steps were necessary to make it happen, including the creation of a climate bank that would promote investments worth more than one trillion euros over the coming decade. She also declared her intention to introduce a carbon border tax to prevent "carbon leakage" or the relocation of carbon-intensive production outside of Europe. This idea was widely applauded by environmentalists, who believe that such a measure will correct competitive distortions and deter countries that might be tempted to abstain from participating in the global climate coalition. "Whether it is Finnish wheat farmers facing drought or French citizens facing a deadly heat wave, we are all feeling quite clearly the effects of climate change," von der Leyen said. "Our most pressing challenge is keeping our planet healthy. The world is calling for more Europe. This is the greatest responsibility and opportunity of our lives."[7]

Indeed, scientists have concluded that hotter summers in Europe are one of the most tangible manifestations of the world's changing weather patterns generated by human activity, which has pumped enormous amounts of greenhouse gases into the atmosphere. In July 2019, temperatures in Paris soared to 109 degrees Fahrenheit—the highest in recorded history—and new heat records were set across France, Germany, Belgium, and the Netherlands. Nuclear reactors were forced to shut down because the water used to cool them became too warm. Health warnings were issued because the dangers of sweltering heat for frail or elderly people were amplified by the lack of air-conditioning in many European cities. The weather alert was triggered by a vast dome of hot air that had traveled from northern Africa and hovered over continental Europe for four days before moving north into Scandinavia and the Arctic region. The record heat levels increased the surface melting of Greenland's massive ice sheet, which covers about 80 percent of the island. A 2018 study found that the ice sheet was already losing three hundred billion tons of ice every year, contributing to an alarming rise in sea levels. Greenland's ice sheet is nearly two miles thick and if all of it were to melt, scientists believe that global sea levels would increase by as much as twenty-four feet, inundating many island nations and coastal regions around the world.[8]

Macron and von der Leyen want Europe to lead the way in establishing a pathbreaking model for the rest of the world in cutting carbon emissions. Two centuries ago, Europe was responsible for 99 percent of global carbon emissions; today it accounts for less than 10 percent, and its share will fall to 5 percent by 2030. Whatever Europe does to address climate change, it will not save the planet unless other countries follow a similar course. Global carbon emissions are still expected to increase by 8.5 billion tons over the next decade even if Europe succeeds in the painful task of cutting its own annual emissions by 1.5 billion tons. If these trends persist, global temperatures will still rise by 3 degrees Celsius or more by the end of the century. Moreover, Europe's laudable goal of curbing its carbon emissions will require economic sacrifices that some nations will not be prepared to make. While many people may share the views of Macron and von der Leyen that Europe must embrace the moral imperative of adopting harsh measures to help resolve the climate crisis, the potential economic backlash could unleash ugly political consequences. The carbon border tax, for example, could further shrink world trade and contribute to a possible recession, which would fuel the anti-Europe arguments of right-wing extremists. "It is ironic that the new leaders of the EU, which has relentlessly championed open markets, will likely trigger a conflict between climate preservation and free trade," said Jean Pisani-Ferry. "But this clash is inevitable. How it is managed will determine both the fate of globalization and that of the climate."[9]

Even more troubling than the issue of preserving free trade is the fear among Central and Eastern European governments that urgent actions taken to tackle the climate crisis will impose much greater hardship on their nations, especially among the rural poor and other disadvantaged sectors of the population. The EU goal to achieve carbon neutrality by 2050, for example, is strongly opposed by Poland, Hungary, Estonia, and the Czech Republic, which fear that they will suffer much greater social and economic dislocation than their wealthier Western and Nordic partners. "We don't want a situation in which caring for the world's climate will happen at the expense of the global economy," said Poland's prime minister Mateusz Morawiecki. "Poland is one of those countries that must first have a very detailed compensation package. We must know how much we will get for modernization."[10] Hungary's prime minister Viktor Orbán also demanded to know how his country's economic interests would be protected under the EU climate change plan, which would require investing up to $300 billion a year in new energy infrastructure. "Let's start to talk about the money!" Orbán said. "We are open, we will negotiate." They were joined in the opposition camp by Czech prime minister Andrej Babiš, who called the EU plan "ecological hysteria" and asked: "Why should we decide 31 years ahead of time what will happen in 2050?"[11]

For the Eastern states that were once part of the Soviet-led communist empire, the climate change issue involves security concerns as well as money. Poland, which still depends on coal to produce 90 percent of the nation's electricity, worries that any radical transformation of its energy profile that diminishes the role of coal will make the country too dependent on Russian gas imports. Given Warsaw's historic animosity toward Moscow, any Polish government seems likely to insist that its basic security interests would be endangered by embracing clean energy sources that would replace coal. Moreover, Poland's concerns about becoming too dependent on Russian energy supplies are shared by other Eastern states that were once in Moscow's orbit, such as Romania, Bulgaria, and the Baltic states.

For these countries, the dilemma is often viewed as a choice between becoming either coal-free or Russia-dependent. For Warsaw, that means an overwhelming number of voters will stick with coal despite high levels of air pollution that claims thousands of Polish lives each year. In other words, any Green Deal for Europe carries risks of further estrangement between East and West.

Across much of Western Europe, the demands for radical measures to address the climate crisis are growing louder. The rise of Green political parties, riding a wave of enthusiastic support from young people such as the Swedish teenage activist Greta Thunberg, who has mobilized millions of climate change activists around the world, is emerging as one of the strongest countervailing forces to right-wing populist nationalists. In the 2019 European elections, Green parties triumphed in the EU's three biggest economies. Led by the soaring popularity of the Greens in Germany, pro-environment parties performed strongly across much of Northern and Western Europe. Up to a dozen European governments, reacting to pressure from their voters, say that they now want to devote at least one-quarter of the EU budget for the next seven years to projects that address the climate crisis. But given the veto powers of Eastern countries, the EU is only going to succeed in its transition to a low-carbon economy through a radical redistribution of financial resources to the most vulnerable areas of Europe. A Green New Deal for Europe, like the one touted by progressives in the United States, would require investing massive amounts in infrastructure, which until recently was resisted by Germany and other Northern countries. If Europe really wants to reach a consensus in order to achieve its climate goals and spur economic growth in the poorer periphery of the continent, its wealthier governments will need to dramatically increase their willingness to commit huge financial resources to public investments related to green technologies.[12]

The climate change controversy is not the only source of growing fissures between Eastern and Western Europe. Resentments are brewing on both sides of the former Cold War divide over differing interpretations of the burdens and responsibilities of EU membership. That argument seems likely to become even more intense when Britain, a net contributor to the EU budget, finally leaves the Union and other countries will be obliged to assume a greater financial burden. Macron and other Western leaders complain that the refusal by Central and Eastern governments to accept their fair share of refugees coming into Europe, mainly through Italy and Greece, betrays the spirit of EU solidarity that has helped to bolster their living standards through the enormous subsidies they have received since they became members. The Western leaders contend that EU membership carries obligations along with benefits. All member states must be willing to accept their duties in implementing European policies. Macron insists that the time has come to curtail the huge regional subsidies being channeled to the Eastern countries unless they reciprocate by accepting their prescribed quotas of immigrants. But Orbán and Jarosław Kaczyński, the powerful head of Poland's ruling Law and Justice Party, insist that they will not open their frontiers to immigrants from the Middle East or North Africa because doing so would endanger national security and dilute the Christian identity of their communities.

Over the past fifteen years, more than 350 billion euros in European Structural and Investment Funds alone have flowed into the ten Central and Eastern European states, according to the European Commission. What were once backward economies mismanaged by decades of communist rule have been transformed into havens of affluence and modernity. In addition to its large infusions of financial support, the EU approved sweetheart tax deals in these countries that attracted investors, financed highways and hospitals, and upgraded universities and digital networks. Brussels also provided them with valuable assistance in shedding the legacy of communist bureaucracy, reforming public administrations and the judiciary, and building up civil society networks with support from Western political foundations. While prosperity remains uneven in the Eastern states, their remarkable rise in living standards helps explain why the Brexit curse did not prove contagious—and why the EU now enjoys overwhelming support among populations from the Baltics to the Balkans in spite of an uncooperative attitude by populist nationalist rulers.

Orbán and Kaczyński have managed to tighten their grip on power in spite of their anti-EU policies by shrewdly manipulating public sentiment into believing that the West has actually exploited the East. An estimated twenty million people have left their Eastern European homelands to work in Western Europe, including Polish laborers who helped reconstruct Berlin, Slovak house cleaners who toil in Parisian luxury apartments, and Romanian farmhands who pick grapes in Burgundy's most prized vineyards. Although these workers may earn more in the West than they could back home, they often feel unfairly treated. Their grievances, in turn, nourish the combative views of right-wing nationalists. The prevailing perspective in the East is that its native workers helped rescue the West from an acute labor shortage that poses a serious economic threat, now and in the future. There is no question that the influx of workers from Eastern Europe has alleviated worker shortages in the West caused by demographic decline; in Germany, for example, annual deaths have outnumbered annual births since 1972. The disparity in wages shows why so many young people in the East still want to leave for the West despite the improvement in living standards since the fall of communism three decades ago. In 2018, Germany's hourly labor costs were six times higher than in Bulgaria and Romania, and more than three times higher than in Poland and Hungary.[13]

Eastern governments also claim that the hemorrhage of skilled talent has inhibited their productivity growth, to the benefit of the West. The EU's newest members are estimated to have poured more than one hundred billion euros of their own money into investments in education and training for the two million young workers (average age thirty) who have moved to Germany over the past ten years. Many highly trained migrants from the East, such as doctors, nurses, and engineers, continue to leave in pursuit of job possibilities in the West because of the considerable income gap. That exodus is perpetuated by the lack of opportunities at home and the lucrative financial incentives to move abroad. This trend, too, could have dire long-term political consequences. The highly educated young people who might serve as an antidote to right-wing nationalists if they stayed home have decided to vote with their feet. In the West, the working and middle classes who fear that their livelihoods will be undercut by a surge of foreign labor coming from Central and Eastern Europe also pose a political risk. Many have become disgruntled voters looking to support right-wing or Euroskeptic parties that want to reinstate national frontiers within Europe and "take back control" from Brussels.

The disaffection between East and West also has roots in the 1989 revolutions that toppled communism. At that time, countries like Poland, Hungary, and the Czech Republic, as well as the Baltic states, felt that they were finally liberated and could rejoin the West, which had long shared their religious and historical traditions. But the utopia they were seeking proved to be an illusion. In many parts of the East, the European Union is perceived as trying to impose a liberal secular lifestyle in which women are encouraged to have fewer children, gays and lesbians are allowed to marry and adopt children, and Muslims from the Middle East and Africa can practice polygamy and other ethnic customs in a multicultural society. Orbán and Kaczyński are lauded by their constituents for fighting back against heathen Western norms and propagating a distinctly nationalist message in favor of church, family, and cultural uniformity. "In 1989, we wanted to be normal, and normality meant living like Western Europeans," said Ivan Krastev, a prominent Bulgarian political scientist. "But imitation breeds resentment. What you see in Hungary or Poland is a return to tradition, and it resembles the kind of resentment you see in the second generation of immigrants, which starts to question its identity."[14]

What troubles Macron and other Western leaders is that Orbán and Kaczyński have sought to entrench themselves in power through authoritarian measures that breach the European Union's democratic values. The two leaders claim that they are only trying to cleanse their administrations of a toxic communist legacy. They accuse Brussels of interfering with their sovereign right to carry out political reforms. After the Polish government changed the composition of the nation's judiciary in 2018, the EU threatened to suspend Poland from the Council of Ministers, the key decision-making body involving Europe's heads of government. The European Parliament also voted to punish Hungary for what it called a "systemic threat" to the EU's basic democratic principles because of Orbán's interference with Hungary's courts, universities, and media to create what he calls an "illiberal democracy."

Neither threat was carried out, as unanimity is required to impose punishment against a transgressor nation. Macron tried insisting instead that if the violations were not halted, then the huge EU subsidies going to Warsaw and Budapest—as much as two billion euros a month for Poland—should be slashed. The European Union, Macron argued, should not be in the business of financing authoritarian regimes. Luxembourg called for Hungary's outright expulsion if it continued with its project to build an illiberal democracy in defiance of EU norms. Frans Timmermans, the European Commission vice president assigned to persuade Poland and Hungary to comply with the European rules, expressed the fear that the antidemocratic tilt by the Eastern governments could pose an "existential threat" to the entire European Union. "We know from our collective European history that you can, through democracy, create autocracy," he said. "Hitler came to power by democratic means—and within weeks he had liquidated democracy and put his opponents in camps."[15] Timmermans believes that the EU's continuing failure to call rejectionist governments to account could embolden further violations by wayward states that ultimately will destroy the credibility of EU treaties and lead to the breakup of the Union.

A North–South split over economic policy also threatens Macron's quest for a more integrated Europe. In the wake of the 2008 global financial crisis and the Greek debt disaster that nearly caused the collapse of the euro, Macron has urged his European peers to approve the creation of a substantial Eurozone budget and other measures that could protect the continent from the threat of future recessions and debt-related shocks. In the longer term, Macron would like to see Europe move toward a fiscal union, starting with adopting a Europe-wide insurance scheme for bank deposits and developing integrated capital markets backed by a large safe asset in the form of a Eurobond. But to Macron's frustration, those ideas have been blocked not just by Germany but by several other creditor nations in Northern Europe. That group, described as the New Hanseatic League, after the federation of city-states that exercised great economic power over Europe in the Middle Ages, includes the Netherlands, Ireland, the Baltic states, and the Nordic states. These smaller EU countries have wielded great influence in taking an uncompromising stand against debt relief for poorer Southern states. That predicament, some economists believe, leaves Europe vulnerable to another major financial crisis, especially if a large country like Italy is forced to default on its debts.

Macron has argued to no avail that Germany needs to abandon its obsession with running permanent fiscal surpluses, which is now enshrined in a constitutional rule requiring all German governments to adhere scrupulously to balanced budgets. Macron contends that it is very much in Germany's own economic interest, as a major commercial power, to ensure the economic well-being of its European trading partners in order to protect its markets and guarantee its own long-term prosperity. But German voters perceive any support of this kind as a zero-sum wealth transfer that takes money out of their own pockets and gives it to spendthrift Southern Europeans. In addition, Germany has been reluctant to spend its huge surpluses on large-scale infrastructure investment projects at home that could help bolster growth prospects for the European economy. And the continuing rejection by Germany and the New Hanseatic countries of debt restructuring plans for Southern Europe has only aggravated the wealth gap between the North and the South. Their leaders claim that Sweden repaired its own banking system, Ireland solved its housing and unemployment crisis, and Denmark has adapted its economy to renewable energies without outside assistance, so Southern Europe should learn to do the same. With Britain leaving Europe, the New Hanseatic nations have become even more assertive in defending their hard-line views. After rejecting Macron's Eurozone proposals at a European Union summit, New Hanseatic leaders were gloating over the demise of his federalist ideas. "2018 was the year when we debated heavily between France and the Netherlands on this idea of stabilization and a Eurozone budget," said Dutch prime minister Mark Rutte. "Both are out of the window. Stabilization is gone. The Eurozone budget is gone."[16]

Macron has been forced to scale back his Eurozone proposals, at least temporarily, in the hope that he will be able to persuade other leaders to take bolder steps in the future. But the New Hanseatics are determined to keep his ideas bottled up to prevent them from ever being put into practice. "Macron's plan started out as an elephant, turned into a mouse, and now that mouse is in a cage," said Wopke Hoekstra, finance minister of the Netherlands.[17] But both Mario Draghi, the former head of the European Central Bank, and his successor, Christine Lagarde, have endorsed Macron's ambitions for a fiscal union, a deposit insurance plan, and a Eurobond asset in order to shore up the future of Europe's single currency. Some experts believe that the potential catastrophe of another global financial crisis may indeed be required in order to convince European leaders to adopt necessary reforms to prevent the future collapse of the euro. Until then, persistent economic weakness in Italy, Greece, and other Southern countries will continue to be used to rally support for populist nationalists who blame Europe's single currency for exacerbating economic inequality between the North and the South.

The polarization of a fragmented Europe over what to do about climate change, immigration, and the need to fortify the EU's single currency will complicate governing for years to come. The paralysis afflicting EU member states because of their conflicting interests over major policy issues feeds into the narrative of anti-European or Euroskeptic parties, which in the 2019 elections secured almost one-third of all seats in the European Parliament. As populist-fueled tensions make it even more difficult for European democracy to function effectively, voters will be increasingly encouraged to look to alternative models of government, such as Orbán's brand of "illiberal democracy" or Putin's authoritarian "strongman" model.[18]

Compounding Europe's dysfunctional management and the surge of populist nationalists has been Britain's delusional execution of its referendum vote in favor of leaving the European Union. In Macron's eyes, Brexit epitomizes the crisis facing Europe. For several months, the French president played the role of bad cop as he urged his fellow European leaders not to postpone the deadline for Brexit. He warned that doing so would prevent any further progress on radical reforms to revive Europe while the continent waited impatiently, as it has done for more than three years, to find out what Britain would do. But Merkel, backed by other leaders who fervently hoped Britain would ultimately change its mind and stay in the Union, procrastinated and offered repeated deadline extensions in the hope of achieving an orderly exit. "You give your friends a chance, and then another one, and then one more," she said in justifying the delays that she hoped would achieve parliamentary approval for the deal. Macron relented but warned that Europe would suffer serious harm because of its indulgent attitude. "We have a European renaissance to manage," he said. "I believe in it very deeply, and I don't want Brexit to come and block us on this."[19]

When Prime Minister Theresa May failed on three occasions to persuade the House of Commons to approve the detailed agreement that her government had painstakingly worked out with the EU, she was forced to resign by intransigent opponents within her own Tory Party. Boris Johnson, her former foreign secretary and a prominent advocate for the Leave campaign, won the succession battle and immediately moved into 10 Downing Street. On his first day in office, Johnson vowed to take Britain out of Europe by the end of October 2019, "no ifs or buts."[20] But Johnson was soon forced to abandon the

Halloween deadline and seek another extension from the European Union to hold rare December elections. Johnson won his gamble by securing a strong majority in parliament to take Britain out of Europe in early 2020.

As Macron had feared, Europe was failing to protect its people from the major shocks of the modern world—in this instance, by becoming trapped in the turmoil of British domestic politics. It was just the kind of ineffectual response that disillusioned voters and drove them into the arms of populist nationalists. While Britain dithered, Macron warned that Europe was becoming distracted and missing opportunities to expand its economic growth and influence in the world. Meanwhile, China, Russia, and the United States were using divide-and-rule tactics to exploit Europe's stasis for their own purposes. Macron became infuriated by the cavalier way in which Boris Johnson and his merry band of "Little Englanders" misled the British people about the impact of Brexit and held the rest of Europe hostage to their whims. "The trap is in the lie and irresponsibility that can destroy the European Union. Who told the British people the truth about their post-Brexit future? Who spoke to them about losing access to the European market? Who mentioned the risks to peace in Ireland of restoring the former border?" Macron wrote in an angry open letter to the citizens of Europe that was published in twenty-eight newspapers. "Nationalist retrenchment offers nothing; it is rejection without an alternative. And this trap threatens the whole of Europe: the anger-mongers, backed by fake news, promise anything and everything."[21]

Macron had believed that it was essential for the EU to take a hard line throughout the Brexit negotiations in order to persuade other member states that might be tempted to follow London's lead that leaving the Union would be a costly and painful experience. The other EU leaders fell in line and gave their unswerving support to Michel Barnier, the former French commissioner who was placed in charge of EU negotiations with Britain. The British debacle removed the threat of France, Italy, Greece, or even the Netherlands heading for the exit. Even the anti-European populist nationalist parties changed their tune about leaving the Union to reforming it from within. The exodus of global banks and corporations, the weakened pound sterling, and the political disarray in Westminster vividly demonstrated the agony that awaited other countries if they tried to follow the British example. In contrast to its squabbles on many other issues, like climate change, immigration, and the Eurozone, the other twenty-seven EU member states maintained a surprisingly unified front throughout the Brexit crisis.[22]

Despite his dismay with the way Brexit has played out, Macron understood the need to keep Britain involved in European security. As the strongest military force on the continent, France will require Britain's continuing support given Germany's pacifist culture and its reluctance to shoulder more of the burden for Europe's defense and security needs. Like his hero Charles de Gaulle, who vetoed Britain's request for entry into the European Common Market in 1963, Macron has always felt that it was illusory to think Britain would sever its dependency on the United States and become fully committed to the European Union. As a pragmatist, Macron hopes that even Boris Johnson will be compelled quickly to abandon his fantasy about building a Global Britain in tandem with America and to recognize that Britain still shares strong interests with Europe. As Macron has explained, these interests include everything from fighting Islamist terrorism at home and abroad to countering Russian cyber-attacks and meddling in Western elections, even to sharing defense technology and the testing of nuclear weapons.

Only after Britain's departure from the European Union can Macron and the new crop of leaders for Europe's key institutions refocus on moving ahead with major reforms that are designed to help Europe compete more effectively on the world stage with China, Russia, India, and the United States. Macron believes that unless Europe moves swiftly to adapt to a new age of big-power competition, it could be fatally challenged by a combination of outside threats, such as the gradual collapse of American security guarantees, Russia's aggressive campaign to destabilize the liberal democratic order, and the hegemonic ambitions of a rising China, as well as the damaging consequences of the climate crisis.

A May 2019 opinion survey conducted in fourteen EU member states by the European Council on Foreign Relations showed that the uncertainty caused by the Brexit fiasco bolstered support for EU membership across the continent. But the survey contains a mordant postscript: in all European countries, the survey found, a majority of people felt that their children's lives will be worse than their own. And despite its newfound popularity, a majority of people also believe that the European Union will fall apart within twenty years.[23]

PART THREE

THE WORLD

CHAPTER 7

DEALING WITH THE DONALD

As Emmanuel Macron and his wife, Brigitte, arrived at the South Lawn entrance to the White House for the first official state visit of the Trump presidency in April 2018, the French leader was prepared for the worst. He had been warned by his ambassador in Washington, Gérard Araud, that Donald Trump would be in no mood to indulge him despite their vaunted "bromance." The lavish welcome was impressive, replete with military bands, color guards, a fife-and-drum corps, and a twenty-one-gun salute. As he climbed out of his limousine, Macron embraced Trump and bestowed kisses on both his cheeks. It was the same way, he later recalled, that Benjamin Franklin and the French philosopher Voltaire greeted each other in 1778. Inside the Oval Office, Trump raved to reporters about how much he liked Macron, who is more than thirty years his junior. As he flicked what he thought was dandruff from the French president's shoulder, Trump declared: "We have to make him perfect. He is perfect."[1]

As the two presidents launched into a forty-five-minute private conversation, followed by a larger meeting with key cabinet officials, Macron turned over in his mind the elaborate arguments he had crafted in English for the contentious issues on their agenda. Ever since their first encounter just two weeks after he took office, Macron had been determined to get along with Trump despite their radically different personalities. As an ultra-pragmatist, Macron said, he realized that it was necessary to establish a trusting partnership with Trump because, almost by default, he had become Europe's chief interlocutor. During my conversations with him, Macron was careful to avoid criticism of Trump's outlandish behavior, saying that he was obligated to work with the elected representative of France's oldest ally. He had quickly grasped Trump's erratic and transactional nature, as well as his affection for strong authoritarian figures. At their May 2017 meeting at NATO headquarters in Brussels, Macron, eager to make a vivid first impression, engaged in a lengthy, white-knuckle handshake with Trump, hoping to send the message that the American president should not mistake his youth and inexperience for weakness: he would be tough and unyielding in defending French and European interests.

Macron had traveled to Washington with an ambitious wish list. He wanted to persuade Trump to abide by the Iranian nuclear deal, maintain the presence of American Special Forces in Syria, and defuse a transatlantic trade war by getting Europe a permanent exemption from steel and aluminum tariffs. Macron thought that he might be able to achieve significant progress on the trade issue. He told Trump that the United States and Europe shared similar problems with a common nemesis, namely China. The most effective approach, he reasoned, would be for the United States and Europe to collaborate on a joint strategy that would persuade China to curtail the subsidies for its steel industry that had so distorted the world market. Macron claimed that the United States and Europe represented nearly half of the global economy in terms of trade and investment flows, and that together they could exert enormous leverage to convince China to halt flagrant commercial abuses, including the theft of intellectual property and discrimination against foreign companies.

"We both know we have a China problem, Donald," Macron said. "So why don't we work together to solve it?"

To Macron's shock and dismay, Trump erupted in a vicious attack on the trade practices of the European Union, and specifically those of Germany. "What do you mean?" Trump exclaimed. "Europe is much worse than China!" He then went on a three-minute rant, according to eyewitnesses, criticizing what he described as the gross injustice he saw in Germany's high tariffs on US automobiles and the easy access to the American market enjoyed by German carmakers like Mercedes-Benz, Volkswagen, and BMW. Later, in a private aside, Trump asked Macron what he thought about Merkel. The French president sensed Trump was trying to sow distrust and kept his own counsel. Trump then interjected that in his view Merkel was "a loser."

Once he calmed down, Trump acknowledged that US trade relations with France were more balanced. He suggested to Macron that they could cut a better deal for their countries if France followed Britain's example in abandoning the Union. "Why don't you leave the European Union?" Trump told him. "We could then reach a bilateral deal on much better terms than you now get as part of the EU." Macron told me that he was momentarily rendered speechless by Trump's outlandish proposal. France is a founding EU member and Macron has been one of the most ardent supporters of a more integrated Europe. "You can well imagine how I reacted," he said.[2] French ambassador Araud, who attended the session, was already well acquainted with Trump's theatrical style, so he was not surprised. He later described Trump's behavior as a vintage performance that was "whimsical, unpredictable, and uninformed."[3]

When the two leaders turned to the Iran nuclear deal, the Joint Comprehensive Plan of Action (JCPOA), Trump attacked the agreement reached under the Obama administration as "insane" and "ridiculous."[4] Macron tried to head him off by acknowledging the deal's shortcomings. He suggested rectifying those flaws by conducting new talks about Iran's ballistic missile program; its destabilizing activities in the region, notably in Syria and Yemen; and a prolongation beyond 2025, when the Iran nuclear deal was set to expire. Macron's "four pillars" plan was designed to preserve and augment the 2015 accord, which, in spite of Trump's opposition, had successfully managed to stop Iran from developing nuclear weapons.

Trump said that he was willing to let Macron pursue new negotiations with Iran to reach an expanded deal, but Macron came away from his White House talks in a sour, pessimistic mood. Even though Trump waited for two weeks to announce his decision to abrogate the agreement, Macron received a clear indication in advance that Trump planned to cancel the deal, "if only because of domestic political reasons." Later, Macron spoke with Iran's president, Hassan Rouhani, about broaching a new deal. He would pursue his mediation efforts with Tehran and Washington for much of the following year, trying to bring together the leaders of two intractable adversaries in hopes of striking a compromise. At one point, Macron was on the verge of arranging a secret meeting between Trump and Rouhani at the United Nations General Assembly in 2018, but Trump waved him off at the last hour, telling Macron that he preferred "to see the Iranians suffer from sanctions a little more."

A year later, in September 2019, Trump told Macron he was eager and willing to meet with Rouhani at the United Nations, but the Iranians demanded some kind of sanctions relief as a sign of good faith. Macron personally tried to broker a meeting during the UN session, telling me that he believed direct dialogue between the leaders of Iran and the United States would be "useful and highly desirable," if only to prevent a future military confrontation that could lead to a devastating war across the Middle East. When a face-to-face encounter proved too complicated, Macron arranged for a secure telephone line to be set up at Rouhani's hotel suite and told Trump to call him on that line at 9:00 p.m. on a Tuesday evening. Macron picked up the phone when Trump called at the appointed hour and then urged Javad Zarif, Iran's foreign minister, to coax Rouhani from his bedroom to speak with Trump. But Zarif reported back that Rouhani was in his pajamas and refused to leave his room. The Iranian leader feared that he was being led into a trap and insisted that some sanctions must be lifted before he would speak with Trump.

Macron's early efforts to establish a dialogue between Tehran and Washington came up short, but he vowed to keep trying. He realized that Trump's ultimate goal was to break the Iranian regime or force its surrender. Macron knew that Trump would never achieve either objective and told him so. Still, Macron persisted in trying to keep the Iran nuclear deal alive and defuse the risks of military conflict. He wanted to prevent Iran's hard-liners from using America's withdrawal to justify cancellation of the agreement and renew their pursuit of nuclear weapons. He was encouraged by his continuing contacts with Rouhani and Trump, who both urged him to keep exploring ways to reach a diplomatic compromise. His role as mediator between Iran and the United States had become an obsessive mission of his presidency. When tensions rose in the Strait of Hormuz after Iran seized an oil tanker in the summer of 2019, Macron reached out to Rouhani and urged restraint, just as he did with Trump. At the G-7 summit meeting in August 2019, hosted by France, Macron renewed his offer to broker a compromise that would address grievances on all sides. He invited Iranian foreign minister Javad Zarif to the summit venue at the Atlantic coastal resort of Biarritz to explore the parameters of a potential deal and the conditions that might be acceptable to the two sworn enemies. France offered a bridge loan worth $15 billion to keep Iran's economy afloat until sanctions were lifted and Tehran could resume selling its oil. The Biarritz negotiations set the stage for Macron's UN shuttle diplomacy a month later that nearly achieved the elusive breakthrough still being sought by all parties. The goal is to have Iran permanently disavow nuclear weapons in return for the permanent lifting of sanctions by the United States and its partners.

"I wanted to be the honest broker of the situation," Macron explained. "But look, I'm not a naive guy. I want to address all the concerns regarding Iran in the region. But if you just kill off the Iran deal without any other option, you open a Pandora's box. You will follow some of the powers in the region who are ready to make war, and you will replicate past mistakes. And so I asked President Trump, 'What is your perspective, do you really want to make war against Iran?' I don't think he wanted to go to this extreme point." After their first discussions about what to do regarding Iran in April 2018, I asked Macron if he made the case to Trump that he might have a more difficult time convincing North Korea to give up its nuclear weapons if he did not honor the Iran deal. Macron agreed with the premise of my question. "I used the same argument. I pushed back. I did my best. I tried to follow a rationale that he can respect," he explained. "But he thinks he is a dealmaker who can find an agreement under his own conditions. It might work in the short term, but it's very insane to think it will work in the mid to long term."[5]

Macron was disappointed that Trump refused to see the logic behind his argument. Trump told Macron that he liked the idea of "getting a bigger and better deal" with Iran and asked him to pursue it, but Macron sensed Trump's lack of seriousness. Just as he struck out in getting Trump to respect the Iran deal, he also failed to persuade Trump to reconsider spurning the Paris agreement on climate change. On Syria, Trump accepted Macron's plea to keep US troops there for a while longer, but later he would unilaterally announce their departure without informing Paris. When Trump betrayed America's Kurdish allies by allowing Turkey to displace the Kurds and set up a buffer zone along its southeastern border with Syria, Macron was angered by the sudden removal of US Special Forces, which left French soldiers dangerously exposed. He also feared that the release of Islamic State fighters of French origin would raise the terrorist threat in France if they should make their way back home. On trade, Trump refused to offer Europe any exemptions from tariffs and even indicated that he was determined to take a tougher stand against Europe than in the past. Macron got nowhere with his argument that the United States and Europe should collaborate in a strategy of standing up to China. Despite these successive rebuffs, the French president insisted that it was necessary to keep talking with Trump, if only to make him aware of the damaging impact of his policies. He declared that France would persist in maintaining a close historic partnership with its oldest ally, which he described as "absolutely critical, in fact fundamental, because we need it."[6]

More than any other leader in Europe, Macron has worked assiduously to court Trump despite their clashing views. Shortly after becoming president, he personally called Trump and invited him to be his special guest at the 2017 Bastille Day celebrations, an honor that Trump genuinely appreciated. Trump admired the grandiose spectacle of vintage tanks rolling down the Champs-Élysées and fighter jets spewing tricolor smoke over the Arc de Triomphe to mark the one-hundredth anniversary of America's entry into World War I. The two presidents visited Napoleon's tomb and later joined their wives for dinner at the Jules Verne restaurant in the Eiffel Tower, where they savored an American-style menu of filet of beef and chocolate ice cream. By the end of his stay, Trump was praising Macron as "a great president, a tough president." Macron's seduction of Trump was so effective that White House advisers would subsequently beg their French counterparts to get their boss to intervene to change the president's mind on controversial issues, including his decision to recognize Jerusalem as Israel's capital.[7]

r reciprocated Macron's hospitality by inviting him
e visit of his administration. That gesture provoked
other allied leaders. Shortly after the Macrons arrived
DC, at the peak of cherry blossom season in April
d his wife flew with them on the Marine One heli-
Vernon for an intimate dinner and a private tour of
ton's home. It was a special privilege rarely accorded
heads of state. The Macrons had done their home-
about America's founding father. They recalled that
ayette became close friends with Washington while
e him in the Revolutionary War. Washington even

was made an honorary French citizen in 1792 by the First French Republic. According to an account of the evening, Trump was fascinated to learn that Washington was a major real estate speculator. He expressed surprise that Washington did not name any of his properties after himself. "If he was smart, he would have put his name on it," Trump said. "You've got to put your name on stuff or no one remembers you." Mount Vernon's chief executive, Doug Bradburn, who served as tour guide, gently reminded Trump that Washington did succeed in getting the nation's capital named after him. "Good point," the president replied with a laugh.[8]

Despite their contrasts in age and personality, Macron and Trump bonded. As they got to know each other over the course of the first year, the two leaders conducted more telephone calls with each other than with any other leader, according to White House and Élysée aides. They indulged in gossip about other leaders and spoke with an easy familiarity about their spouses, rather than dwelling on the details of policy matters. Trump was particularly intrigued by the symmetry of Brigitte being twenty-four years older than Macron while Trump was twenty-four years older than his wife, Melania. "She looks in such great shape," Trump exclaimed when he first met Brigitte, then sixty-four. The Macrons took Trump's brazen personal remarks in good humor, even if they seemed taken aback by the American's casual intimacy. Nonetheless, the hugging and hand-holding between the two presidents reflected not just the tactile nature of each man but also genuine affection. An Élysée aide likened the rapport between them to that of a diligent son and a wacky father.

Among his European peers, Macron became known as "the Trump Whisperer." The label reflected perhaps a touch of disdain mixed with envy for his easy access to the Oval Office occupant. His political opponents at home sought to depict him as Trump's poodle. Macron rejected their criticism by insisting that it was important to sustain a dialogue with Trump even if he did not change his mind on issues important to Europe. "Every personal relationship is unique,"

Macron explained. "We may be very different in our own styles, but we have some things in common, in that we are mavericks within our political systems."

When confronted by Trump's intransigence on global issues, Macron learned to circumvent his opposition by appealing to other constituencies. After Trump withdrew the United States from the Paris climate change accords, Macron released a video address to the American people calling on US scientists, engineers, and "responsible citizens" to discover a second homeland by coming to live and work in France. He invited the chief executives of major American corporations to dinner at the Versailles Palace and lobbied them to support the environmental goals of the Paris accords in defiance of the Trump administration's action.

On the last day of his state visit, Macron went to Capitol Hill and directly challenged Trump on virtually every major issue during an impassioned speech to both houses of Congress. On the sixtieth anniversary of the day when Charles de Gaulle had appeared before American legislators in 1958, Macron was greeted warmly with a three-minute standing ovation as he entered the House chamber. Macron's cross-party appeal was evident throughout his fifty-minute address, as lawmakers from both sides of the aisle joined in frequent applause as he presented his arguments. His speech attacked the very basis of Trump's America First policies as he pleaded with Congress to keep the United States engaged in world leadership. He warned against the temptation to succumb to "isolationism, withdrawal, and nationalism," which "would not douse but only inflame the fears of our citizens."

Macron urged the United States to preserve the international institutions created with American leadership after World War II. Calling on the United States and its European allies to reinvent "a new breed of strong multilateralism" to shape the twenty-first century world order, Macron denounced Trump's decision to impose steep tariffs on steel and aluminum and argued that the problems of global trade could not be solved by "massive deregulation and extreme nationalism." He warned the legislators that Trump's path of confrontation would cause incalculable damage to the vital interests of both America and Europe. "Commercial war is not the proper answer," Macron said. "At the end of the day, it will destroy jobs, increase prices, and force the middle class to pay. It is not consistent with our mission, with our history, with our current commitments to global security."[9]

As he was leaving the House chamber, Macron was mobbed by lawmakers from both sides of the aisle who congratulated him for his stirring defense of multilateralism. At least two senators, Bob Corker, a Republican from Tennessee, and Chris Coons, a Democrat from Delaware, were heard to tell him, "I wish you were our president." Then Macron's cell phone rang. It was Trump calling to express his enthusiasm for what he called "a great speech" and to say how impressed he was by the way Macron had rallied support from both Republicans and Democrats. The French president expressed incredulity that Trump would praise him so effusively for a speech in which he had bluntly criticized so many of Trump's America First policies. One of Macron's diplomatic aides later explained the paradox: "It shows that in Trump's world, words don't really matter. What counts is the performance and how the message plays with the audience."[10]

Despite Macron's warm welcome from Congress and other well-wishers in Washington, he departed without any clear signs that his friendly overtures to Trump had paid any significant dividends. He thought that Trump might be willing to give him a little time to prod Iran toward new negotiations until, on May 8, Trump abruptly declared that the United States would no longer abide by the Iran nuclear agreement. Macron lamented Trump's decision and had warned him repeatedly that leaving the agreement would further damage America's credibility in the world. "Other world powers, just as sovereign as us, have decided not to respect their own word," Macron said. Continuing with cold realism, he added, "If we accept that other great powers, including friends who have been with us in the darkest hours, put themselves in the position of deciding for us our diplomacy, our security, while putting us at severe risk, then we are no longer sovereign, and we can't credibly face public opinion."[11]

Rather than recoil from Trump in the wake of such setbacks, Macron kept insisting that it was important to maintain an open dialogue with him. He understood the exasperation felt by many European leaders, notably Germany's chancellor Angela Merkel, who confided to aides that it was stressful for her just to be in the same room with Trump.[12] Macron saw Trump as the raw manifestation of resurgent populist nationalism in America. The frustrations and votes of his supporters, who shared similar grievances with their far-right counterparts in Europe, helped carry him into the White House, and Trump was now determined to sustain the fervor of his electoral base. French diplomats explained that Macron, in his analytical way, saw Trump not as a renegade but as the representative of a unique lineage in American history dating back to President Andrew Jackson. "The Iran decision is the best illustration of the Jacksonian moment the United States is now going through," François Delattre, France's ambassador to the United Nations at the time, told me. "It is a strange mix of unilateralism and isolationism. This does not come out of the blue. Whether we like it or not, this school of thought is very much part of American history. This disengagement started before President Trump, and I tend to believe it will last after him."[13]

What troubled Macron most about his conversations with Trump was his cavalier disregard toward the importance of the transatlantic relationship and its impact on the global economy. Annual trade between Europe and the United States is worth more than $1.3 trillion, and their combined commerce and investments account for nearly half of the global economy. Yet Trump insisted on seeing Europe as an adversary rather than a collection of tried-and-true allies. Even if the United States had been a strong supporter of the European Union since the beginning, Trump said, he perceived the bloc more as "a foe" in terms of "what they do to us in trade." The day after EU leaders held a summit in June 2018 to discuss the trade conflict with Washington, Trump attacked them at a rally in North Dakota, telling his audience that "the European Union was set up to take advantage of the United States."[14]

After the state visit, Macron reported back to his fellow European leaders that he saw in Trump the character of a bully who would take advantage of those too weak to fight back. At a gathering of EU leaders in Sofia, Bulgaria, shortly after his Washington visit, Macron said that Trump was unwilling to exempt Europe from steel and aluminum tariffs and threatened to impose further hardship by slapping penalties on European auto imports. As the world's leading commercial bloc, he said, the European Union should refuse to "negotiate with a gun to its head" and be ready to retaliate unless Trump backed down. The EU leaders agreed unanimously to tell the Trump administration that negotiations could start only if the United States granted a permanent tariff exemption. "What we demand are no conditions and no limits and to go back to the situation before," Macron said. "The condition for all talks is to lift all threats and tariffs, without mention of a time limit." Unless the United States accepted those terms, the European Commission, which handles trade talks on behalf of the bloc, would be authorized to impose a 25 percent tariff on more than $3 billion worth of American goods coming into Europe.[15] The European leaders also said that they would not follow America's example but instead would support the Iran nuclear deal as long as Tehran adhered to its terms. They vowed to protect their companies' doing business with Iran by setting up an alternative financing program, called INSTEX (Instrument in Support of Trade Exchanges), to circumvent American sanctions.

It was Europe's most aggressive challenge to the United States since the 2003 Iraq War, when Germany and France refused to join the United States and Britain in the military invasion to topple Saddam Hussein. George W. Bush had resented them for staying out of the conflict and refused to acknowledge the fact that the French and German leaders turned out to be correct in their predictions of disaster in Iraq, but they regarded Trump's belligerence toward them as far worse. Europe's exasperation over the Trump administration's bullying tactics was best expressed by Donald Tusk, the president of the EU Council, who remarked that Europe's patience with Trump's "capricious assertiveness" was finally exhausted. "With friends like that, who needs enemies?" Tusk asked. "Thanks to him, we have got rid of all illusions. He made us realize that if you need a helping hand, you will find one at the end of your arm."[16] Europe decided to move ahead with commercial talks with other countries, and it concluded its largest trade deal ever with Japan in July 2018; that agreement, by some measures, will create the largest free trade area in the world and cover one-quarter of the global economy. The bloc also pushed ahead with free trade pacts with Mexico, Canada, Vietnam, and Singapore and stepped up negotiations with a long list of other countries. Europe's trade offensive "fits the notion that you don't need the US to do open trade," observed Pascal Lamy, former director-general of the World Trade Organization and a close Macron ally.

As Macron expected, Trump proved to be a prickly and temperamental partner at G-7 and NATO summits. On the eve of the G-7 meeting in June 2018 hosted by Canadian prime minister Justin Trudeau, Macron telephoned Trump to have a candid discussion with him about trade and immigration issues. He stressed the need for Europe and the United States to project a show of unity, even if they could not immediately resolve their differences. He found Trump in a foul mood and unwilling to rescind American tariffs on steel and aluminum imports, which Macron criticized as "illegal" and a "big mistake." They also clashed on how the United States and NATO forces could help stop a renewed surge in refugees trying to cross the Mediterranean Sea from Libya. Macron thought that he could speak his mind in telling Trump that he was alienating America's closest allies by announcing unilateral decisions to impose tariffs that would only trigger retaliation and a possible trade war. But Trump launched into a tirade about the United States being constantly exploited by its allies through disadvantageous trade deals and by institutions like NATO in which allies did not pay their fair share.

The call ended acrimoniously, with Trump warning Macron that he would not be pushed around by other Western leaders who were intent on undermining him. Macron described the call as "not just bad, but terrible from start to finish."[17] After their conversation, Macron released a tweet aimed directly at Trump just hours before the G-7 summit. "The American president may not mind being isolated, but neither do we mind signing a 6-nation agreement if need be." Pressed for comment by journalists at the summit, Macron told them, "Nobody is forever."[18]

Trump's behavior at the G-7 summit demonstrated his contempt for the multilateral institutions that Macron and other allied leaders desperately hope to salvage. During the summit, Trump complained that US allies were stealing from America. "We're the piggy bank that everybody's robbing, and that ends," he said. Trump kept repeating his standard refrain that the international order was stacked against the United States. He declared that the World Trade Organization, NATO, and the EU were all "bad for America" because they acted in ways damaging to American interests. He singled out Merkel as a target for his scorn, telling a European prime minister that he could not tolerate the German chancellor because "that woman embodies everything that I hate." At one point during the summit proceedings, Trump tossed a couple of Starburst candies across the table at her and said, "Here, Angela. Don't say I never gave you anything."[19]

Trump decided to leave the summit early, skipping a discussion of climate change on the last day. In a fit of pique, he withdrew his endorsement of the summit's final declaration—which the White House had previously approved—in support of "free, fair, and mutually beneficial trade." In a hostile tweet sent from Air Force One after he left, Trump ripped into Justin Trudeau and accused the Canadian prime minister of misleading the public about what transpired at the summit. "Based on Justin's false statements at his news conference, and the fact that Canada is charging massive tariffs to our US farmers, workers and companies, I have instructed our US representatives not to endorse the communique as we look at tariffs on automobiles flooding the US market."

Based on their unpleasant phone conversation ahead of the G-7 meeting, Macron realized that Trump had been intending all along to disrupt the two 2018 summits in order to mobilize his political base ahead of the November midterm elections. In light of how contentious a subject trade had been between the United States and Europe at the G-7 summit, he was convinced that Trump would throw an even bigger tantrum at the NATO meeting in Brussels a month later over the shortfalls in defense spending by the European allies. In a prescient tweet right after their heated argument over the phone, Macron wrote: "If this was the mood music before the G-7, imagine how bad things will be at next month's NATO summit." He was right.

In the days ahead of the 2018 NATO summit meeting, Trump told his top national security officials that he did not see the point of the Western military alliance. He complained that NATO no longer served its original purpose and was seriously depleting American resources. He also questioned NATO's Article 5, which commits member states to help defend any other member that comes under attack. Trump asked, why should American soldiers be sent to protect the Balkan country of Montenegro, NATO's newest member? His frustrations with the alliance had grown in the first two years of his presidency as many European members, notably Germany, failed to reach an agreed-upon goal of spending 2 percent of their gross national product on defense spending.[20]

Even before the NATO summit started, Trump chastised Germany at a breakfast with NATO secretary-general Jens Stoltenberg. With television cameras rolling, Trump claimed that Germany was "totally controlled by Russia" because of its growing dependence on Russian gas with the construction of the Nord Stream 2 pipeline. He accused the Berlin government of doling out billions of dollars to Russia to build the pipeline while shirking its NATO commitments by devoting little more than 1 percent of its GDP to defense and continuing to rely on the United States for its security. "I have to bring it up, because I think it's very unfair to our country," Trump said as Stoltenberg listened in a state of shock. The video footage played out on American television with the desired political effect of Trump depicting himself to his voters as insisting that rich European allies carry more of the burden for their own defense and relieve some of the costs to the American taxpayers. A flurry of Trump tweets reinforced his message, which sounded to some allies like blackmail.

When Trump missed most of the first day's session, many leaders breathed a sigh of relief, thinking that they had escaped the worst of his wrath. On the second day, the presidents of Ukraine and Georgia were invited as special guests at the start of the meeting to make their case for joining NATO. Trump arrived late, holding a single piece of paper with figures citing the shortfalls in defense spending by NATO states. He interrupted the presentations of the other leaders and launched into a verbal barrage against those he labeled as deadbeats and free riders on American security protection. Merkel and Macron were so appalled that they left their seats to plead with Stoltenberg to declare an emergency session and ask the embarrassed Ukrainian and Georgian representatives to leave the room.[21]

Macron warned Stoltenberg that he was in danger of allowing the NATO session to turn into another fiasco like the G-7 meeting. Stoltenberg took their advice and cleared the room of guests and staffers. Then he allowed Trump to finish his twenty-minute harangue. Trump blasted NATO's new headquarters, built at a cost of $1.4 billion, as a colossal waste of money. He went down his list and addressed each leader individually, berating those he felt were not doing enough. He attacked Merkel yet again for what he called Germany's shameful reluctance to spend more on its own defense while getting rich by exporting BMW and Mercedes-Benz luxury cars to American consumers.

Other European leaders jumped in to defend her. Lithuania's president, Dalia Grybauskaitė, praised Merkel for her leadership in achieving European unity on sanctions against Russia. Denmark's prime minister, Lars Løkke Rasmussen, reprimanded Trump for his "bombastic statements" and noted that the Danish military had suffered casualties in the US-led mission in Afghanistan that were proportional to those of Americans. In emotional language, Rasmussen told the president that he had attended many funerals of Danish soldiers and that he could not accept Trump telling him Denmark was not doing enough for NATO.[22]

Stoltenberg feared that the meeting would dissolve in anger and turmoil. The only way to bring the session to a peaceful end, realized Prime Minister Mark Rutte of the Netherlands, was to offer Trump some way of declaring victory. Rutte told Trump that he should be pleased that since he took office the NATO allies had collectively raised their defense budgets by more than $70 billion. Stoltenberg seized the moment and thanked Trump for his leadership in highlighting the spending issue. He then brought the meeting to a merciful close. Trump left the room to announce to waiting journalists that the summit was a rousing success. He claimed that NATO governments had agreed to consider doubling their spending commitment to 4 percent of GDP. Macron then came out and publicly denied that any such commitment had been made. As other NATO leaders emerged from the room shaken and troubled by the erratic behavior of the American president, Trump departed for Britain to prepare for a meeting four days later in Helsinki with Vladimir Putin. In his parting shot in Brussels, Trump told journalists that his controversial performance demonstrated that he was, in fact, "a very stable genius."[23]

Trump's boorish behavior at both summits in 2018 convinced Macron that everything had to be done to prevent any further presidential blowups before Trump wrecked the Atlantic alliance. A year later, at the 2019 G-7 summit hosted by France, Macron sought in advance to defuse a Trump outburst by declaring that there would be no final communiqué from the leaders of the world's major industrialized democracies. "Let's be honest," Macron said before the meeting convened. "Nobody reads the communiqués which are the result of interminable bureaucratic haggling. And those who do bother to read them are only looking for points of disagreement."

Shortly after Trump arrived on Saturday for the three-day summit in Biarritz, Macron pulled him aside for a two-hour private lunch, with no aides present. Macron told Trump how he intended to orchestrate every aspect of the summit, including his secret initiative to bring Javad Zarif to the summit venue to explore a way out of the impasse on the Iran crisis. They agreed on the same objectives: to prevent Iran from ever possessing nuclear weapons and to contain it from provoking further instability in the region.

Trump appreciated Macron's solicitude and declared that the lunch was "the best and most productive meeting we have ever had." The Trump Whisperer thus managed to preserve a pretense of unity among the seven leaders—but not before Trump complained that it was time to bring Russia back into the group. He said Vladimir Putin's presence would be useful for any discussions about what to do in Iran, North Korea, and Syria. The other leaders objected that Putin had done nothing to rectify his annexation of Ukraine or his support for separatist rebels in eastern Ukraine, let alone restore democracy to Russia. Trump shrugged off their opposition and declared that he would in all likelihood invite Putin to the next summit in 2020, to be hosted by the United States.

Over the course of several months, following private talks with Merkel and other leaders, the French president concluded that their constant frustration in dealing with Trump and his unpredictable behavior was slowly bringing EU governments around to Macron's view that they had arrived at a critical juncture in the history of the Atlantic alliance. There was a growing recognition, even among the most ardent pro-American states, that Europe needed to think and act more strategically in order to protect its collective interests from being exploited by larger powers like the United States, Russia, and China. EU leaders understood that in the realm of trade at least, Europe, as the world's leading commercial bloc, already possessed the size and the clout to defend its strategic interests on an equal footing with friends and foes alike.

Several prominent chief executives of American corporations lobbied the White House to find a resolution to its battle with the EU over tariffs because the stakes were so enormous. For their companies, Europe accounted for 56 percent of their global earnings in 2017, and more than 60 percent of America's total foreign assets, or a stunning $16 trillion, were sunk in Europe. On the other side, Europe's total investments in the United States exceeded $2.6 trillion, more than four times the level of comparable investments from Asia. It was clear that the risks for the global economy were too perilous for an all-out trade war to break out between Europe and the United States, as Trump eventually realized.[24] When he entered the Oval Office on July 25, Jean-Claude Juncker, president of the European Commission, reminded Trump of the futility of tit-for-tat trade wars that only inflict harm on both sides. "If you want to be stupid," he told Trump, "then I can be stupid, as well."[25]

The transatlantic trade truce reflected Macron's conviction that Europe can make its voice heard when dealing with the United States, China, and Russia only from a position of strength. Macron has been a driving force in prodding the European Union to ensure that American technology giants like Amazon and Facebook pay their fair share of taxes in the countries where they operate, rather than be allowed to siphon off their profits into tax havens. A French law, which Macron wanted to see adopted by other European nations, was passed in 2019 that imposed a 3 percent tax on digital service companies whose global revenues surpass $800 million. That measure, which targeted about two dozen companies, predominantly American, enabled the French government to collect more than $500 million in extra taxes. It also infuriated President Trump. He accused Macron of engaging in protectionist behavior by unfairly discriminating against US companies in demanding they should pay higher taxes in France. For the first time in the long American relationship with France, the United States launched an investigation of the French tax using the same mechanism the Trump administration employed in placing sweeping tariffs on China. Trump also threatened to retaliate by slapping new tariffs on French wine imports. A truce was reached at the G-7 summit in Biarritz in which France promised to reimburse the taxes once an international tax treaty was developed and Trump dropped his threat of imposing tariffs against French wine. But the issue is likely to remain a recurring source of conflict. French finance minister Bruno Le Maire cited the need to stand up to digital giants that were becoming too unmanageable and eluding the control of sovereign states by seeking to escape from paying their fair share of taxes. He pointed out that the American digital behemoths were paying average tax rates of less than 10 percent, compared to 23 percent for more traditional companies. "We're being confronted with the emergence of economic giants that are monopolistic and that not only want to control the maximum amount of data, but also escape fair taxes," Le Maire said. "It's a question of justice."[26]

The European legislation in the digital sector reflects a new determination to use the continent's commercial clout to compete with other big powers in defending its values and interests. Macron was particularly vocal in accusing the United States of seeking to weaponize the dollar's unique status as the world's reserve currency in which most global commerce is transacted. American efforts to extend the territorial reach of its sanctions against Iran by threatening to punish European companies that do business with Tehran triggered an angry backlash in Europe. Many European companies, faced with the loss of their access to US capital markets, felt that they had no other choice but to withdraw from any transaction with Iran because they could not afford the costs of being excluded from American markets. The Iran sanctions crisis convinced Macron that the euro should acquire greater clout in global markets and, if necessary, challenge the dollar's role as the dominant trading currency in order to end what Charles de Gaulle called "America's exorbitant privilege."

In the arena of military security, Europe's continuing dependence on the United States has become a serious vulnerability in the post–Cold War era. With the renewal of big-power competition among the United States, China, and Russia, Macron has made his push for greater defense cooperation within Europe—to diminish its reliance on the United States—the centerpiece of his blueprint to develop a more assertive role for Europe. "We have to rethink the strategy of blocs that has dominated the world," Macron told me. "The United States is still an important ally, but we in Europe must become more sovereign and independent in taking care of our own security and defense."[27] In his call for a "European renaissance," Macron insists that France and its EU partners can achieve "strategic autonomy," or mastery over their own destiny, only by shedding their dependence on outside powers. "Europe can no longer entrust its security to the United States alone," Macron told France's top diplomats in August 2018 at a conference where they had gathered to discuss the future of France and Europe's foreign and security policy. "It is up to us to assume our responsibilities and to guarantee European security and, thereby, sovereignty."[28]

A good example of Europe's lack of control over its own fate occurred in October 2018, when Trump decided that the United States should withdraw from the Intermediate-Range Nuclear Forces (INF) Treaty, which had prohibited the deployment of medium-range nuclear missiles in Europe for the past three decades. "When I see President Trump announcing that he's quitting a major disarmament treaty which was formed after the 1980s Euromissile crisis that hit Europe, who is the main victim? Europe and its security," Macron said in a radio interview marking one hundred years since the end of World War I. "It shows why peace in Europe is still precarious."[29]

Macron used the occasion of the centennial anniversary of the Great War's armistice to call for the creation of "a true European army" to protect against a variety of threats, including in cyber-space and from China, Russia, and the United States. He invited more than sixty heads of state to Paris to show the solidarity of their support for the international order that had kept the peace in Europe for seven decades. Trump denounced Macron's proposal for a European army as "very insulting" to the American soldiers who had defended Europe from fascism and communism. Macron later sought to clear up any misunderstanding by telling Trump he merely wanted Europe to take greater responsibility for its own defense—as Trump himself had been urging Europe to do for years.

The anniversary took place just after the Republicans had lost control of the House of Representatives to the Democrats, and Trump arrived in Paris in a dyspeptic state. He refused to join other heads of state in a march under drizzling skies to the Arc de Triomphe, preferring to ride in his limousine, as did Putin. Trump was further angered by Macron's address. "Patriotism is the exact opposite of nationalism," Macron said in his speech. "Nationalism is a betrayal of patriotism by saying: 'our interest first, who cares about the others?'" Recalling the rivalries that led to World War I, Macron warned that "old demons" were reappearing and that "giving in to the fascination for withdrawal, isolationism, violence, and domination would be a grave error for which future generations would very rightly hold us responsible."[30] Trump, who was not asked to speak at the event, listened to Macron's short address through an earpiece wearing a scowl on his face.

Trump flew back to Washington from his two-day stay in Paris infuriated with the way Macron had treated him as window dressing. Once safely home, he unleashed a Twitter barrage against Macron. He mocked the French president's low approval ratings and France's high unemployment levels. He also ridiculed Macron's aspirations for Europe to build its own army. "It was Germany in World Wars One and Two—How did that work out for France? They were starting to learn German in Paris before the U.S. came along. Pay for NATO or not!" he tweeted.

Macron refused to respond in kind. But he insisted that he would not be deterred by Trump's hostility from pursuing his goal of a continental army to achieve security independence for France and Europe and thus guarantee their sovereignty. "At every moment in our history, we have been allies," Macron said, alluding to two centuries of partnership between France and the United States. "But to be an ally is not to be a vassal."[31]

The heart of the dispute, as Macron sees it, is that Europe will never be able to reach its full potential as a sovereign and unified force in the world until it can ultimately jettison its reliance on American security commitments. "Europe is finally realizing that before saving the world, it needs to save itself from the assault of its former protector, the United States," Sylvie Kauffmann, editorial director of the French newspaper *Le Monde*, told me. "It is at last accepting the idea that its reliable uncle has turned into a bully."[32] In many respects, Macron has stood as the only leader in Europe who seems prepared to push ahead with a truly independent vision in the twenty-first century. France has become the only autonomous military power on the European continent, with its own aircraft carrier, nuclear deterrent, and seat on the UN Security Council. By contrast, many European countries, particularly Poland and the Baltic states, are reluctant to cut their security ties to the United States because they believe that Washington remains their best form of insurance against Russian aggression. But as doubts have grown about the durability of American protection, Macron has become convinced that Europe must learn to defend its own interests, even in defiance of its closest partner, the United States.

During his state visit to Washington in April 2018, Macron presented with great fanfare a small oak tree to Trump as a living gift in honor of the world's oldest alliance. It had been transplanted from Belleau Wood, the World War I battlefield sixty miles east of Paris where nearly two thousand US Marines died while fighting invading German forces. The tree was placed in quarantine, since it was an imported sapling, after which it was supposed to be replanted on the South Lawn of the White House. But the European sessile oak, less than five feet tall, died in exile within a few weeks because its roots were apparently damaged. The tree's demise came as the once-flourishing bromance between Trump and Macron was rapidly wilting because of their conflicts over Iran, climate change, trade, and security issues. Despite Macron's claims to the contrary, it was hard to avoid the metaphorical symbolism of the dead tree.

CHAPTER 8

PARTNERSHIP WITH PUTIN?

The black limousine carrying Russian president Vladimir Putin rolled up to the red carpet at the entrance of the ornate seventeenth-century Palace of Versailles. As he waited to greet the first foreign head of state he had invited to France, Emmanuel Macron replayed in his mind the elaborate plan he had conceived. He had taken office as France's president two weeks earlier, and he was acutely aware that first impressions could be decisive. He had recently engaged in a memorable white-knuckle handshake with Donald Trump, pumping his arm vigorously even as Trump sought to pull away. "It wasn't innocent, it was a moment of truth," Macron said later. "One must show that you will not make small concessions, even symbolic ones."[1] Because he understood Putin's ardent desire to be treated like a czar, Macron had chosen to stage their first meeting in the sumptuous setting of Versailles to celebrate the three-hundredth anniversary of Peter the Great's visit to the child

king Louis XV. He knew that Putin would challenge him, and he
was prepared to punch back.

As Putin emerged from his limousine, Macron stepped forward
with a brisk, one-word greeting: "Bienvenue!" They then began three
hours of intense discussions. Even before his election, Macron had
recognized that there was an opening for France to become a new
pivotal power, one that was willing to speak with all parties and use
diplomatic dexterity to find solutions to the most vexing problems.
He was well aware that any path to success would involve close cooperation with Russia. In his initial private talks with Putin, Macron
refrained from complaining about Russian meddling in French elections and Putin's blatant support for his far-right challenger, Marine
Le Pen. Instead, he extolled Russia's historical and cultural connections to the West, embodied by Peter the Great. "We must find ways
to anchor Russia in Europe and the West," Macron told me. "I know
all the faults and bad traits of Putin, but we have an historic opportunity because he is a man of Saint Petersburg who looks toward Europe, much more than many people realize."[2]

Macron sought to channel his discussions with Putin into how to
break the stalemates over Ukraine and Syria. He had been warned by
German chancellor Angela Merkel—with whom he had met in Berlin on his first day in office two weeks earlier—that Putin was an inveterate liar. Merkel had met or spoken with Putin on more than one
hundred occasions since the Ukraine crisis erupted in 2014. When
he vehemently denied that Russian soldiers had been dispatched to
Crimea or eastern Ukraine, she showed him photographic evidence
of their presence. Yet Putin persisted in denying reality and claimed
that the pictures were fakes. Macron did not want to start their relationship by getting into arguments over truths and falsehoods. He
knew that Putin's singular obsession was to persuade the West to lift
the economic sanctions that were imposed after Russia's annexation
of Crimea in 2014. Macron acknowledged that lifting sanctions and
increasing trade and investment would be in the mutual interests of
both Russia and France, but Putin needed to take the initiative to

break the impasse in Ukraine by withdrawing Russian troops and allowing free and fair elections. Putin adamantly refused, which did not surprise Macron, but at least he consented to convene a new round of peace talks with Ukraine in the presence of French and German leaders—a four-power conclave known as the "Normandy format," after the location where the first talks were held.

On Syria, where Russian troops had intervened to prop up the regime of Bashar al-Assad, Macron suggested that he was prepared to tolerate Assad's presence in power at least until free elections could be organized as part of any political settlement. But he insisted that unlike US president Barack Obama, France would uphold its "red line" against any use of chemical weapons on civilians and vowed to strike back in retaliation if that happened. Putin seemed more conciliatory than usual. He agreed that French and Russian forces in Syria needed to work closely together to defeat Islamist terrorist groups and maintain Syria's territorial integrity. They arranged to hold regular consultations among their forces on the ground to coordinate military operations and exchange information about the location and movements of terrorist groups. For Macron, the first conversation with Putin achieved his main goal: agreement that France would help serve as a mediator and strive to bring Russia closer to the West, though Macron made it clear that he would not back down on matters of principle or break with the Western consensus on sanctions.[3]

After they concluded their talks, Macron escorted Putin through the famous Gallery of Battles, which celebrates French military victories, including those of Napoleon's armies over Russia. In that grandiose setting, Macron used their joint press conference to show that even though he was a thirty-nine-year-old neophyte who had never held elective office before winning the French presidency, he was determined not to be a pushover. Macron flattered Putin by declaring that "no essential issue can be handled today without talking to Russia." But he did not try to mask their differences over Ukraine and Syria and characterized their get-acquainted conversation as "extremely frank and direct."

He then used a reporter's question to launch a fierce barrage of criticism at Putin that Russian media outlets like RT and Sputnik had engaged in spreading propaganda during the French election campaign. "They acted as organs of influence that spread defamatory untruths about me and my campaign," Macron declared as a stunned Putin looked on. "They did not behave as journalists, but as agents of influence and lying propaganda; no more, no less. And I will not give an inch on this." Putin did not react to Macron's denunciation of the Russian media, but he expressed outraged denial when asked if the Kremlin approved a massive wave of cyber-attacks against Macron in the days ahead of the election. He also insisted that even though he had welcomed Macron's opponent Marine Le Pen to the Kremlin during the campaign, his gesture of hospitality was not intended to influence the outcome of the French election. "If Madame Le Pen asked to meet us, why would we refuse her?" Putin said. "The more so since she always publicly spoke out for developing relations with our country. It would be strange for us to refuse her."[4]

Macron came away from his first meeting with Putin feeling that it was more vital than ever for him to take the lead for Europe in nurturing a new dialogue with Moscow. Merkel was exhausted and disillusioned by her frequent and inconclusive dealings with Putin. Even though they spoke each other's languages fluently, Merkel and Putin could never overcome a chasm of mistrust rooted in their personal histories: Putin had been a KGB officer stationed in Dresden as the Berlin Wall fell, and Merkel was a scientist turned dissident who had become the leader of a reunited Germany. Trump's rapport with Putin was complicated by suspicions about his controversial business dealings in Moscow and the investigation led by Special Counsel Robert Mueller into whether his campaign colluded with Russia to swing the 2016 US presidential election in his favor. Macron believed that only he, and France, were in a position to persuade Putin to abandon his hostility toward the West and his fanciful notion of creating a rival Eurasian bloc of nations that would establish an alliance of authoritarian regimes with China.

Macron sought to use his affable early relations with Trump to convince the United States to begin easing sanctions against Russia. He warned that cutting off aluminum imports from Russia could damage important European industries such as automobiles and aerospace. Russia is the world's largest producer of aluminum outside of China, and shortages in the world market had already led to dramatic price increases of more than 30 percent.[5] Besides the economic relief that would result from lifting sanctions, Macron also hoped to encourage Putin to make political concessions on Syria and Ukraine. Yet following the meeting in Versailles, Macron knew that he had failed to convince Putin to show more flexibility in resolving those conflicts.

Then, in March 2018, came news that Sergei Skripal, a former Russian double agent working with British intelligence, and his daughter had been poisoned by a rare nerve toxin in the town of Salisbury, England. They were found slumped on a park bench and rushed to a local hospital, where they were treated just in time to survive. The toxin was identified as Novichok, a highly lethal substance that had been fabricated in the former Soviet Union. Video cameras had caught two Russians, later linked to the military intelligence arm known as GRU, entering Britain and making their way to Salisbury. The attack was reminiscent of the 2006 poisoning of Alexander Litvinenko, a Russian dissident whose tea had been spiked with polonium, a highly toxic radioactive substance. He later died in a London hospital. Once the evidence proved Russian involvement beyond any doubt, British prime minister Theresa May announced the expulsion of twenty-three Russian diplomats and pleaded for support from the United States and the European allies.

Despite misgivings about the impact on relations with Russia, Macron and Trump would eventually concur about "the need to take action to hold Russia accountable." At first, both leaders were dubious about May's demands for a coordinated allied response and wanted to see more conclusive evidence that the assassination attempt was ordered by the Kremlin. Once Macron became convinced, he persuaded Trump that it was absolutely necessary for the United States

and Europe to stand together against the intolerable use of chemical
weapons against private citizens on British soil. Trump was reluctant
to condemn Putin because he had just called him to offer congrat-
ulations on his recent election to a fourth term as president. He did
not raise the Skripal attack with Putin and suggested perhaps it was
merely another case of "spy games." But May insisted that Britain had
definitive proof of the Kremlin's involvement and it was a matter of
trust and solidarity among allies. Trump, May, Macron, and Merkel
then agreed to blame Russia in unison, citing "no other plausible ex-
planation" for the poisoning attempt. With the United States finally
on board to take punitive action, other European nations soon agreed
to coordinate expulsions. In all, more than one hundred Russian diplomats would be sent home from over twenty countries.[6]

The Skripal poisoning created such outrage in the West that Macron was tempted to suspend his efforts to build a more cooperative
partnership with Moscow. He was coming under mounting political
pressure at home to cancel a forthcoming visit to the Saint Petersburg
International Economic Forum, which Putin had invited him to attend as his guest of honor. Macron's foreign minister, Jean-Yves Le
Drian, reminded Macron of his "red line" strictures against the use of
chemical weapons in Syria. Le Drian argued that the Skripal poisoning jeopardized the security not only of one of France's main allies
but also of France and Europe, because a lethal nerve agent—traced
by careful analysis to its Russian origins—had been used in flagrant
violation of international laws against chemical weapons. But Macron concluded that cutting off ties and ostracizing Moscow would
harm French and Western interests by breaking off cooperation with
the Kremlin in dealing with global hot spots.

The next crisis was not long in coming. Less than two weeks
after the Western expulsions of Russian diplomats over the Skripal
poisoning, French intelligence reported that Syrian military planes
were dropping barrel bombs containing chlorine gas on the town of
Douma. More than forty men, women, and children had been killed
in what the intelligence sources described as a massacre of innocents.

Macron wasted no time in deciding that France had to take action. "The red line has been crossed," he declared. He began coordinating a military response with the White House, while at the same time sending a clear message that Moscow should keep its distance and not get involved. He spoke to Trump every day in the week following the Syrian attack as they considered the proper course of action and what targets should be hit. US Defense Secretary James Mattis urged caution because of the risks of a confrontation with Russian and Iranian forces. It was decided that the allied air strikes should be carefully circumscribed to focus on three chemical weapons facilities: a scientific research center outside Damascus that was used in the production of the weapons, and two chemical weapons facilities west of Homs that produced the nerve agent sarin and served as a military command post.[7] More than one hundred missiles were launched against the Syrian targets, more than twice as many as the United States had unleashed a year earlier in retaliation for the use of chemical weapons by Assad's regime.

Just hours before the air strikes, Macron called Putin to reassure him that the Western attacks would be orchestrated so that they did not hit Russian or Iranian targets. He found Putin in a curiously relaxed mood. The Russian leader said that he would naturally condemn the strikes "in the most serious terms" but also promised to ensure that his forces stayed out of the way. He also assured Macron that he would not take any military action in response—contradicting the belligerent warnings issued by his military leadership in previous days. Macron told Putin that France, the United States, and Britain did not want to trigger a broader conflict but felt compelled to show their determination to halt any further use of chemical weapons. Macron hoped that the message would not only deter the Assad regime from using chemical weapons in the future but also resonate in the Kremlin in the aftermath of the Skripal poisoning.

In the days leading up to the air strikes, opinion polls showed that the French public was skeptical about the purpose of such an attack. Macron claimed that Syria's use of chemical weapons made

France morally obligated to intervene by participating in the Western air strikes. "We cannot tolerate the normalization of the employment of chemical weapons, which is an immediate danger to the Syrian people and to our collective security," he said. In the end, a majority of the French people backed his action, with criticism mainly coming from the political extremes, including Jean-Luc Mélenchon of the far-left France Unbowed Party and Le Pen's far-right National Rally. For Macron, the crisis provided further justification of his policy of maintaining open channels of communication with both Trump and Putin, even at the risk of not always achieving his goals. The outcome of the Syrian air strikes, he felt, vindicated his belief that France should continue to pursue its mission as a pivotal power that could work in tandem not just with its allies but also with its adversaries.

A few weeks later, Macron went ahead with his trip to the Saint Petersburg economic forum. Putin seemed genuinely grateful, welcoming him as the forum's guest of honor along with Japanese prime minister Shinzō Abe. He greeted Macron's wife, Brigitte, with a huge bouquet of roses, then gave them a personal tour of the sumptuous Constantine Palace outside Saint Petersburg, a former imperial retreat whose magnificent gardens open up to the Baltic Sea. Macron and his wife paid homage to the victims of the three-year Nazi siege of Saint Petersburg, then known as Leningrad, in which Putin's parents suffered greatly. Macron continued his frequent appeal for Russia to recognize its Western roots and find ways to reconcile with the United States and Europe. He lauded Russia's great literary tradition and recalled Fyodor Dostoevsky's praise for Russia's enduring partnership with Europe when he gave an 1880 speech in honor of Pushkin. "Russia is an inalienable part of Europe," Macron said. "I am perfectly aware of Russia's irreplaceable role in solving international problems. Mistakes have been made in the past. We must work to remove our divisions on many issues, so let us gather around the table to talk about these things. If we miss this moment, we may lose it forever."[8]

In their private discussions, Macron urged Putin to continue his support for the Iran nuclear deal that Trump had just walked away from. He was pleased when Putin assured him that Russia saw the importance of maintaining the integrity of the agreement since preserving economic benefits for Iran was the best way to discourage Tehran from restarting its nuclear program. They both deplored Trump's decision to leave the agreement, which they felt Trump was doing for purely domestic reasons. "He is making good on his electoral promises, so he is a victor domestically," Putin said. "But if this deal is destroyed, many will lose."

Taking aim at the Trump administration, Putin contended that Trump's threats to impose tariffs on steel and aluminum exports from Europe were tantamount to the kind of sanctions that Russia had been enduring. "Now you know how we feel," he observed in a smug aside to Macron. Later, he would elaborate on Russian television about his "I told you so" moment, saying that the Europeans were getting a taste of the way the United States had long treated Russia. "In essence these [tariffs] are sanctions. What, did they annex Crimea?" Putin asked. He said that the Europeans probably felt that America's "counterproductive policies" would never affect them. "No one wanted to listen, and no one wanted to do anything to stop these tendencies. So here we are."[9]

In his public appearance at the Saint Petersburg forum, where he was seated next to Macron, Putin warned that the global trading order was suffering "a systemic crisis" in which the rules that had governed world commerce for decades were being subverted. "We are now talking about a completely new era of protectionism, defended by references to national interests," Putin said. "These kinds of random sanctions are extremely damaging as more and more attempts are made to circumvent the rules. The current situation in the world is such that everybody is playing soccer with the rules of judo. So what we have is neither soccer nor judo. It's chaos."

Macron made no effort to rebut Putin's sharp criticism of American policies. He was still bristling over the failure of his long courtship with Trump to produce solid results. He avoided direct criticism of Trump but insisted that recent events had shown yet again that

it was time for Europe to regain its full sovereignty, including responsibility for its own military, energy, and financial security. He
condemned the American use of extraterritorial laws that threatened
foreign firms with sanctions if they engaged in trade with Iran. Patrick Pouyanné, the chief executive of the French oil giant Total SA,
which signed a $2.6 billion investment deal with Russia for an Arc-
tic natural gas facility, said that the American sanctions had made
it impossible for Total to continue working in Iran, so they had to
drum up new business elsewhere. "I cannot run a company like Total
under threats in which I'll have no access to the US banking system,
no access to US shareholders, no access for myself as CEO to the US
territories," Pouyanné said.[10]

Total had already committed to investing more than $9 billion in
Russia for other energy projects. Macron predicted that France would
soon overtake Germany as Russia's biggest investor. Indeed, despite
the impact of Western sanctions against Moscow, French–Russian
economic exchanges were thriving. Putin said that more than five
hundred French companies were active in his country, employing
about 160,000 Russians, and bilateral trade exceeded $15 billion a
year. But without significant progress in resolving Russia's political
conflicts with the West, the promise of greater prosperity and economic expansion for both sides would remain elusive. After his stay
in Saint Petersburg, Macron spoke confidently about a "convergence
of positions" with Putin, notably on Iran. But on other issues there
were no signs that Putin was ready to budge. He refused to acknowledge Russia's culpability in shooting down a Malaysian jetliner over
Ukraine that killed 283 passengers and 15 crew members. He also
showed no willingness to take fresh steps to explore political solutions
to conflicts in Syria and Ukraine. Just a week before the forum took
place, Putin had inaugurated a new land bridge designed to establish
a permanent connection between Russia and Crimea.

Nonetheless, Putin was eager to build upon his new relationship
with Macron, pressing his claim that Russia could become "a natural ally" for Europe even as Trump attacked the European Union
as "a foe" of the United States because of its trade practices. When

the Blues, the French soccer team, qualified for the World Cup soccer championship, Putin congratulated Macron and invited him to Moscow to watch the final. A soccer enthusiast since his youth, Macron eagerly accepted. He joined Putin in the VIP box, leaping to cheer and roar his approval with every goal scored by the French team. When the Blues defeated Croatia 4–2 to win the World Cup, Macron descended onto the field to embrace the French players and celebrate with them despite a drenching rainstorm. He would later describe that experience as his happiest moment as president.

More than any other European leader, Macron has maintained open channels of communication with Putin in the hope of luring Russia back toward a cooperative relationship with the West. Five days ahead of the G-7 summit of major democracies that France hosted in August 2019, Macron invited Putin to his summer residence on the Mediterranean coast for several hours of discussion about how to move forward with their search for peaceful resolutions of conflicts over Iran, Ukraine, and Syria. Russia had been expelled from the group after its annexation of Crimea in 2014, but Macron believed that it was important to sustain a dialogue with Putin. They both agreed that efforts to lift sanctions against Russia were enhanced by the new opportunity for peace in Ukraine offered by the election of Volodymyr Zelenskiy as its president. Macron brushed aside criticism that he was seeking to normalize relations with Putin while Russia continued to violate human rights. France supported the return of Russia to the Council of Europe, Macron said, not as a reward but in order to give Russian citizens access to the European Court of Human Rights. He also claimed that European interests were not served by isolating Russia or pushing Moscow into China's embrace. "It will take time to resolve our misunderstandings, but I strongly believe that we need to keep trying," Macron told Putin. Europe's quest for strategic autonomy, he stressed, could only be attained once its relations with Russia were "profoundly reinvented."[11]

After two years in office, Macron continues to struggle in his chosen role as a pivotal balancing power trying to serve as a bridge connecting rival parties in the world. He has realized how steep a learning curve he faced when he became president since he had never before engaged in serious political or diplomatic negotiations. He had never studied international relations, nor had he cultivated a mentor to coach him in the intricacies of statecraft. But Macron is a voracious reader of history and literature who effectively trained himself in diplomacy once in office. He visited twenty-seven countries during his first year as president, eagerly absorbing all he could learn about the world. Despite his peripatetic travels and vaunted skills at seducing his interlocutors, Macron has failed to make much headway in persuading the leaders of the United States and Russia to align their policies with those of France and Europe. Macron could never get either Trump or Putin to reciprocate in the ways he wanted. He found Trump rudely dismissive of his views and those of America's other allies because the American president bases his decisions on faulty preconceptions and domestic politics. For his part, Putin has always been suspicious and probing for vulnerabilities in their discussions. Macron admits that he quickly realized in his dealings with the Russian leader that "you must never display weakness with Putin, or he will ruthlessly exploit you."

Macron has displayed remarkable resilience in pursuing his international vision for France despite his frequent setbacks. He says that he bases much of his strategy for French foreign and security policy on ideas first outlined by President Charles de Gaulle. "Our role everywhere is to be a mediating power," Macron told the conference of French ambassadors gathered at the Élysée Palace. "A diplomatic, military, cultural, educational, national, and European power, and always to be a mediator . . . meaning that France never stops making itself heard, but that it always seeks to build alliances on this basis. It is not a compromising power, not a middling power, but a mediating power; one which seeks to build this very international order which alone will enable us to make globalization a little more human and humanist."[12]

Macron says that France's fight against terrorism will remain his top strategic international priority throughout his presidency. The nation was traumatized in 2015 when 130 people were massacred in the Bataclan Theater by Islamist terrorists. That tragedy was followed by an attack in Nice eight months later in which 80 people died when a deranged Tunisian immigrant drove a truck through crowds gathered on a seaside promenade to celebrate Bastille Day. Preventing more such attacks is why Macron has relentlessly pushed for a durable peace settlement in Syria. With genuine passion, he explained his firm belief that if civil war in Syria continues for years, radicalized recruits from Europe will be attracted to the Islamist cause, provoking further waves of desperate refugees from the Middle East seeking entry into the European Union. "This is why Europe needs to build a new architecture of collective security with both Russia and Turkey," Macron said. "It's complicated with Turkey because of the pan-Islamic ambitions of President Erdoğan, which pose a problem for me because his views are so anti-European."[13] Macron said that it is well past time for the European Union to drop the pretense that membership in the Union may eventually be extended to Turkey, which has been knocking on Europe's door for more than four decades. The only sensible solution, he said, is for Europe to establish long-term strategic partnerships with Russia and Turkey, its two most important neighbors on the eastern periphery.

Macron pushed hard to convene a four-nation summit meeting in Istanbul in October 2018 that brought the leaders of France, Germany, Russia, and Turkey together to discuss a political resolution to the Syrian conflict and the refugee crisis that it created. Macron's urgent concern was the risk that a Syrian-Russian onslaught against Islamist fighters holed up in the northern province of Idlib, home to three million people, would trigger another human catastrophe that would send hundreds of thousands of refugees streaming into Turkey and then toward Europe. Just as Putin and Erdoğan had weaponized the Syrian refugee problem in 2015 for their own purposes, Macron feared that they might try to use the Idlib standoff to foment political instability in Europe by stoking anxieties about another major refugee exodus. That was the last thing that Macron, Merkel, and other European leaders wanted to see, since another massive wave of refugees arriving on Europe's doorstep could help populist national-ists and their xenophobic policies achieve broader support from vot-ers across the continent.

Putin and Erdoğan had earlier agreed to a tenuous cease-fire, but mounting pressures on both sides suggested that it could quickly fall apart. Turkey had long backed rebels who were seeking to overthrow Assad and was worried that Russia, as Assad's principal ally, would use its superior airpower to devastate one of the last Islamist rebel strongholds in northwestern Syria. In private conversations with Ma-cron, Putin stressed that he was coming under enormous pressure from his military commanders to give the signal to annihilate the positions of Hayat Tahrir al-Sham, formerly known as the al-Qaeda affiliate in Syria. The Russian military leadership believed that up to five thousand Russian-speaking fighters were holed up with the group, mainly from Chechnya, Dagestan, and other Muslim regions in Central Asia. They believed that an all-out onslaught would con-solidate Assad's hold on power and eliminate any future terrorist threat for Moscow from Russian-speaking Islamist fighters. Putin told Macron that he had received information that these fighters were preparing to use chemical weapons in a final battle for Idlib. Ma-cron replied that according to French intelligence reports, Assad's forces were making the same preparations and had deployed chemi-cal weapons repeatedly in the past. That was all the more reason, Ma-cron argued, for Russia to show restraint with its airpower and ensure that Assad's forces were held in check.

The Istanbul summit succeeded in shoring up the cease-fire by persuading Russia and Turkey to pull back all forces and heavy weap-ons to create a demilitarized zone running ten miles into rebel terri-tory. "Russia and Turkey have negotiated an agreement that must be strictly implemented," Macron told reporters after the summit. "We will all be extremely vigilant to ensure that these commitments are met and that the ceasefire is stable and sustainable. We are counting on Russia to exert very clear pressure on the [Syrian] regime."[14] But those hopes, as with so many efforts to broker peace in Syria, would prove highly premature.

What was most striking about the Istanbul summit was the absence of the United States. America's retreat from the Middle East, first under Barack Obama and then under Trump, had shifted power and influence toward Russia and Iran. Macron had warned Trump during their meetings in April 2018 that further American withdrawal from the region would damage the strategic interests not just of the United States but of all Western democracies. Trump told him that he was determined to remove American forces, first from Syria and Iraq, then from Afghanistan. Macron urged him to reconsider the huge stakes involved. "US soldiers have made a tremendous contribution in Syria," Macron explained to me, describing the argument he made to Trump and referring to several hundred American Special Forces who were operating in eastern Syria. "You cannot say I will not accept the [Iran nuclear] agreement because it does not take account of Iranian activity in the region, and then leave Syria right after you think the war with the Islamic state is over. It's inconsistent, and I think he agreed with that."[15] But Trump's patience did not last long. To Macron's surprise, and with no advance warning, Trump declared in December 2018 that American forces would leave the region as soon as feasibly possible. Trump's abrupt decision also stunned American military commanders. Defense Secretary James Mattis soon offered his resignation because of Trump's decision to leave the field of battle in the Middle East. After coordinating so closely with Trump on Syria, where French and American forces had worked well together, Macron expected at least to receive an early alert from Trump. It never came.

Instead, Macron's first conversation about Syria in the new year was with Putin. On January 2, Macron called Putin to discuss the possible collaboration of French and Russian troops in the wake of an American departure. A week later, Trump finally called Macron, who was still furious over what he viewed as an embarrassing betrayal by the Americans.[16]

Macron's frustrations with Trump and his inconclusive talks with Putin about how to achieve stability in the Middle East reinforced his conviction that Europe needed to regain its sovereignty and explore new ways to guarantee its own security in the twenty-first century. With doubts growing about American commitments to shield Europe and Russia violating restrictions on intermediate-range missiles, Macron approved a change in strategic doctrine that could extend France's nuclear deterrent force to protect German territory in the event of an armed attack. With Britain's looming exit from the European Union, France would become the sole remaining nuclear power on the continent. Macron was prepared to extend the French nuclear deterrent to other European partners in order to reassure them about potential Russian aggression. But conventional and nuclear forces were part of a previous generation's calculus of power. Emerging as major new threats in the growing tensions between Russia and the West were "gray zone" tools of aggression that were cheap but highly effective in undermining the political stability of Western democracies.

Macron recognized that technology was transforming the nature of military conflict and that artificial intelligence would soon amplify new ways to wage war. The massive and coordinated hacking operations used by Russia to interfere in American, French, and other European elections highlighted the vulnerability of Western democracies to clandestine attacks by clever adversaries. Although Macron believed that Trump was in fact correct in his frequent harangues about Europeans needing to spend more for their own defense, he realized that purchasing more troops, tanks, bombs, and submarines would not protect Europe from cyber-attacks and disinformation campaigns. If Europe was ever going to achieve an enduring strategic partnership with Russia, there would have to be a greater level of cooperation and understanding with Moscow about the uses and abuses of advanced technologies in the future. As one of the West's youngest and most consequential leaders, Macron felt comfortable thinking in terms of the next three decades, unlike most of his peers.

Thirty years after the fall of the Berlin Wall, Macron believes that the world is poised at a new inflection point, one where artificial intelligence and advanced technologies may transform the power relationship between Russia and the West.

Under Putin, Moscow has refined hybrid methods of undermining key institutions in the West and managed to achieve high-impact results at very little cost by using Western commercial digital platforms that are readily available to the public. Russia's success in exploiting Western technology calls to mind the famous quote from Lenin: "The capitalists will sell us the rope with which we will hang them." Russia has piggybacked on American, European, and Chinese technology, in both hardware and software, to use platforms such as YouTube and Twitter to disseminate false information for propaganda purposes and to disrupt Western elections by hacking into weakly protected databases of governments or political parties.

Given its dwindling population and shrinking oil revenues, Russia may feel that it has no choice but to double down on asymmetric warfare methods that are increasingly driven by artificial intelligence in order to fulfill Putin's strategy of extending Russia's influence more widely across Europe. Despite repeated denials by the Russian government of any involvement in cyber-attacks, Russia-backed hackers have continuously targeted France and Germany to spread false information during election campaigns while continuing traditional espionage efforts that use electronic devices to collect classified intelligence from deep inside Western governments. French and German investigators, with help from Estonia, have followed the perpetrators time and again back to the same troll factory in Saint Petersburg.

Putin and his military strategists have expressed amazement at how effective their methods have been in sowing discord and disarray across Europe. The Kremlin's financial and political support for right-wing populist nationalist parties, such as France's National Rally, the Northern League in Italy, Austria's Freedom Party, Hungary's ruling Fidesz Party, and the Alternative for Germany, has targeted voter resentments in its disinformation campaigns. Moscow has capitalized on the failure of mainstream parties in the West to respond effectively to public anxieties about the impact of immigration on national identity, the growing divide between rich and poor, and the frustrations of young people seeking sustainable employment. These social problems are exploited by Moscow's social media campaigns in ways that elicit a sympathetic response from aggrieved groups in the West. In the Baltic states, for example, Moscow has frequently used social media campaigns to stir up protests among ethnic Russians in Latvia and Estonia who complain about not being allowed to vote or receive full citizenship rights.

Putin enjoys further leverage in his dealings with European leaders because of the importance of Europe's trade with and investment in Russia, the levels of which are nearly ten times those of the United States. Russia's disinformation strategy has generally sought to deepen political divisions across Europe by supporting the causes of both right- and left-wing populist parties against the ruling establishment, often through clever social media campaigns ahead of elections. When Macron and other Western leaders have vehemently objected to Russia's actions, Putin has responded either by denying responsibility for any such attacks or by claiming that Russia is merely engaging in retaliation against Western propaganda. Even as domestic unrest grows in Russia, Putin's campaign to restore Russia's big-power status has proved immensely popular at home.

Russian cyber-attacks, even those that failed, have raised urgent questions about what the West should do about them. Some experts say that the Atlantic alliance's failure to develop an effective deterrent strategy is tacit acknowledgment that the West is already engaged in similar actions and that countermeasures could backfire by inflicting further damage on any governments that retaliate. Other experts caution that Moscow would simply use any response as a pretext to escalate the conflict by ramping up attacks on infrastructure and other sensitive targets. Keith Alexander, a former director of the National Security Agency, has pointed out that at the very least, the unabated attacks by Russia show that "the West's approach to cyber security is not working." He believes that when it comes to cyber-warfare, "we still have not figured out how to establish real collective defense."[17] The question of whether cyber-attacks fit the classic definition of warfare remains unresolved, making it difficult to invoke international law in justifying retaliation or coming to the defense of allies under attack, as prescribed by NATO's Article 5. This gray zone of aggression short of conventional or nuclear conflict has made it imperative to create new laws and institutions that could prevent such methods from escalating into regional or global wars.

Macron believes that the best way to fight cyber-threats is through a global governance scheme that would bring together not just governments but also private-sector companies to police the internet. At the Paris Peace Forum that he convened in November 2018, Macron urged world governments and leading technology companies to pledge their support for a new set of common principles that would guide behavior in cyber-space. More than 50 governments, 90 nonprofit organizations, and 130 private corporations, including Microsoft, Cisco, IBM, Samsung, Siemens, Facebook, and Google, endorsed Macron's call for "trust and security in cyber-space" and the need to develop universal rules to govern the internet and ensure cyber-security. This international accord, which falls short of a legal treaty of the kind that bans the use of chemical and biological weapons, will operate through the Internet Governance Forum under the supervision of the United Nations secretary-general.

Macron's abiding faith in multilateralism may seem naive, but he insists that a "collegial approach" among rival governments and information technology giants to prevent abuses in cyber-space is the only feasible way to regulate conflicts. He emphasizes the importance of business involvement because, with half of humanity now using online services, the largest digital companies have more clout than governments in determining how to stop hacking attacks, digital theft, and other cyber-intrusions. Macron realizes how complicated it would be for such a utopian plan to succeed; like any arms control agreement, it could work only when the most powerful players are willing to cooperate and to trust each other. His biggest challenge is to convince Putin, Trump, and Xi Jinping to cede national sovereignty in a domain that would require global supervision in order to succeed. Russia, China, and the United States have so far refused to sign up.[18]

Macron knows that his efforts to build a strategic partnership with Putin have fallen short of his goals but understands that his long-term aspirations will take at least a decade to achieve. Putin has refused to pull his forces out of Ukraine, rejected any compromise in his support of the Assad regime in Syria, and declined to accept responsibility for assassination attempts against Russian dissidents on foreign soil in spite of overwhelming evidence to the contrary. He has claimed that Russia can ignore the West and build a new authoritarian alliance with China. But at some point Putin may realize that his two biggest strategic challenges emanate from the south and the east, not from Europe and the United States. Islamist revolutionaries are still active and fomenting rebellion across the southern tier of Russia, while China's Belt and Road Initiative will circumvent Russia even as the huge Chinese population encroaches on Siberian territory in the east.

Macron seems determined to keep talking to Putin in spite of the Russian leader's professed disdain for Western liberal democracy. The French president is convinced that Russia will eventually turn back toward Europe because that's where so much of its culture and history remain embedded. "Russia has no choice," Macron said. "Its population is shrinking, it has an enormous land mass spreading across nine time zones that it cannot defend alone, and its economy is no bigger than Spain's. Ever since Peter the Great, Russia has looked to the West to protect its interests, and I am convinced it will do so again in the future."[19] That is why at each of his meetings with Putin, Macron makes a point of reciting the names of famous Russians, such as Dostoevsky, Pushkin, and Peter the Great, who all believed that Russia's destiny lies with Europe.

CHAPTER 9

CHINA'S BUYING

After years of misery, Portugal's Socialist prime minister António Costa finally had some good news to report. At a gathering of European Union leaders in Brussels in June 2017, he proclaimed with great satisfaction that at last "the years of sacrifice are over." Costa described the remarkable recovery Portugal had achieved in rising from the depths of a debilitating recession after the 2008 financial crisis, which sent unemployment levels soaring and nearly caused the collapse of its banking system. He then explained the secret to the country's apparent economic miracle. His government had sold off— mainly to China—the crown jewels of the nation's infrastructure for about $12 billion. Costa's peers gave him a rousing ovation. They complimented his wizardry in guiding Portugal's economy back to good health, even comparing him and his finance minister to national soccer hero Cristiano Ronaldo.

Emmanuel Macron was troubled, however, by the appearance of a Faustian bargain. During a break, he approached Costa and asked him if he had thought about the long-term consequences of ceding such enormous control over his nation's economy to China. "You're a socialist, António, so I never thought you would privatize such important parts of the economy," Macron said. "Where did you get this idea of selling off everything to China?" Costa looked across the room and pointed at German chancellor Angela Merkel. "From her," he said. Costa then explained that Portugal was left with no choice when Germany demanded the sale in 2011 of Portugal's infrastructure assets in return for Berlin's support of a 78 billion euro ($95 billion) loan from the International Monetary Fund, the European Commission, and the European Central Bank (known as "the troika").[1] Even though its debt troubles were not as serious as Greece's, Portugal was forced to pay a high price for the troika's rescue package. The Lisbon government was compelled to adopt painful austerity measures that hiked taxes and imposed drastic cuts in health, education, and welfare.[2] At Germany's behest, Portugal was required to sell as many state-owned companies as possible to the highest bidder. When European bids were not forthcoming, China swooped in like a vulture capitalist to pick off the most valuable pieces at fire-sale prices.

China's takeover of Portugal's national electricity grid and its power utilities is just one element in a divide-and-conquer strategy that is rapidly turning Beijing into a powerful political and economic force in Europe. In 2009, China acquired control of the port of Piraeus, outside Athens, when the troika prodded the Greek government to sell off its assets. China then launched plans to build a high-speed train system from Greece through Budapest and Belgrade to transport its goods into Europe's most affluent regions. The Beijing government also established the "16+1" dialogue with Central and Eastern European nations, which were eager to attract Chinese investments to support new infrastructure projects. By exploiting the competing desires of EU member states for its investments, China gained important leverage over the bloc, which is its largest trading partner. Chinese investors have already bought up banks, ports, energy companies, and high-tech manufacturers across the continent.

The Swedish carmaker Volvo, the German robotics company Kuka, and Luxembourg's Banque Internationale have all fallen into Chinese hands.

Macron views China's relentless rise as a significant geopolitical event that will shape the lives of his generation. He realized upon taking power that France was the only European nation capable of developing a political, economic, and military strategy to cope with China's evolving superpower status. With America's retreat from global leadership and Merkel distracted by political difficulties at home, Macron by default became Europe's most prominent leader. He has appealed for China's cooperation and welcomed Beijing's support for the Paris climate change accord as well as its continued backing of the Iran nuclear deal after Trump pulled out. At the same time, he recognizes that China poses a serious challenge to the international order, and not just on trade and investment issues. China's aggressive actions in the South China Sea and its threats to freedom of navigation have prompted Macron to expand France's naval presence in the Indo-Pacific region and upgrade its defense relationships with Australia, India, and Japan.

Macron is acutely aware that France needs to be joined by the rest of Europe in concerted efforts to acquire sufficient leverage to deal effectively with the China challenge. After years of complacency, Europe is slowly awakening to the risks of China's aggressive pursuit of its advanced technologies and key infrastructure assets. American intelligence experts have alerted their European counterparts to the dangers of China's encroachment. The annual "National Security Strategy," published by the US government, warned in late 2017 that "China is gaining a strategic foothold in Europe by expanding its unfair trade practices and investing in key industries, sensitive technologies, and infrastructure."[3] In 2018, China's investments in Europe would grow to levels nine times greater than its investments in the United States.[4] Over the past ten years, China has bought or invested in assets in Europe worth more than $320 billion, according to *Bloomberg*.[5]

During his first state visit to China in January 2018, Macron projected himself as Europe's leading voice who wanted to chart an equitable relationship with the emerging superpower. He quoted Charles de Gaulle, who is widely revered in China for declaring in 1964 that France would become one of the first countries to recognize the People's Republic: "France is and will continue to be the power at the heart of Europe that will lead the dialogue with China." Ever the seducer, Macron flattered his Chinese hosts by speaking a few words in Mandarin, and he offered President Xi Jinping the unprecedented gift of a horse from the elite French Presidential Guard. Macron had learned that Xi expressed admiration for the majestic horses that carried the 104 guards who escorted him during a previous trip to Paris in 2014. Macron personally selected the eight-year-old brown gelding named Vesuvius that he presented to the Chinese leader; the animal was then placed in strict quarantine, as is customary under Chinese law.[6]

Macron began his China visit with a stop in Xi'an, home to the famed Terracotta Army and the most populous and prosperous city in the world during the golden age of the Tang dynasty. Macron appreciated the symbolism of Xi'an, which marked the eastern departure point of the ancient Silk Road that Xi is seeking to resurrect with his Belt and Road project. Macron chose the ancient imperial capital as a dramatic stage from which to deliver a blunt message to the Chinese government: China must open up its markets to foreign companies, just as Europe has welcomed Chinese investors, or Europe will be forced to apply new restrictions on Chinese trade and investment. "I came here to tell China about my determination to bring the Europe-China partnership into the twenty-first century," Macron told his audience in a speech that ran for more than an hour. "I want us to define together the rules of a balanced relationship in which everyone will win."

Macron warned that Europe was running out of patience with China's lack of reciprocity when it came to foreign investments, intellectual property rights, competition, and access to public markets.

"The ancient Silk Roads were never only Chinese," Macron said. "The new roads being built must not only go in one direction." He expressed his personal support for China's Belt and Road Initiative, but stressed that its execution "must meet our own plans as well."[7] It was a message that he repeated with firm conviction on subsequent visits to China, as he did in Shanghai in November 2019.

In Beijing, Xi offered Macron and his wife the honor of a private tour of the Forbidden City, the imperial palace that served as the political home of China's rulers for five centuries. The two leaders also visited a start-up incubator and China's space academy before attending an elaborate state dinner with the customary toasts to Chinese-French friendship. Macron promised to return every year to China and said that he hoped to build a strong personal partnership with Xi. In spite of such diplomatic niceties, Macron left his hosts in no doubt that unless China adopted a more welcoming attitude toward European companies, he and other European leaders would start to impose restrictions on Chinese investors. Macron's own impressions from his trip were decidedly pessimistic. He came away thinking that China would not budge unless confronted by a serious challenge from a united Europe, even as EU leaders were struggling to reach a consensus on how to counter China's lopsided advantages.[8]

"We must be wary of any Chinese strategy that could exploit us," Macron told me. "Control of maritime routes, cables, infrastructure, and transport in Europe: this is not compatible with our interests. Chinese policy in this context is hegemonic, and we must push back. China is like a player of Go; it is extremely strategic in its thinking and not just mercantile." Macron said he was all in favor of political and economic dialogue with China, but to be an effective partner Europe needed a cohesive strategy with four aims: containment in the Indo-Pacific region, action on climate change, avoidance of too much debt in Africa, and respect for sovereignty in Europe. This last point, Macron said, was extremely important in order to prevent China from acquiring too much leverage over Europe.[9]

Macron returned home thinking that Europe needed to adopt more robust defensive policies rather than making fruitless efforts to compel China to change its ways. Xi's consolidation of power showed that the core features of China's dictatorship were not going to change. The Chinese people would continue to be subject to systematic repression of human rights, as well as strict censorship of the media and the internet. The Chinese government, under the tight control of the Communist Party, would persist in its massive interventions in the economy while sustaining the uneven playing field for foreign companies. For years Western nations had deluded themselves into thinking that China's rapid economic development would inexorably create political pressures to move toward their own model of free market democracy. Instead, China was blazing its own path by fortifying its authoritarian, one-party system. At the same time, China was exploiting the gullibility of the West by ruthlessly pursuing nationalistic trade and investment policies and engaging in the theft of intellectual property. Xi's consolidation of power and the aggressive nature of his "Made in China 2025" industrial policy—the aim of which is to dominate ten key high-tech sectors within a decade—had already rushed European hopes for political and economic liberalization.[10]

Macron believes that Europe needs to respond urgently to China's strategic challenge by fighting back with similar methods, such as curbing the sale of European companies and their technologies as long as China denies equal access to its markets. In contrast to the United States, which shies away from industrial policies, France and Germany advocate the creation of European industrial champions that would receive preferential treatment in the EU marketplace, in the same way China favors its state-owned enterprises over foreign competitors. In addition to backing European companies over outside competitors, Germany now wants to shield entire sectors from Chinese acquisition, including aircraft, finance, telecommunications, trains, energy, and robotics.

Other European states have staunchly opposed the French and German plans in the belief that they would establish a "fortress

Europe" walled off from competition and thus innovation. They also fear that such a strategy would only fan the flames of protectionism and further damage the global economy. A test case arose when Germany's Siemens and France's Alstom tried to combine their rail assets with the ambition of becoming a European industrial giant that could compete in global markets. The merger would have created the world's second-largest rail company with combined revenues of $17 billion, yet it would still have been only half the size of China's state-owned CRRC Corporation. Macron argued that Europe needed to create more industrial titans, such as the aeronautics company Airbus, to ensure that its firms were not squeezed out of their own markets by the growing power of Chinese and American companies, but EU antitrust commissioner Margrethe Vestager opposed the merger on the grounds that it would stifle competition within Europe's rail industry. She expressed doubts that Chinese rail companies would bother to enter the European market in the near future and scorned the notion that Europe could best nurture its future industrial champions by suppressing competition in the marketplace.[11]

When the European Commission backed up Vestager's decision despite intense political pressure from Paris and Berlin, France's finance minister, Bruno Le Maire, and Germany's economy minister, Peter Altmaier, expressed outrage with the rejection of the merger. They said that Europe needed to awaken to the China threat and change antitrust laws that were clearly obsolete because they no longer corresponded to the current nature of global markets. The alternative, they warned, was to see their own citizens continue to lose more jobs as Chinese firms invaded European markets, a trend that, if not stopped, would inflict serious damage on political stability. Yet Vestager refused to back down, saying that European regulations clearly stated that consumer choice must be protected in order to keep prices in check by ensuring there was enough competition in the marketplace.

Macron appealed to Jean-Claude Juncker, the wily politician who served for eighteen years as prime minister of Luxembourg before becoming president of the European Commission in 2014. Juncker shared Macron's alarm about China's increasingly brazen intrusions into Europe. He had formulated an EU-wide investment-screening process to thwart China from acquiring control of valuable technologies in Europe but had been forced to cede final authority for all decisions to national governments. Macron was not alone in his complaints about the unfair nature of the Chinese-European relationship. Other European governments were coming forward with more tales of abuse. Germany's intelligence agency even accused China of mining the personal data of German politicians and diplomats. Despite incessant demands from EU leaders, China still refused to offer equal treatment to European companies in China. Moreover, if Europe's ports, rail networks, and energy grids were controlled by China, the entire continent could be relegated to quasi-colonial status.

In March 2019, shortly before Xi embarked on a trip to Rome and Paris, the European Commission published its most alarming assessment to date of Europe's relationship with China. The Commission is responsible for handling trade negotiations for all twenty-eight EU members, so its words carry weight in these matters. The Commission's strategy paper declared that "the European Union and China were committed to a comprehensive strategic partnership, yet there is a growing appreciation in Europe that the balance of challenges and opportunities that China presents has shifted."[12] The Commission called for all member states to rally behind a unified approach toward China that would be "more realistic, assertive and multi-faceted."

The European Commission concluded that Europe should no longer treat China as a developing economy but confront it as an "economic competitor in pursuit of technological leadership" and as "a systemic rival promoting alternative models of governance." The strategy paper noted that China had impeded Europe's fight against climate change as a major exporter of coal-fired power plants. It also criticized China's human rights policies, which had taken a dramatic turn for the worse under Xi's presidency, for instance, in its treatment of Chinese lawyers and journalists. The paper cited China's "large military maneuvers" as a new source of anxiety for Europe, not just in the South China Sea but also in Europe's own neighborhood, including the Arctic region. China had conducted joint military exercises with Russia in the Black Sea, the Mediterranean Sea, and the Baltic Sea, including missile tests off the coast of Kaliningrad, to the consternation of Poland and three Baltic states that are EU and NATO members. In addition, several European think tanks reported that China was engaged in hacking and other cyber-activities to influence politics in Europe.

The European Commission paper reserved its toughest criticism for China's attitude toward Europe on trade and investment. The Commission demanded that China "deliver" on its past commitments to curtail industrial subsidies as prescribed by the World Trade Organization and to complete a bilateral investment treaty with the European Union by 2020. The negotiations had dragged on for seven years, and the EU was concerned that China was trying to delay any deal as long as possible. Finally, the Commission urged member governments to follow a ten-point plan that would coordinate policies within the European Union "in order to exert more leverage in pursuit of its objectives." Only by taking a unified approach, it concluded, could European governments hope to achieve reciprocal access to the Chinese market and persuade Beijing to remove huge subsidies for local companies and cumbersome restrictions on foreign firms.

Shortly after the paper was released, at an EU summit meeting convened to discuss Europe's strategy toward Beijing, Macron hailed the Commission's hard-nosed proposals as a welcome transformation in Europe's thinking about the emerging superpower. "The time of European naiveté has ended," Macron declared. "For many years we had an uncoordinated approach and China took advantage of our divisions."[13] But other leaders were not so sure. Prime Minister Costa of Portugal warned that it would be a mistake to discriminate against

China if it encouraged protectionist policies. Then Italy's prime minister, Giuseppe Conte, who was planning to meet with President Xi
in Rome the following day, announced that his populist-led government would break ranks and become the latest participant in the Belt
and Road Initiative. The new display of European unity toward the
China challenge had survived less than a day.

Macron was irate, but Conte defended his government's decision
as "fully legitimate, and it is justified precisely in the light of our national interests."[14] Italy's government was desperate to lure Chinese
investments to help pay for its ambitious reform programs, such as
basic income contracts for the poor, but was divided over whether
to encourage China to buy up key assets. "If it is a question of helping Italian companies to invest abroad, we are willing to reason with
anyone," said Matteo Salvini, the powerful interior minister who led
the right-wing Northern League Party that governed at that time in
coalition with the populist Five Star Movement. "If it is a question
of colonizing Italy and its companies by foreign powers, then no."[15]
For his part, China's leader sought to quell fears about the intentions
of his government and said there was "mutual trust" between Rome
and Beijing. "There is no conflict of interest between us and we both
know how to respect each other's concerns," Xi said on his official
visit to Italy, where he was received with military honors and sere-
naded by the Italian tenor Andrea Bocelli at a lavish state banquet.

A major attraction of Italy's deal with Beijing is that Rome
wants to secure China's cooperation in Africa. Beijing enjoys significant influence with key African governments, and Italy is eager to
gain China's help in curtailing illegal human trafficking across the
Mediterranean. Conte tried to reassure other EU leaders that all investments by China would be "carefully monitored" and that Italy's security and strategic infrastructure would be protected. Along
with a dozen Central and Eastern European states that are seeking
to benefit from Chinese investments, Rome hopes that Beijing will
funnel large sums of money into Italy to upgrade its antiquated road,
rail, and port infrastructure. China has already bought up stakes in

the ports of Venice, Genoa, and Trieste. Whether those hopes can be fulfilled, given skepticism about China's expanding debt burdens, remains open to question. But for Xi, it was a symbolic diplomatic coup to persuade a founding EU member state that belongs to the G-7 group of large industrialized countries to endorse his initiative. Most of all, Xi succeeded in fending off a determined bid by Macron and the European Commission to counter his divide-and-conquer strategy toward Europe.

From Italy, Xi traveled to France for what promised to be a diplomatic showdown with Macron, who had become China's most prickly European partner. Ever since his trip to Xi'an and Beijing in January 2018, Macron had emphasized the need for two-way commercial relations between Europe and China. If China would not agree to open its markets as broadly as Europe had done, the French president insisted, Europe should start closing its doors in similar ways so that an equitable partnership could be established. For example, Macron led Europe's push to shut off the EU's public procurement contracts, worth nearly $3 trillion, to Chinese bidders as long as Beijing continued to deny a slice of its mammoth projects to European companies. The Europeans had made similar complaints about such discrimination with the United States, which restricted many public procurement offerings to American firms.[16]

President Xi sought to mollify his hosts in Paris by lavishing on French companies billions of dollars in new trade contracts, which Macron's government hoped would go a long way toward rectifying a lopsided commercial imbalance in Beijing's favor. China agreed to buy up to three hundred new Airbus passenger planes, nearly twice as many as China intended when the contract was first discussed during Macron's visit to China. The aviation deal came as a huge boost to the fortunes of Airbus, a French-German-led consortium that had been lagging well behind its American rival Boeing until two fatal crashes resulted in the grounding of all 737 MAX planes, once Boeing's most profitable aircraft. Xi also announced that China would lift its previous import restrictions on French beef, poultry, and cheese products. (China had banned imports of Brie, Camembert, and Roquefort because they contain bacteria that the Chinese thought were harmful, until the French proved otherwise.) In all, more than a dozen commercial and government contracts were signed, worth close to $40 billion. China also promised greater access to its consumers for France's high-class fashion and consumer products. The Chinese offer came just as Galeries Lafayette, the iconic French department store, was planning to launch a massive expansion of its franchise in China, which accounts for about one-third of the world market in luxury goods.[17]

Xi and Macron also discussed how France could expand cooperation with China to develop its nuclear power industry by building a plant to reprocess China's spent nuclear fuel. France has one of the world's most advanced nuclear power industries; more than 70 percent of the country's electricity is furnished by nuclear power plants scattered around the country. Since nuclear power plants release very little if any emissions into the atmosphere and China is one of the world's biggest polluters, both leaders believed that French collaboration in China's nuclear energy sector would serve as the archetypal example of a "win-win" deal that would enable China to expand its electricity capacity and curtail its impact on climate change. One of China's newest nuclear reactors, Taishan 1, is a French project, and a second unit will soon be commissioned.

Although helping China with its nuclear program might be seen as a contradiction of Macron's argument that Europe should restrict Beijing's access to its advanced technologies, the French president stressed that in this case benefits outweighed risks in terms of addressing global climate challenges. But other European leaders would later point out what they saw as the hypocrisy in Macron's attitude after he criticized them for courting Chinese investments. "We cannot act as if these initiatives do not exist, because the new Silk Roads are the most important geopolitical concepts in recent decades," Macron told French ambassadors in a review of his China policy. "We should not give in to any kind of guilty or short-term fascination: it is a vision of globalization that has its virtues in terms of stabilizing certain regions, but it is a hegemonic system."[18] Macron later told me that he came away from his conversations with China's powerful leader convinced that Xi has a clear perspective on where he wants to take China and does not seem to care about consequences for other nations. "Xi has a coherent strategic vision for China's global leadership in the future," Macron said. "He is rebuilding an empire, and he is prepared to be very aggressive in terms of pushing the limits of international law."[19]

Macron sought to convey an image of European unity by inviting Merkel and Juncker to join him at the table for his discussions with Xi on his last day in Paris. He noted that the West's openness to trade and investment had helped bring seven hundred million Chinese out of poverty, but warned that it had also "generated deep transformations and tensions in our society which led to the need for legitimate protection"—a reference to the serious loss of industrial jobs in Europe and America. At a press conference after their talks, Macron cited the unprecedented nature of the four-way talks as a demonstration of the common responsibilities shared by Europe and China in sustaining the multilateral system. "No single country can redefine the rules of the international game," Macron said, alluding to Trump's rejection of the Paris climate change accord and the Iran nuclear deal. The French president acknowledged that "the order of things has been shaken" by America's unilateralist drift, and so he was pleased that Xi had promised to uphold both agreements. China then reaffirmed its support for Europe's insistence that the World Trade Organization remain the key foundation of the rules-based multilateral trading system, a position at odds with the United States. For his part, Xi said, "a prosperous Europe corresponds with China's vision for a multipolar world," and it was necessary to move forward together in spite of mistrust on both sides. "We cannot let natural suspicions get the better of us," Xi said. "We cannot always be guarded against each other and worry that they may do something behind our backs."[20]

Macron's efforts to project an image of European unity by inviting Merkel and Juncker to join their talks on global governance backfired when other EU leaders expressed their annoyance with what they saw as his attempt to usurp authority in orchestrating European policy toward China. Several EU governments, especially those in Central and Eastern Europe, rebuffed Macron and said that they would continue to "court" China by offering further enticements to lure Chinese investment.

There can be no doubt that Beijing's growing economic clout is deepening East–West divisions within Europe and exerting political influence over governments that have gladly welcomed Chinese investments. In 2018, Greece blocked an EU statement in the United Nations criticizing China's human rights record, and Hungary rejected an EU letter denouncing the torture of detained lawyers in China. Hungary, Greece, Croatia, and Slovenia—all beneficiaries of China's investments—also softened an EU statement condemning China's actions and legal claims in the South China Sea. In contrast to the criticism he often hears from his EU partners, Hungary's prime minister, Viktor Orbán, is clearly pleased that he does not receive any lectures from China about his illiberal policies that threaten democratic values. Nor does Orbán feel that he needs to apologize to Macron or anybody else for his country's "Eastward Opening" toward China. "We see the world economy's center of gravity shifting from west to east, from the Atlantic to the Pacific region," he explained. "This is not my opinion—this is a fact."[21]

China has spurned Macron's warnings and continued its shopping spree buying up strategic assets across Europe, including companies prized for their research and development in robotics, artificial intelligence, medical devices, alternative energy vehicles, aviation, big data, and cybersecurity.[22] Once Chinese producers gain access to European know-how, they can quickly drive European competitors out of business. Europe used to be a leader in manufacturing solar panels; in 2001, five of the ten leading companies were European. By 2018, eight of the top ten companies were Chinese, the other two being

Canadian and South Korean. China has now set its predatory sights on Europe's elite companies in robotics, automobiles, and aviation. Chinese companies purchased Kuka, Germany's renowned robotics firm that employs fourteen thousand people, for more than $5 billion and invested another $2 billion in the automobile giant Daimler. In Italy, Chinese investors bought up the tire-maker Pirelli and acquired large stakes in energy companies like Eni, Enel, and CDP Reti. In Britain, China made a large-scale investment in the Hinkley Point nuclear power plant, hoping to glean valuable insights for its nuclear projects back home. Once a firm is acquired by a Chinese company, European suppliers are often abandoned in favor of Chinese supply chains, leading to further losses in European jobs.

In Portugal, where China has spent billions of dollars on energy projects, health services, insurance, real estate, and media properties, Chinese investors hope to use their presence there as a strategic platform from which to expand their reach into Brazil, Angola, Mozambique, and other former Portuguese colonies. The relationship between Lisbon and Beijing reflects an ironic reversal from the days when Portuguese traders settled in Macau in the sixteenth century and eventually dominated its economy. "Ten years ago, we were building the airport in Macau and an entire economic infrastructure there," said Sérgio Martins Alves, secretary-general of the Portugal-China Chamber of Commerce and Industry. "Now, it is the opposite. The Chinese have taken control of our major assets."[23]

A backlash against China's aggressive buying of European assets is starting to gain momentum. Besides Macron, other politicians and business executives across the continent are calling for urgent measures to protect Europe's sovereignty, industrial independence, and security interests from Chinese incursions. "In a world with giants like China, Russia or our partners in the United States, we can only survive if we are united as the EU," said Germany's foreign minister Heiko Maas. "And if some countries believe that they can do clever business with the Chinese, then they will be surprised when they wake up and find themselves dependent."[24] When China attempted a takeover of the manufacturing firm Leifeld Metal Spinning, which makes uniquely high-strength metals used in the automobile, space, and nuclear industries, the German government blocked it on strategic grounds.

In the most high-profile case to date, European governments have been agonizing over whether to give China an opportunity to install the next generation of mobile telephone equipment. After pressure from the United States, several European governments have balked at allowing the Chinese company Huawei to build the 5G infrastructure because of fears that it could compromise their national security. Yet other European governments have decided to adopt Huawei's system because they found it to be the cheapest option with the best technology. The United States, Canada, Australia, and New Zealand have refused to allow Huawei to build the next generation of telecom networks on national security grounds. But some European politicians claim that such anxieties are overblown and that excluding Chinese suppliers from the 5G rollout will deprive consumers of the chance to purchase the most advanced systems at the best available price. Britain concluded that it could manage the security risks with Huawei and defied American warnings.

American intelligence officials have toured European capitals to warn governments about the kinds of security risks they would face by allowing Huawei to supply the superfast 5G services that will enable a new generation of digital products and services. Huawei is the world's largest telecommunications equipment manufacturer and has worked with German partners such as Deutsche Telekom for many years. China's 2017 national intelligence law, which requires "citizens and companies to support, cooperate and collaborate in national intelligence work," has raised fears that Huawei could be asked by the Chinese government to incorporate "back doors" into equipment that would allow Beijing authorities access for spying or sabotage purposes.[25]

Germany's foreign and interior ministries, after consulting with the United States and other allied nations, have sought to prevent

Huawei and other Chinese suppliers from participating in the bidding process for 5G contracts in Germany. American diplomats have warned the European allies that Washington will be forced to restrict the sharing of intelligence with any country that chooses to install Huawei's 5G systems. America's alarmist posture is based on the potentially dramatic impact of the rollout of 5G technology on both economies and modern systems of warfare. The enormously faster broadband speeds of 5G systems—up to ten gigabits per second, or ten times faster than 4G systems—will transform our lives in ways that few people can imagine. With such advanced technology, it is very likely that pilotless fighter jets, smart missiles, and automation in nearly all aspects of everyday life will become commonplace.

While some European governments challenged the American arguments, others took them seriously. Once an ardent suitor of Chinese investments, Poland grew suspicious about adopting the Chinese 5G technology after the Warsaw government arrested the Chinese regional director of Huawei for alleged espionage activities. The European Commission expressed qualms that becoming too reliant on either Chinese or American digital technology could pose a risk to Europe's strategic autonomy but left the choice to national governments. "5G networks will provide the future backbone to our societies and economies, connecting billions of objects and systems, including sensitive information and communications technology systems in crucial sectors," a Commission strategy paper says. "To safeguard against potential serious security implications for critical digital infrastructure, a common EU approach to the security of 5G networks is needed."[26]

Germany's 5G debate showed that Europe is belatedly becoming more sensitive to concerns that business interests must not be allowed to outweigh security needs in the fields of digital technology and artificial intelligence. In his annual State of the European Union Address in 2018, European Commission president Juncker declared that Europe cannot run the risk of behaving like "naive free traders" in sectors that affect its vital security interests. He laid out a proposal for a foreign investment screening process that would help oversee future investments and foreign acquisitions for the twenty-eight EU nations that involve matters of strategic security. The European Parliament adopted legislation to create an alert mechanism for future foreign investments involving dual-use technologies, but the final decision on whether to approve or veto such investments will be left in the hands of national governments. The strategic challenge facing Western democracies in their dealings with China will not soon go away: it is already emerging as a top priority on the transatlantic agenda as the United States and Europe both struggle to contain China's growing power.

The United States and its European allies have tried to coordinate their strategies toward China for well over a decade, but without much success. The fact that China now looms as an alternative political model to Western democracy raises the stakes for both the United States and Europe as they search for ways to tame its behavior. China is not just an economic rival or a military threat. It has emerged as the avatar of revisionist authoritarian regimes that seek to disrupt the liberal international order dominated by the United States and its European allies for more than seven decades.

The Huawei case shows that in the absence of a unified approach to China among EU member states, Europe could easily become trapped on the sidelines of a new era of big-power competition between the United States and China.

Macron and other European leaders have pleaded for greater coordination across the Atlantic in dealing with the China threat. At $36 trillion, the combined economies of the United States and Europe are almost three times that of China, which would provide tremendous leverage for the West at the negotiating table. A letter in June 2018 signed by all twenty-eight EU ambassadors in Washington cited China's market distortions as one of the principal areas where the United States and Europe should cooperate. The two sides share similar goals toward China in that they seek reciprocal openings to the Chinese economy and a reduction by Beijing to trade barriers and state subsidies to favored companies.

But Trump has proved to be an unreliable ally. Instead of enhancing American clout by collaborating with Europe on a joint strategy toward China, he has pursued his own trade war with Beijing while stoking tensions with the EU by imposing tariffs on European steel and aluminum.

Europe's geopolitical limitations have compelled Macron to act on its behalf by expanding France's military presence in China's neighborhood. With Britain leaving the European Union, France is the only European power with a significant presence in the Indo-Pacific region. France has deployed more than seven thousand troops in the area to maintain security over its five territories, including New Caledonia and French Polynesia, which are populated by more than 1.5 million French citizens. Besides protecting its overseas territories and citizens, France has adopted a robust approach to preserving freedom of navigation through frequent naval patrols in the South China Sea under the 1982 United Nations Convention on the Law of the Seas. Macron has made several official visits to the region to emphasize France's "Pacific pivot" and its enhanced security relationships with Japan and Australia. In 2016, France struck a $40 billion deal with Australia to supply twelve new submarines. Paris has also signed defense cooperation pacts with Australia, Japan, and India that Macron says should serve as "the heart of a new axis of democracies in the Indo-Pacific." The agreements promise a huge windfall for French defense industries; as part of their fortified military relationship, France has sold six submarines to India for $3.75 billion and thirty-six Rafale fighter jets for $8.8 billion.

Macron told me that the new strategic partnership linking France, Japan, Australia, and India will serve as an important reminder to China of the geopolitical reach of Europe's universal values defending basic human rights. "France is developing its Indo-Pacific strategy and will expand its naval and military presence in the region as a way of saying to the Chinese, without hostility or aggression, that 'it's not your backyard.'"[27] Macron believes that if Europe hopes to be a significant player in a new era of big-power competition, it needs to act boldly and decisively in defense of its own values and interests. Europe also needs the military and strategic assets to do so, however, and for now France is the only continental power with such capacity. In that sense, Macron's strategic initiative to cultivate partners in the Indian and Pacific Oceans and help them contain China is also designed to send a message to Washington: the United States must realize that France and Europe can serve as valuable allies not just in the defense of their own continent but in other parts of the world as well.

CHAPTER 10

MACRON ALONE

On a bright sunny day that illuminated Paris in all its breath-taking beauty, Emmanuel Macron seemed to carry the weight of the world on his shoulders. He had spent the previous hour reviewing with his top security advisers the various hot spots where France maintains vital interests. A new Indo-Pacific strategy designed to protect freedom of navigation and more than a million French citizens living in that vast oceanic region would require more ships and sailors, as well as the presence of France's sole aircraft carrier. Another refugee exodus might engulf Turkey and Europe if Syrian president Bashar al-Assad's army, backed by Russian air power, staged a devastating final assault on the enclave of Idlib, where thousands of die-hard Islamist fighters were holed up. The Strait of Hormuz, where 20 percent of the world's oil supply flows out of the Persian Gulf, had become a confrontation zone between Iranian gunboats and Western tankers. In the Sahel region of Africa, Islamist militants were making territorial gains that would need to be repulsed by French forces.

After defense minister Florence Parly and other advisers hauled away their classified maps and charts, I was invited into the private office. Macron and I shook hands and sat down. The French president was clearly primed to talk geopolitics.

As a Western leader in his early forties, I asked him, how did he envision what the world might look like three decades into the future, and how did he intend to shape it? Macron said that he had thought long and hard about the future. During his first twelve months in office, he traveled more than one hundred thousand miles to nearly every continent to acquire a firsthand understanding of a changing world. He explained, in precise and elegant French, that Europe needed to pursue a three-part strategy to cope with the challenges of the next generation and find its rightful place in a new multilateral world order. The return of big-power competition in the world had caught Europe off guard. He believed that Russia, China, and the United States had an interest—each for different reasons—in under-mining, if not breaking up, a more integrated Europe, maximizing its global influence through shared sovereignty. Too many Europe-ans had become resigned to the pessimistic view that their continent would never be able to stand up to the other major powers in de-fending its values and interests. The absence of leadership at a critical time in shaping Europe's future role in the world contributed to this malaise. Macron was trying on his own to fill the political vacuum left by the declining power of Angela Merkel, the tumult surround-ing Brexit, Poland's hostility to the EU, and the economic troubles of Italy and Spain. He shared General de Gaulle's worldview that Europe alone must ensure its full sovereignty and independence. But he was repeatedly frustrated in persuading other European leaders to embrace that perspective and think in terms of a global strategy.

The most consequential event that Macron saw transforming to-day's world was the evolving duopoly between China and the United States. The calling into question of Western values and leadership by the rise of China and the retreat of the United States will lead, in Macron's view, to further deterioration of Western civilization unless Europe can establish itself as a third force. "It's not just the global impact of a trade war. It's the threat of two different forms of hegemony confronting Europe and the rest of the world," Macron explained. "On one hand, we have the American model enforced by the extraterritoriality of its laws and finance, along with its military might, which can impose its will on allies. On the other, we have the Chinese form of hegemony which is being built through the new Silk Road and commercial leverage over regional partners, in Asia, Africa, Russia, and even parts of Europe." Faced with the competing hegemonies of the two superpowers, Macron said, Europe has a special responsibility to defend international law by building *une alliance de bonne volonté* (an alliance of goodwill) with democracies like Canada, India, South Africa, Australia, South Korea, and Japan.[1]

Now that the world is entering a new age in the wake of the post–Cold War era, Macron said, the first priority of a new global strategy for Europe should be rethinking the structures of its existing partnerships. In his Sorbonne speech six months after taking office, Macron declared that Europe must comprehend that "the gradual and ineluctable disengagement by the United States" would persist beyond the Trump presidency and that seven decades of reliance on the American security umbrella were now over. "The United States will remain an important ally, but we in Europe must regain our strategic autonomy by becoming more sovereign in taking care of our own defense," Macron told me. "That's why I engage in judo with Trump."

The judo reference helps explain Macron's approach to diplomacy. He believes that France cannot fulfill its ambitions as a mediating power without maintaining open and friendly relations with all parties. Macron may strongly disagree with Trump's policies, such as his positions on trade and the Iran nuclear deal, but the French president believes that it is important to cultivate a close personal rapport in order to exploit any opportunity to nudge the American position in what he views as the right direction. He will not resist Trump's pushing and prodding until the right moment, which will be when he feels he can flip Trump to a more amenable stance. As in judo, passive or accommodating behavior in diplomacy may not be a sign of weakness but rather a tactical move to outfox an opponent.

Macron genuinely fears that unless Europe awakens to its geopolitical challenges, the entire political integration project that Europe has been cultivating over the past seventy years could collapse. "It's what I firmly believe," Macron told me. "Empires and civilizations can vanish, as we saw at the end of World War I (with the demise of the Hapsburg and Ottoman Empires). We are much too complacent, believing that we can drift along as we have in recent years without serious consequences. But history shows that Europe (as a collective project) can also disappear. I believe Europe must have a vision as a political community, not just as a commercial market. And Europe can only be a political power in the world when it knows how to protect itself."[2]

Macron realizes that big-power leaders such as Putin, Xi, and Trump only respect competitors who demonstrate strength. Unless Europe becomes more assertive in carving out its own role in the world, the continent may be doomed to serve as a minority partner of China or the United States. Hence Macron's gloomy prediction that "Europe could disappear." He is determined to compel Europe to take greater responsibility for its own defense in the twenty-first century and move away from its dependency on the American security umbrella. This quest is absolutely crucial to the long-term revival of a more integrated and successful Europe that can shape its future role on the world stage. He is encouraged by the decision of Norway, Sweden, Finland, Greece, and Estonia—countries on the periphery of Europe—to join his European Defense Initiative, which would enable European nations to intervene in conflicts without the participation of the United States and NATO. But there is still a long way to go to achieve Europe's sovereignty over its own security. "I am investing in my French forces, and I defend the idea of an independent European army and security policy while being a true ally and partner of the United States," Macron said. "But when the United States pulls out of international agreements like the Iran nuclear deal and the Paris climate change accords, we need to look toward other powers who share our ideals." He also rejected Trump's demand that in doing more for its own defense, Europe should buy more equipment from the United States, rather than investing in its own armaments industries. "Strategic autonomy means that we in Europe will decide how we should allocate our resources, because our long-term security depends on it."

The second part of Macron's global strategy for Europe emphasizes the need to build new partnerships with key neighboring powers such as Russia and Turkey. Europe has become estranged from both countries for understandable reasons, but its long-term security interests will eventually require some kind of reconciliation. Macron believes that Europe must do everything possible to prevent Russia from becoming locked into a long-term alliance with China and should encourage the restoration of closer relations between Moscow and the West. Its declining economy, shrinking population, and huge uninhabited land mass stretching across eleven time zones have made Russia an obvious target for China's strategic plans. Europe, he said, has no interest in seeing its relationship with Moscow become a frozen conflict because Russia has become aligned as a junior partner in a big-power coalition with China. The West's policy of isolating Russia has failed, and new efforts must be made to convince Moscow that its destiny lies in the West, not in the East.

To disprove Putin's conviction that Europe acts like a mere vassal of the United States, Macron believes that Europe should demonstrate greater strategic autonomy by asserting its independence and should not feel obligated to seek Washington's approval for its own initiatives. The first step he took in nurturing a better partnership with Russia was brokering negotiations between Kiev and Moscow, with mediation by Paris and Berlin, to seek a durable solution to the Ukraine crisis. At the G-20 summit in Osaka, Japan, in June 2019, Macron held an intense private conversation with Putin to reinforce his message that despite their different values and interests, liberal democracies and authoritarian regimes should find ways to maintain a constructive dialogue. There is no reason for Europe to approach a new partnership with Moscow from a position of weakness, Macron believes, since it is much wealthier (Europe's economy is more than ten times greater than Russia's) and it is hardly militarily inferior (with annual defense spending that runs four times higher than Russia's).

Macron believes that Turkey is the other key player on Europe's frontier. Even though Turkey's president, Recep Tayyip Erdoğan, has spurned democratic reforms and embraced an authoritarian model, Ankara will be an important partner in building a cooperative security architecture with Europe. Turkey serves as Europe's gateway to the Middle East and thus can act as a potential bulwark against instability. Erdoğan's willingness to block the exodus of Syrian refugees heading toward Europe, in exchange for cash and visa guarantees for his people, served as a positive sign that Turkey can play a helpful role even though its hopes for eventual membership in the European Union are now off the table. "We cannot build Europe on a long-term basis without thinking about our relationship to Russia and Turkey, in an uncompromising way and without being naive," Macron said. "Erdoğan's pan-Islamic ambitions pose a serious problem for me, but we must find a way to anchor these countries to Europe. These are two powers which are vital to our collective security. The histories of their people are connected with Europe, and so together we must reinvent a future strategic partnership."

The third part of Macron's global strategy focuses on building a new kind of partnership with Africa in the twenty-first century. There are more than one hundred million French speakers in Africa, and fourteen nations use the CFA franc as their financial currency. That currency is guaranteed by the French treasury, as part of a colonial legacy, and its use is contested by many Africans who feel that it hurts their exports because the franc is chronically overvalued. On his visits to several African states, the French president has articulated a new postcolonial vision: "There is a new generation in Africa that has no personal connection to the colonial past, so we have an opportunity to build a new partnership without historical complexes." In Macron's opinion, the time has arrived to establish a more equitable relationship between the two continents. He is convinced that Africa could become one of the most remarkable transformational stories of our time and believes that a revitalized relationship with a new African generation can enhance Europe's leverage on the world stage. As a goodwill gesture, Macron promised to return artifacts of African heritage from French museums to their countries of origin, a move that would help quell an enduring source of resentment between Europe and Africa. He also has paid tribute to the estimated two hundred thousand African soldiers who fought in the trenches on behalf of France during World War I. Yet the future, in Macron's view, holds the most enticing promise for Africa's engagement with Europe because of the talent and ambitions of its youngest generation.

Africans under the age of thirty represent over 70 percent of the continent's population. They want to break Africa's depressing cycle of rampant corruption and defective governance, which has resulted in failing states vulnerable to exploitation by outside forces, including terrorist groups. Many of them possess a new determination to pull their continent out of its perpetual misery toward a more peaceful and prosperous destiny. While the populations of Europe, China, Russia, and Japan are shrinking, Africa is growing at a rapid rate and looms as the world's next great economic frontier. Of the world's ten fastest-growing economies in 2018, six were African, according to the World Bank. The United Nations predicts that over the next decade the world's ten fastest-growing cities will all be African.

With a median age of just nineteen, the continent's population is expected to double to more than two billion people by 2050, and then double again by the end of the century, when one out of three humans will be African.[3] Despite its attractive growth opportunities, the challenges facing the continent are enormous. Africa suffers from a raft of troubles, including Islamist terrorism, ethnic warfare, overpopulation, rapid urbanization, and disease. Demographers predict that as many as 450 million young Africans in coming decades may

seek entry into Europe. Nigerians are now the largest source of immigrants flocking into Italy, and the current wave of people coming
from Africa might just be a prelude to a much greater future surge.
Of the 2.2 billion people who are expected to be added to the global
population by 2050, 1.3 billion will be Africans, about the size of
China's population today.[4]

No other continent suffers more from the pernicious effects of
the climate crisis than Africa, especially in the Sahel region, where
drought, famine, and civil wars have devastated the band of ten
countries located south of the Sahara. Lake Chad, which provides
water and food for millions of people, may soon dry up, provoking
a massive exodus for which the continent is unprepared. Macron is
clear: "We must act urgently because so many problems are culmi-
nating in Africa at the same time. We need new and innovative ap-
proaches to improving health, education, and economic development
to help Africa succeed, or the human trafficking and illegal immigration that directly affects Europe will just get much worse."

If Africa can surmount its problems, the continent offers bounti-
ful possibilities that could lift millions of people out of a miasma of
endemic poverty, corruption, epidemics, and ethnic warfare. Macron
believes that a key factor in Africa's potential success will be the fate
of its women, who yearn for better educational and entrepreneurial
opportunities. If a larger proportion of young women can be liberated
from being confined to squalid homes and saddled with too many
children, Macron thinks that Africa could achieve enormous progress
within a generation. Europe's own security is at stake because it needs
to ensure that Africa's young people can aspire to a better life and not
become disaffected or attracted to radical Islam. More and more Africans, especially those with skills and the means to pay for the trip, are
tempted to make the crossing into Europe. But their departure will
only worsen a brain drain that sucks the most talented and motivated
people away from their native continent.

Experts believe that, paradoxically, the migration flows toward
Europe are likely to increase even if Africa prospers. Some studies

predict that by 2050 the number of Afro-Europeans could rise from 9 million at present to 150 million or even 200 million—or one-quarter of Europe's population. Macron is familiar with the work of contemporary Africa scholars, such as Stephen Smith at Duke University and Alex de Waal at Tufts University, who cite ancient patterns of trade and migration across the Mediterranean as a reason why Europe should deal with its demographic crisis by accepting the gradual integration of Africa and Europe. A "Fortress Europe" has already proved to be a failure in stemming the tide of illegal immigrants, so the best alternative may be to embrace the long-term prospect of growing integration between the two continents, especially as African migrants become a significant part of the European workforce.

Because of its history and proximity, Europe is uniquely situated to develop a more interdependent future partnership with Africa. But Europe has been rapidly losing ground to China, for whom the new Silk Road crossing the Mediterranean Sea into Africa provides controllable access to the continent's vast resources. The intense competition between Europe and China over the fate of Africa threatens to become one of the next geopolitical crises of the century unless Europe wakes up and recognizes the vast potential of the African continent. Macron laments the fact that some EU leaders have dismissed his ideas as an attempt by France to draw its European partners into costly efforts to share the postcolonial burdens of providing security and development aid to Africa. He insists that it is critical for Europe to understand that its future strategic interests are at stake and could soon be overwhelmed by the Beijing government's aggressive designs on the southern continent. "China can play a beneficial role in the development of Africa, but if it seeks a new form of colonialism by extracting its wealth in raw materials and piling more debts on these countries, it could lead to the bankruptcy and destabilization of much of the continent," Macron said. "Right now, China is engaged in a kind of commercial exploitation that must be brought to an end or it will be very damaging in the long run."

Macron also believes that an effective global strategy for Europe must extend beyond geopolitics. The impact of digital technologies and artificial intelligence will soon grow exponentially, extending far beyond the control of governments. These extraordinary developments can be harnessed for the benefit of humanity only if governments include more innovative and unconventional players in the search for solutions. Macron is convinced that corporations and civil society have acquired much greater importance for global governance because they already circumvent the power and control of nation-states. One consequence of their growing influence must be assuming greater responsibility for their actions, just as government behavior is supposed to be constrained by international law.

As the world's largest commercial bloc, with more than five hundred million citizens, the European Union has discovered that it can wield extraordinary clout by setting standards and regulations that eventually become global norms. Macron has applauded vigorous antitrust action by the European Commission to prosecute American digital giants like Google, Facebook, and Amazon for abusing their dominant positions in the European market. Europe is flexing its muscles as an economic and regulatory superpower in other ways as well. In 2016, the European Parliament approved the General Data Protection Regulation (GDPR), which made fundamental changes in the handling of the data of all European citizens across every sector, from banking and private pensions to health care and social media. Corporations that do not protect an individual's data as prescribed by GDPR can be subject to heavy fines. France, Germany, and other European states have adopted laws that can punish social media companies if they do not banish hate speech from their online platforms within twenty-four hours of its appearance there, with fines up to $1.5 million per day. These measures seek to block content that encourages terrorism, hatred, violence, racial insults, religious discrimination, and child pornography. Macron would like to go even further by making online platforms legally responsible for disseminating fake or slanderous information. But other European governments are reluctant to take steps that they fear will inhibit freedom of expression, no matter how objectionable the content might be.

Macron's profusion of ideas to endow Europe with an effective global strategy has overwhelmed some of his European peers, who claim that their scope and volume make his policy suggestions too much to contemplate, let alone execute. A Slovakian minister compared Macron's blizzard of proposals to climbing Mount Everest without an oxygen mask. Since he became France's president, the list of Macron's policy plans designed to transform Europe into a more powerful and integrated player on the world stage has been nothing short of stunning:[5]

- An EU military intervention force and budget in place by 2020
- A European agency for the protection of democracies to defend against cyber-attacks
- A European climate bank to finance the transition to a carbon-neutral economy
- A European intelligence academy to train officials
- A European civil protection force for responding to disasters
- A European public prosecutor for terrorism and organized crime
- A European public asylum office for joint processing of claims
- A European frontier police force
- A carbon frontier tax levied on imports into the European Union
- A European innovation agency for research into artificial intelligence
- EU subsidies to support the development of electric vehicles
- The targeting of American technology companies with a value-added tax
- A bigger EU budget to fund investment and cushion economic shocks
- An overhaul of EU agriculture policy and a new EU food inspection force
- Accelerated harmonization of corporate tax bases

- Gradual harmonization of corporate tax rates and social security contributions
- A guaranteed minimum wage adapted to each country
- An offer to all young Europeans to spend six months as a student or apprentice in another EU country
- Creation of new European universities based on networks of institutions
- A series of national and local conventions to discuss Europe's future
- Half of European Parliament members chosen from EU-wide lists by 2024
- A much smaller European Commission, with no more than fifteen commissioners
- A multispeed Europe, with Britain offered associate status
- A new European trade prosecutor to ensure that competitors abide by EU rules
- A French-German industrial cooperation treaty to harmonize corporate regulations

Macron realizes that the sheer number of European proposals he has put forward since taking office may be difficult to digest, but he believes that it is better to have too many ideas than too few. He often says that building a stronger, more dynamic Europe is the flip side of his commitment to modernizing France. Macron is determined not to back down in either case. "The deep transformation of France that I am undertaking does not work without a new stage of the European project," Macron said. "That's why the French elected me." He also wants to stimulate other EU leaders to think more deeply about developing a long-term strategic vision that will guide Europe's evolution. He has encouraged them to put forward their own proposals if they do not agree with his suggestions. Europe, he says, cannot afford further delays in becoming a more integrated continent. It is already engaged in a race against time to catch up with the United States and China, particularly when it comes to the next generation of new technologies.

The rapid rise of artificial intelligence, for example, threatens to leave Europe languishing behind its competitors and make it vulnerable to American and Chinese domination. Macron has urged Germany and other EU members to join France in pouring massive resources into artificial intelligence research. Unless Europe makes urgent investments in cloud computing and artificial intelligence, its share of the world's GDP, which is now at 22 percent, will rapidly decline.[6]

Macron has achieved only limited success in prodding his peers to embrace the need for radical change. The reluctance shown by many EU leaders to embrace a more integrated continent is not just due to a lack of imagination. Many of them, including Merkel, believe that European voters do not wish to see further steps taken toward a more unified Europe. To the contrary, they believe that public opinion in many parts of Europe wants more sovereign powers to be returned to national governments. Those European leaders, Macron says, show a willingness to follow rather than shape public attitudes. Many of them seem prepared to adopt populist policies if doing so would be the most effective way to help their moderate parties cling to power and prevent extremists from entering government. As part of their anti-EU crusade, populist nationalists claim that governance must be pursued at the lowest common denominator so that laws and regulations are brought closer to the daily lives of the people. To Macron's annoyance, some of Europe's mainstream leaders seem to share this perspective.

Macron argues that Europe's biggest challenges arise from issues that transcend national frontiers, such as climate change, aging populations, immigration flows, and the digital revolution. That is why he believes that Europe's leaders cannot afford to "sleepwalk" through their current set of crises but must fight back against populist extremists and persuade voters that optimal solutions to their most vexing problems can only be achieved at a European level. He contends that three centuries of Western hegemony have drawn to a close and a new world order is slowly emerging. Western dominance began with the Age of Enlightenment in eighteenth-century France.

It was then reinforced by Britain's leadership of the industrial revolution in the nineteenth century and culminated with America's military and economic power in the twentieth century. Macron insists that with that era now over, Europe must act urgently to secure the primacy of democracy and fight back against authoritarian tendencies gaining momentum at home and abroad.

"The profound crisis in Western democracy is at the heart of my battle for Europe," Macron declared emphatically. "We cannot afford any sense of complacency or futility. Our democracies are in serious trouble because we have not managed to reduce income inequalities in our society made worse by globalization. That is why Europe must prove it can serve as a humanist model for the world in making far-reaching reforms, whether in terms of education, creating jobs for young people, or scaling up our research into new technologies. Otherwise, voters will be tempted to turn to the shortsighted and dangerous ideas of the nationalists, which often bring wars and destruction in their wake."

The root of the problem, he said, lies in growing social and economic inequalities that have generated fear and resentment about deteriorating living standards in Western societies. "The crisis we are now experiencing can lead to war and the disintegration of our democracies," Macron said in a June 2019 speech in Geneva, Switzerland, marking the one-hundredth anniversary of the International Labor Organization. "Something is not right when capitalism only works for the benefit of a privileged few. When a majority of people do not get to share in economic progress, they can become attracted to authoritarians who will tell them democracy no longer protects them against the inequalities of a capitalism that has gone mad."[7]

How Europe copes with its economic inequalities will have an enormous impact on its goal of serving as an exemplary model of social democracy in a world that is turning toward more authoritarian styles of governing. Yet how can Europe align behind that aspiration, Macron asks, when some EU member states, such as Hungary, Poland, and perhaps even Italy, are moving toward illiberal or authoritarian governments, with the apparent consent of their voters? Macron believes that Europeans with strong democratic convictions have a solemn obligation to speak out against such transgressions, as he has done. More than any other European leader, with the possible exception of Angela Merkel, Macron has tirelessly advocated the need to forge a united Europe that will uphold humanist values. France must lead, he says, because the traditions in favor of a tolerant, open, caring, and educated society took root during the Age of Enlightenment, which served as the founding inspiration of Western democracy.

As Europe suffers the consequences of its inaction, Macron hopes that his EU partners will start to recognize the need for Europe to shape a common approach to the outside world. He has openly challenged the intrusion of outside forces that he claims are seeking to disrupt Europe's internal politics, citing the activities of Trump's former adviser Steve Bannon as an example. "For the first time, I see connivance between nationalists and foreign interests whose aim is to dismantle Europe," Macron said. Bannon is not alone in trying to manipulate Europe's constellation of forces. The governments of Russia, China, and the United States are all trying to shape Europe's political course. Their interference should serve as ample warning that Europe needs to speak more loudly and firmly with one voice to defend its own values and interests. As Sweden's former prime minister Carl Bildt contends: "Europe has no choice but to become a serious player in this new age of great power competition, or else it will become a playground for the ambitions of others."[8]

Some EU heads of government question whether Europe should even aspire to become a great power in competition with the United States, China, and Russia. They believe that Europe should remain strictly a commercial power and that its trade strategy toward the outside world, along with its regulatory powers, should be sufficient to ensure its vital interests. But Macron claims that this view would enable outside powers to exploit Europe's internal divisions, as has occurred with China. "If we do not have our own global strategy,

China will continue to exploit us," Macron told me. "It becomes a problem for our own sovereignty when China acquires control of maritime routes, infrastructure, and transport in Europe. This is not compatible with our interests. We need to be strong and united to push back against great powers." The alternative, he said, is to see Europe lapse back into a diverse collection of small and medium-sized states with a five-century history of conflicts and rivalries that led to a succession of devastating wars. That scenario would betray the wise and courageous vision of the European Union's founders, who vowed never again to allow their countries to become a perpetual battleground for competing national interests.

In the wake of World War II, with the continent lying in ruins, an extraordinary array of statesmen began constructing British prime minister Winston Churchill's vision for a postwar United States of Europe based on democratic principles. Their aim was to prevent future catastrophes like World War II, which killed an estimated seventy-five million people, about 3 percent of the world's population in 1940. In Germany, Konrad Adenauer and Walter Hallstein sought to banish Germany's blood-soaked history with an irrevocable commitment to a peaceful Europe. In France, Robert Schuman and Jean Monnet set in motion the European Coal and Steel Community, which would pool vital basic materials so that wars could be rendered physically impossible. In Italy, Altiero Spinelli and Alcide De Gasperi conceived plans for closer economic integration in Europe as a prelude to eventual political unity. Johan Willem Beyen of the Netherlands, Paul-Henri Spaak of Belgium, and Joseph Bech of Luxembourg created the Benelux customs union, which started the peaceful dismantling of national frontiers in Europe.

All of Europe's founders had suffered personally at the hands of Nazi or Fascist dictatorships. They would later regret the fact that they and their allies did not take action sooner, when warning signs were flashing red well before the worst of the war's carnage and destruction became apparent. History's lessons seem firmly etched in Macron's mind as he ceaselessly urges his European peers to join him in pushing for a bold leap toward greater integration. Macron told me that he genuinely fears that EU leaders may lose a race against time to prevent the populist nationalist tide from engulfing them all and destroying the dream of a unified Europe assuming its proper place in the pantheon of big powers. The rise of authoritarian China, the frequent meddling in European politics by an aggressive Russia, and the retreat by the United States from global leadership into self-absorption have all signaled the demise of the postwar international order.

As he struggles in lonely isolation to push Europe forward, Macron is often reminded of Jean Monnet's clarion warning that "as long as Europe remains divided, it will be weak and a constant source of conflict." He is genuinely anguished and perplexed by the reluctance of his European peers to appreciate the profundity of Monnet's ominous message. He wants them to join him in defending liberal values and stronger European governance before it is too late. The European Union's remarkable success in terminating centuries of bloodshed and building supranational forms of governance that set an example for the rest of the world was the principal reason it was awarded the Nobel Peace Prize in 2012.

Whether Macron can restore momentum to the cause of a more integrated Europe that punches above its weight in the world remains uncertain. If he succeeds, he could infuse new life into Europe's ambition to serve as a shining beacon of democracy, freedom, and prosperity at a time when the authoritarian temptation is stronger than at any point since the 1930s. But if he fails, then Europe risks becoming irrelevant or worse, particularly if hate-mongers and demagogues assume power and try to reverse policies designed to bring the continent closer together. In that event, Macron may have served, tragically and reluctantly, as the last president of Europe.

ACKNOWLEDGMENTS

I am grateful to many people for their assistance in writing this book. Any work of contemporary political history involves many unforeseen twists and turns. I was fortunate to receive excellent support in my efforts to make this chronicle about the presidency of a dynamic and important European leader as timely as possible. Above all, I am grateful to Emmanuel Macron and his staff at the Élysée Palace for their cooperation. The French president was generous in taking time from a peripatetic schedule to share his thoughts and feelings about France, Europe, and the world at large. During the course of our conversations, I came to appreciate his keen insights as well as the complex difficulties that a modern leader faces in juggling many demands to serve his people in a fair and equitable manner.

I wish to thank friends and colleagues on both sides of the Atlantic for their wise counsel and other forms of support that enabled me to write this book. In Paris: Nathalie Baudon, Alice Baudry, Clément Beaune, Laurent Bigorgne, Jim Bittermann, Edward Cody, Daniel Cohn-Bendit, François Delattre, Olivier Duhamel, Ismaël Emelien, Philippe Étienne, Barbara Frugier, Bernard Guetta, Pierre Haski, François Heisbourg, Pierre-André Imbert, Yves-André Istel, Sylvie Kauffmann, Aurélien Le Chevallier, Enrico Letta, Nikolaus

Meyer-Landrut, Alain Minc, Dominique Moïsi, Cédric O, Sophie Pedder, Jean Pisani-Ferry, Jonathan Randal, Alan Riding, Elaine Sciolino, Maurice Szafran, John Tagliabue, Paul Taylor, Justin Vaïsse, Hubert Védrine, and Dominique de Villepin.

In Berlin: Niels Annen, Thomas Bagger, Markus Ederer, Joschka Fischer, Wolfgang Ischinger, Stefan Kornelius, Friedrich Merz, Michael Naumann, Cem Özdemir, Lars-Hendrik Röller, Norbert Röttgen, Wolfgang Schäuble, Volker Schlöndorff, Peter Schneider, Steffen Seibert, and Paolo Valentino. In Brussels: Michel Barnier, Reinhard Bütikofer, Natalia Drozdiak, Karel De Gucht, Jan Hromádko, Matt Kaminski, Ursula von der Leyen, Simon Lunn, Philippe Maze-Sencier, Giles Merritt, Marc Otte, Martin Selmayr, Jamie Shea, and Stefano Stefanini. In Washington, DC: Gérard Araud, Celia Bélin, Sidney Blumenthal, Richard Burt, Christian Caryl, Derek Chollet, Nelson Cunningham, Karen Donfried, James Goldgeier, Ben Haddad, Fiona Hill, Jim Hoagland, Fred Kempe, Charles Kupchan, Emmanuele Lachausse, James Mann, Mack McLarty, Dan Morgan, John Ritch, Elaine Shannon, Julianne Smith, Constanze Stelzenmüller, Strobe Talbott, Nicolas Véron, Thomas Wright, and Karen De Young. Last but not least, I would like to express sincere gratitude to my editor and publisher at PublicAffairs, Clive Priddle, as well as to Peter Osnos and my agent, Gail Ross, for their encouragement and steadfast support.

NOTES

1. A FAST START

2. LA RÉSISTANCE

1. Alissa J. Rubin, "Emmanuel Macron Is Inaugurated as France's President," *New York Times*, May 14, 2017.

2. Author's background interviews with Élysée officials, Élysée Palace, Paris, November 8–10, 2018.

3. Author's interview with Emmanuel Macron, Élysée Palace, Paris, February 22, 2019.

4. Anne-Sylvaine Chassany, "Life in Emmanuel Macron's Inner Circle," *Financial Times*, May 3, 2018.

5. Author's interview with Jean Pisani-Ferry, Paris, May 22, 2018.

6. Adam Plowright, "Macron Won't Stop Until He Has Cured the French Malaise," *Times of London*, April 7, 2018.

7. Author's interview with Alain Minc at his office in Paris, February 28, 2018.

8. "The Political Philosophy of Emmanuel Macron" (interview), *Le 1*, July 8, 2015.

9. Author's interview with Hubert Védrine, Paris, October 29, 2018.

10. Author's interview with Ismaël Emelien, Élysée Palace, Paris, March 2, 2018.

11. Harriet Agnew, "Emmanuel Macron Unveils Overhaul of Health Care System," *Financial Times*, September 19, 2018.

12. Ingrid Melander, "No Kid Left Behind: Macron Tries to Fix France's Education System," Reuters, July 5, 2018.

13. Adam Nossiter, "Emmanuel Macron's Unwanted New Title: President of the Rich," *New York Times*, November 1, 2017.

14. Author's background interviews with presidential advisers, Élysée Palace, Paris, March 1–2, 2018.

15. Agnew, "Emmanuel Macron Unveils French Anti-Poverty Strategy."

16. Emmanuel Macron, State of the Nation Address to the Senate and National Assembly, July 9, 2018, transcript provided by Élysée Palace.

17. Author's interview with Pierre-André Imbert, Washington, DC, April 12, 2018.

18. Author's interview with Emmanuel Macron, Élysée Palace, Paris, February 22, 2019.

19. Ibid.

20. Author's interview with Dominique de Villepin at his home in Paris, November 9, 2018.

1. James McAuley, "Low Visibility," *New York Review of Books*, March 21, 2019.

2. Alissa J. Rubin, "Hundreds of Thousands in France Protest Taxes by Blocking Roads," *New York Times*, November 17, 2018.

3. Alissa J. Rubin, "Macron Inspects Damage After Yellow Vest Protests as France Weighs State of Emergency," *New York Times*, December 1, 2018.

4. Author's background interviews with presidential advisers, Élysée Palace, Paris, February 18–19, 2018.

5. Adam Nossiter, "Tear Gas and Water Cannons in Paris as Grass-Roots Protest Takes Aim at Macron," *New York Times*, November 24, 2018.

6. James McAuley, "France Suspends Fuel Tax After Weeks of Unrest," *Washington Post*, December 4, 2018.

7. Raphaëlle Bacqué, Ariane Chemin, and Virginie Malingre, "Depuis la crise des 'gilets jaunes,' la vie à huis clos d'Emmanuel Macron," *Le Monde*, December 22, 2018.

8. Author's background interviews with French government officials and diplomats, Élysée Palace, Paris, November 8–9, 2018.

9. Pinault interview with *Le Monde*, June 22, 2018.

10. Pigasse interview with *Les Echos*, June 21, 2018.

11. Interview with President Emmanuel Macron, TF1, November 15, 2018.

12. Cédric Pietralunga and Alexandre Lemarié, "'Gilets jaunes': Emmanuel Macron peaufine sa stratégie de sortie de crise," *Le Monde*, December 22, 2018.

13. Ibid.

14. Author's interview with senior French diplomat, Paris, March 10, 2019.

15. Author's interview with Emmanuel Macron, Élysée Palace, Paris, February 22, 2019.

16. "Emmanuel Macron Tries to Buy Off His Critics," *Economist*, December 13, 2018.

17. Adam Nossiter, "Macron Vows Order Without Compromise in Rebuke to Yellow Vest Protests," *New York Times*, December 31, 2018.

18. Adam Nossiter, "France's Yellow Vests: A Populist Movement Following Its Own Playbook," *New York Times*, December 5, 2018.

19. Institut Montaigne and Elabe, "The Yellow Vest Protesters: The Tip of the French Social Crisis?," March 28, 2019, www.institutmontaigne.org/en /blog/yellow-vest-protesters-tip-french-social-crisis.

20. Harriet Agnew and Ben Hall, "'Look at Me, I Exist': French Protesters Send Message to Macron," *Financial Times*, December 7, 2018.

21. Institut Montaigne and ELABE, "The Yellow Vest Protesters."

22. "Spreading Like Poison," *Economist*, February 23, 2019.

23. Robert Zaretsky, "Les Miserables vs. Macron," *Foreign Policy*, November 26, 2018.

24. "La Lettre d'Emmanuel Macron Aux Français," *Le Monde*, January 14, 2019.

3. THE GREAT CONVOCATION

1. "Macron lance le grand débat national: 'Il ne doit pas y avoir de tabou,'" *Le Monde* and *Agence France Presse*, January 15, 2019.

2. Noemie Bisserbe, "Macron Tries to Channel Yellow Vest Anger into 'Great Debate,'" *Wall Street Journal*, January 15, 2019.

3. Cédric Pietralunga, Aline Leclerc, and Patrick Roger, "Emmanuel Macron lors du 'grand débat': Ce qui remonte, c'est la fracture sociale," *Le Monde*, January 16, 2019.

4. Ibid.

5. Adam Nossiter, "Can Macron Talk the Yellow Vests into Submission? He Will Try," *New York Times*, January 23, 2019.

6. Author's interview with Emmanuel Macron, Élysée Palace, Paris, February 22, 2019.

7. Julia Amalia Heyer, "France's Golden Boy Learns How to Fight: Macron Debates His Way out of the Yellow Vest Crisis," *Der Spiegel*, March 29, 2019.

8. James McAuley, "Can Macron's Grand Debates Address Yellow Vest Concerns in France?," *Washington Post*, January 24, 2019.

9. Victor Mallet, "Emmanuel Macron Scents Revival as France's Great Debate Ends," *Financial Times*, March 15, 2019.

10. "The Great National Debate: A First Step Toward Reconciliation?," interview with Olivier Duhamel, Institut Montaigne, January 18, 2019.

11. Author's interview with Jean Pisani-Ferry, Café de Flore, Paris, February 18, 2019.

12. Virginie Malingre, "Face à une soixantaine d'intellectuels, Macron défend son projet de 'démocratie délibérative,'" *Le Monde*, March 19, 2019.

13. Ibid.

14. Renaud Thillaye, "Is Macron's Grand Débat a Democratic Dawn for France?," Carnegie Europe, April 26, 2019.

15. Virginie Malingre, "Notre-Dame de Paris: 'Nous la rebâtirons tous ensemble,' promet Emmanuel Macron," *Le Monde*, April 16, 2019.

16. "France Agonizes over the Flames That Devastated Notre Dame," *Economist*, April 16, 2019.

17. Rym Momtaz, "Macron Draws Parallel Between Notre Dame and Political Turmoil," *Politico*, April 16, 2019.

18. Joshua Robinson and Stacy Meichtry, "Notre Dame Rebuilding Draws Yellow Vest Ire," *Wall Street Journal*, April 20, 2019.

19. Noemie Bisserbe, "French Protesters Hang Up Their Yellow Vests," *Wall Street Journal*, June 16, 2019.

20. Adam Nossiter, "Macron, Chastened by Yellow Vest Protests, Says 'I Can Do Better,'" *New York Times*, April 25, 2019.

21. Ibid.

22. Virginie Malingre, "Comment Macron prépare sa rentrée," *Le Monde*, July 29, 2019.

23. Helene Fouquet, "Macron Takes an 'Enchanted' Literary Break Before G-20 Reality Check," *Bloomberg*, November 29, 2018.

24. Emmanuel Carrère, "Orbiting Jupiter: My Week with Emmanuel Macron," *Guardian*, October 20, 2017.

25. President Emmanuel Macron, speech to the European Parliament, Strasbourg, France, text provided by Élysée Palace, April 20, 2018.

4. THE POPULIST MENACE

1. Angela Giuffrida, "Europe's Far-Right Leaders Unite with a Vow to Change History," *Guardian*, May 18, 2019.

2. Viviene Walt, "Why Italy's Matteo Salvini Is the Most Feared Man in Europe," *Time*, September 13, 2018.

3. Christopher Caldwell, "Macron vs. Salvini: The Ideological Battle for Europe's Future," *Spectator*, September 8, 2018.

4. Ryan Heath, "Europeans Love the EU and Populists, Too," *Politico*, May 23, 2018.

5. Yascha Mounk and Roberto Stefan Foa, "Yes, People Really Are Turning Away from Democracy," *Washington Post*, December 8, 2016.

6. Ryan Heath, Maïa de la Baume, and Jacopo Barigazzi, "Macron and Salvini Face Off over Continent's Future," *Politico*, July 19, 2018.

7. Michel Rose and Gavin Jones, "France's Macron Warns of Populism 'Leprosy,' Italy Hits Back," Reuters, June 21, 2018.

8. Cédric Pietralunga, "Macron: 'Je ne céderai rien sur nos valeurs,'" video interview with Macron on Twitter, *Le Monde*, August 29, 2018.

9. Robert Zaretsky, "Only Macron Can Save Europe, Says Macron," *Foreign Policy*, October 23, 2018.

10. James Politi, Anne-Sylvaine Chassany, and Tobias Buck, "Macron Hits Out at Italy After Migrant Boat Is Turned Away," *Financial Times*, June 12, 2018.

11. Heath et al., "Macron and Salvini Face Off over Continent's Future."

12. Ben Hall, "Macron vs. Salvini: The Battle over Europe's Political Future," *Financial Times*, December 28, 2018.

13. Giuseppe Fonte, "Italy and EU End Latest Standoff on African Asylum Seekers," *Reuters*, July 30, 2019.

14. Ishaan Tharoor, "France and Italy's Feud Is a Sign of Battles to Come," *Washington Post*, February 8, 2019.

15. Author's interview with Paolo Gentiloni, Washington, DC, February 6, 2019.

16. World Bank, "Climate Change Could Force over 140 Million to Migrate Within Countries by 2050," March 19, 2018.

17. President Emmanuel Macron, New Year's address to the French people, text provided by Élysée Palace, November 2, 2018.

18. President Emmanuel Macron, speech at University of Ouagadougou, Burkina Faso, text provided by Élysée Palace, November 28, 2017.

19. Valentina Pop and Giovanni Legorano, "The EU's New Headache: Skeptics Are Poised to Gain Power from Within," *Wall Street Journal*, May 22, 2019.

20. Author's interview with Emmanuel Macron, Élysée Palace, Paris, September 12, 2019.

21. Hannah Roberts and Henry Foy, "Salvini Under Fire for Taped League Meeting with Russians," *Financial Times*, July 9, 2019.

22. Bruno Waterfield, "Putin, Johnson, and Farage Will Destroy Us, Says EU Chief," *Times of London*, May 21, 2019.

23. Mary Fitzgerald and Claire Provost, "The American Dark Money Behind Europe's Far Right," *New York Review of Books*, July 10, 2019.

24. Cas Mudde, "The Far Right May Not Have Cleaned Up, but Its Influence Now Dominates Europe," *Guardian*, May 28, 2019.

5. TROUBLES ACROSS THE RHINE

1. Stefan Wagstyl, "What Macron Achieved on Brief Visit to Merkel in Berlin," *Financial Times*, May 16, 2017.

2. Author's background interviews at the Chancellery in Berlin and the Élysée Palace in Paris, November 12–15, 2018.

3. Ibid.

4. Author's interview with Emmanuel Macron, Élysée Palace, Paris, February 22, 2019.

5. Marcus Walker, "Emmanuel Macron's New Deal for Europe Faces Old German Doubts," *Wall Street Journal*, May 7, 2017.

6. Andreas Kluth, "The Euro Must Be Fixed or Dropped," *Handelsblatt*, November 22, 2018.

7. Leonard Schuette, "One Year Since Macron's Sorbonne Speech: Plus Ça Change?," Center for European Reform, October 25, 2018.

8. Anne-Sylvaine Chassany, Guy Chazan, and Mehreen Khan, "Impatient Macron Presses Merkel on Eurozone Reform," *Financial Times*, March 16, 2018.

9. "Germany and France: Differences of Style and Substance Are Straining the Relationship," *Economist*, May 26, 2018.

10. Nico Fried and Stefan Kornelius, "Merkel über Macron: Es gibt Mentalitätsunterschiede zwischen uns," interview with Chancellor Angela Merkel, *Süddeutsche Zeitung*, May 15, 2019.

11. David M. Herszenhorn, "Macron Declares 'Decision Time' for Europe and Says France Is Now Waiting for Germany," *Politico*, May 18, 2018.

12. Gabriela Galindo, "Le Maire: EU Falling Apart Before Our Eyes," *Politico*, June 19, 2018.

13. Joschka Fischer, "Waiting for Germany," *Project Syndicate*, April 27, 2018.

14. Author's interview with Norbert Röttgen at the German Marshall Fund Forum, Brussels, March 10, 2018.

15. Author's conversation with Daniel Cohn-Bendit, Washington, DC, October 3, 2018.

16. Author's interview with Dominique Moïsi, Brussels, September 3, 2018.

17. Anne-Sylvaine Chassany and Guy Chazan, "Eurozone Reform: Solving the Franco-German Puzzle," *Financial Times*, June 27, 2018.

18. Klaus Brinkbäumer, Julia Amalia Heyer, and Britta Sandberg, "Interview with Emmanuel Macron: 'We Need to Develop Political Heroism,'" *Der Spiegel*, October 13, 2017.

19. Kim Willsher, "Leaders Visit Historic Site Where Germany Signed Armistice in 2018," *Guardian*, November 10, 2018.

20. Tom Fairless, "Macron, Merkel Show Unity on Defense and Security," *Wall Street Journal*, November 18, 2018.

21. Katrin Bennhold and Steven Erlander, "Merkel Joins Macron in Calling for a European Army 'One Day,'" *New York Times*, November 13, 2018.

22. "Macron and Merkel Renew Their Vows, but Underlying Relations Are Troubled," *Economist*, January 17, 2019.

23. "A Conservative German Response to Macron's EU Vision" (editorial), *Financial Times*, March 11, 2019.

24. Jürgen Habermas, "What Macron Means for Europe," *Der Spiegel*, October 26, 2017.

6. EUROPE IN PIECES

1. Author's interview with Emmanuel Macron, Élysée Palace, Paris, September 12, 2019.

2. Ibid.

3. Charlemagne, "Europe's Gaseous Political Alliances," *Economist*, June 22, 2019.

4. Jim Brunsden, "European Union's System Failure," *Financial Times*, July 2, 2019.

5. Jim Brunsden and Ben Hall, "How Emmanuel Macron Won the Battle over the EU's Top Jobs," *Financial Times*, July 5, 2019.

6. David M. Herszenhorn and Jakob Hanke, "Macron Warns of 'Institutional Dysfunction' if EU Can't Fill Top Jobs," *Politico*, June 27, 2019.

7. Ursula von der Leyen, president of the European Commission, opening statement to the European Parliament Plenary Session, Strasbourg, France, press release from European Commission, July 16, 2019.

8. Henry Fountain, "Europe's Heat Wave, Fueled by Climate Change, Moves to Greenland," *New York Times*, August 2, 2019.

9. Jean Pisani-Ferry, "The Coming Clash Between Climate and Trade," *Project Syndicate*, July 31, 2019.

10. Rochelle Toplensky, "EU 2050 Climate Target Blocked by Eastern Nations," *Financial Times*, June 20, 2019.

11. Jo Harper, "EU Climate Goals Ditched as Warsaw and Budapest Dig In," *Deutsche Welle* news service, June 26, 2019.

12. Martin Sandbu, "Europe's Green Surge Matters More Than the Rise of the Far Right," *Financial Times*, June 5, 2019.

13. Federico Fubini, "The Roots of European Division," *Project Syndicate*, May 17, 2019.

14. Author's interview with Ivan Krastev, Washington, DC, May 8, 2019.

15. Michael Peel and Ben Hall, "Can the EU Solve Its Autocrat Problem?," *Financial Times*, May 22, 2019.

16. Bjarke Smith-Meyer, "Rutte Declares Eurozone Budget Dead," *Politico*, June 21, 2019.

17. Martin Sandbu, "Macron Holds on to Hope for Shrunken Eurozone Budget," *Financial Times*, June 24, 2019.

18. Andrea Kendall-Taylor and Alina Polyakova, "Populism and the Coming Era of Political Paralysis in Europe," *Washington Post*, May 24, 2019.

19. Victor Mallet and Alex Barker, "Macron Plays Bad Cop to Merkel's Good Cop on Brexit," *Financial Times*, April 11, 2019.

20. George Parker, Robert Wright, and Jim Pickard, "Boris Johnson Vows to Leave the EU in 99 Days," *Financial Times*, July 24, 2019.

21. See, for instance, "Emmanuel Macron's Letter to the Citizens of Europe," *Le Monde*, March 5, 2019.

22. Kathleen R. McNamara, "Despite the Brexit Chaos, Europe Did Not Collapse Like Dominoes," *Washington Post*, April 12, 2019.

23. European Council on Foreign Relations, "Despite Record Support for EU, Europe's Voters Fear Collapse," survey based on YouGov polling, May 16, 2019.

7. DEALING WITH THE DONALD

1. Julie Hirschfeld Davis and Katie Rogers, "Le Bromance: Trump and Macron, Together Again," *New York Times*, April 24, 2018.

2. Author's interview with Emmanuel Macron and background talks with French diplomats, Washington, DC, April 25, 2018.

3. Author's interview with Gérard Araud, Washington, DC, June 7, 2018.

4. Peter Baker and Julie Hirschfeld Davis, "Trump Signals Openness to a 'New Deal' to Constrain Iran," *New York Times*, April 24, 2018.

5. President Emmanuel Macron, briefing with journalists following his meeting with President Donald Trump, Washington, DC, April 25, 2018.

6. Ibid.

7. Gilles Paris, Marc Semo, and Solenn de Royer, "Macron-Trump: Des amis sans affinités," *Le Monde*, April 22, 2018.

8. Eliana Johnson and Daniel Lippman, "Trump's Truly Bizarre Visit to Mt. Vernon," *Politico*, April 10, 2019.

9. "French President Emmanuel Macron Addresses US Congress," April 25, 2019, transcript provided by French embassy, Washington, DC.

10. Author's background conversations with French diplomats, Paris, April 2018.

11. President Emmanuel Macron, speech at the awarding of the Charlemagne Prize, Aachen, Germany, May 9, 2018, transcript provided by Élysée Palace.

12. Author's background interviews at the Chancellery and Foreign Ministry in Berlin, November 2018.

13. Author's interview with François Delattre, New York, June 2018.

14. Gabriela Galindo, "Trump: EU Was Set Up to Take Advantage of the United States," *Politico*, June 28, 2018.

15. Ian Wishart and Gregory Viscusi, "EU Hardens Against Trump with United Stand on Trade and Iran," *Bloomberg News*, May 17, 2018.

16. "EU's Tusk Asks: With Friends Like Trump, Who Needs Enemies?," Reuters, May 16, 2018.

17. Author's background interviews with Emmanuel Macron and senior French diplomats, Élysée Palace, Paris, June 2018.

18. Mary Papenfuss, "France's Emmanuel Macron Throws Down Trump Twitter Gauntlet: G7 Can Be G6," *Huffington Post*, June 8, 2018.

19. Anne Applebaum, "Trump Hates the International Organizations That Are the Basis of US Wealth, Prosperity, and Military Power," *Washington Post*, July 2, 2018.

20. Julian E. Barnes and Helene Cooper, "Trump Discussed Pulling US from NATO, Aides Say Amid New Concerns over Russia," *New York Times*, January 14, 2019.

21. Author's background interviews with senior NATO officials, Brussels, July 2018.

22. David M. Herszenhorn and Jacopo Barigazzi, "Very Stable Trump? European Leaders Beg to Differ," *Politico*, July 12, 2018.

23. Ibid.

24. Joseph Quinlan, "Investors Are Ignoring the Perils of a Transatlantic Divorce," *Financial Times*, June 19, 2018.

25. Valentina Pop and Vivian Salama, "Juncker's Trade Pitch to Trump: I Can Be Stupid as Well," *Wall Street Journal*, July 26, 2018.

26. Liz Alderman, "France Moves Toward Digital Tax, Stoking Fight with White House," *New York Times*, July 11, 2019.

27. Author's interview with Emmanuel Macron, Élysée Palace, Paris, February 22, 2019.

28. President Emmanuel Macron, speech delivered to French ambassadors, Élysée Palace, Paris, August 27, 2019.

29. Interview with President Emmanuel Macron, Europe One radio, November 6, 2018.

30. President Emmanuel Macron, speech delivered at the Arc de Triomphe, November 11, 2018, transcript provided by the Élysée Palace communications service.

31. French television interview with President Emmanuel Macron aboard the aircraft carrier *Charles de Gaulle*, November 14, 2018.

32. Author's interview with Sylvie Kauffmann, Paris, February 20, 2019.

8. PARTNERSHIP WITH PUTIN?

1. François Clemenceau, "Ma poignée de main avec Trump, ce n'est pas innocent," *Le Journal de Dimanche*, May 28, 2017.

2. Author's interview with Emmanuel Macron, Élysée Palace, Paris, September 12, 2019.

3. Author's background interviews with senior French officials, Élysée Palace, Paris, June 3–4, 2019.

4. "France's Macron, Alongside Putin, Denounces Two Russian Media for Election Meddling," Reuters, May 29, 2017.

5. Neil Hume, Guy Chazan, and Harriet Agnew, "Europe in Diplomatic Push to Ease Russia Sanctions," *Financial Times*, April 20, 2018.

6. Author's background interviews with senior French officials, Élysée Palace, Paris, June 3–4, 2019.

7. Helene Cooper, Thomas Gibbons-Neff, and Ben Hubbard, "US, Britain, and France Strike Syria over Suspected Chemical Weapons Attack," *New York Times*, April 13, 2018.

8. Katie Polglase and Laura Smith-Spark, reporting from Saint Petersburg, CNN, May 25, 2018.

9. Anton Troianovski, "Trump's Tariffs Teach Europe a Lesson, Putin Says," *Washington Post*, June 7, 2018.

10. Anatoly Kurmanaev, "Macron's Outreach to Putin Tests US Relations," *Wall Street Journal*, May 25, 2018.

11. Marc Semo, "Entre Macron et Poutine, l'amorce d'un réchauffement," *Le Monde*, August 19, 2019.

12. President Emmanuel Macron, speech delivered to French ambassadors, Élysée Palace, Paris, August 27, 2019.

13. Author's interview with Emmanuel Macron, Élysée Palace, Paris, September 12, 2019.

14. "Russia, Germany, France, and Turkey Call for Lasting Ceasefire, Constitutional Meeting for Syria," Reuters, October 27, 2018.

15. Author's interview with Emmanuel Macron, Washington, DC, April 25, 2018.

16. Ibid.

17. Keith Alexander, "A Transatlantic Alliance Is Crucial in an Era of Cyberwarfare," *Financial Times*, September 4, 2018.

18. Author's background interviews with French government officials, Élysée Palace, Paris, May 27–29, 2019.

19. Author's interview with Emmanuel Macron at Élysée Palace in Paris, September 12, 2019.

9. CHINA'S BUYING

1. Author's background interviews with senior French diplomats, Élysée Palace, Paris, November 6–8, 2018.

2. Peter Wise and Ben Hall, "Portugal: A European Path out of Austerity?," *Financial Times*, April 9, 2019.

3. The White House, "National Security Strategy of the United States of America," December 2017, www.whitehouse.gov/wp-content/uploads /2017/12/NSS-Final-12-18-2017-0905.pdf.

4. Eric Brattberg and Etienne Soula, "Is Europe Finally Pushing Back on Chinese Investments?," Carnegie Endowment for International Peace, September 14, 2018.

5. Andre Tartar, Mira Rojanasakul, and Jeremy Scott Diamond, "How China Is Buying Its Way into Europe," *Bloomberg*, April 23, 2018.

6. Michel Rose, "Macron Seeks to Woo China's Xi with 'Horse Diplomacy,'" Reuters, January 8, 2018.

7. Helene Fouquet and Ting Shi, "Macron Tells China New Silk Road Can't Be One-Way Street," *Bloomberg*, January 8, 2018.

8. Author's background interviews with French government officials, Élysée Palace and French Foreign Ministry, Paris, November 8, 2018.

9. Author's interview with Emmanuel Macron, Élysée Palace, Paris, February 22, 2019.

10. Philippe Legrain, "The EU's China Conundrum," *Project Syndicate*, April 5, 2019.

11. Alex Barker and David Keohane, "EU Steps Up Siemens-Alstom Scrutiny Amid Split over China Threat," *Financial Times*, January 11, 2019.

12. European Commission and High Representative of the Union for Foreign Affairs and Security Policy, "EU-China: A Strategic Outlook," March 12, 2019, https://ec.europa.eu/commission/sites/beta-political/files /communication-eu-china-a-strategic-outlook.pdf.

13. Michael Peet, Victor Mallet, and Miles Johnson, "Macron Hails 'End of Europe Naiveté' Towards China," *Financial Times*, March 22, 2019.

14. Miles Johnson, "Xi Jinping Welcomes Italy's Plan to Join China's Belt and Road Initiative," *Financial Times*, March 20, 2019.

15. Ibid.

16. Rym Momtaz, "Macron Steals Trump's Thunder with Chinese Airbus Order," *Politico*, March 25, 2019.

17. Adam Nossiter, "Behind the Niceties of Chinese Leader's Visit, France Is Wary," *New York Times*, March 25, 2019.

18. President Emmanuel Macron, remarks at a conference of French ambassadors, Élysée Palace, Paris, August 27, 2019.

19. Author's interview with Emmanuel Macron, Élysée Palace, Paris, September 12, 2019.

20. Victor Mallet, "EU Leaders Urge China to Open Up Domestic Market," *Financial Times*, March 26, 2019.

21. James Kynge and Michael Peel, "Brussels Rattled as China Reaches Out to Eastern Europe," *Financial Times*, November 27, 2017.

22. Philippe Le Corre, "EU Moves to Protect Interest Against Predatory China," *Financial Times*, November 26, 2018.

23. Laurens Cerulus and Jakob Hanke, "Enter the Dragon," *Politico*, October 4, 2017.

24. "China's Xi Pushes New Silk Road," *Deutsche Welle*, March 25, 2019.

25. Noah Barkin, "German Officials Sound China Alarm as 5G Auctions Loom," Reuters, November 13, 2018.

26. European Commission and External Action Service, "EU Strategy Plan for Relations with China: 10 Point Action Plan," press release, March 12, 2019.

27. Author's interview with Emmanuel Macron, Élysée Palace, Paris, September 12, 2019.

10. MACRON ALONE

1. Author's interview with Emmanuel Macron, Élysée Palace, Paris, February 22, 2019. Unless otherwise noted, all quotes from Macron in this chapter are from this interview about his geopolitical strategy.

2. Author's interview with Emmanuel Macron at the Élysée Palace, September 12, 2019.

3. David Pilling, "The Scramble for Business in Africa," *Financial Times*, September 24, 2018.

4. Charlemagne, "The Rebirth of Eurafrica," *Economist*, September 22, 2018.

5. Anne-Sylvaine Chassany, "Emmanuel Macron Makes Radical Appeal for More Powerful EU," *Financial Times*, September 26, 2017.

6. Joschka Fischer, "Who Will Win the Twenty-First Century?," *Project Syndicate*, July 30, 2019.

7. "A Genève, Macron dénonce les dérives d'un 'capitalisme devenu fou,'" *Agence France Presse*, June 11, 2019.

8. Carl Bildt, "From Plaything to Player: How Europe Can Stand Up for Itself in the Next Five Years," European Council on Foreign Relations, July 19, 2019.

INDEX

William Drozdiak is a nonresident senior fellow at the Brookings Institution's Center on the United States and Europe and a senior adviser for Europe with McLarty Associates, an international strategic consultancy firm based in Washington, DC. He is the author of *Fractured Continent: Europe's Crises and the Fate of the West.* Drozdiak worked for two decades as a senior editor and foreign correspondent for the *Washington Post.* Before joining the *Post,* Drozdiak was the US State Department correspondent for *Time.* He has written extensively about international relations for many other publications, including articles in *Foreign Affairs, Foreign Policy, Newsweek,* and the *Financial Times.* He lives in Washington, DC.

PublicAffairs is a publishing house founded in 1997. It is a tribute to the standards, values, and flair of three persons who have served as mentors to countless reporters, writers, editors, and book people of all kinds, including me.

I. F. STONE, proprietor of *I. F. Stone's Weekly*, combined a commitment to the First Amendment with entrepreneurial zeal and reporting skill and became one of the great independent journalists in American history. At the age of eighty, Izzy published *The Trial of Socrates*, which was a national bestseller. He wrote the book after he taught himself ancient Greek.

BENJAMIN C. BRADLEE was for nearly thirty years the charismatic editorial leader of *The Washington Post*. It was Ben who gave the *Post* the range and courage to pursue such historic issues as Watergate. He supported his reporters with a tenacity that made them fearless and it is no accident that so many became authors of influential, best-selling books.

ROBERT L. BERNSTEIN, the chief executive of Random House for more than a quarter century, guided one of the nation's premier publishing houses. Bob was personally responsible for many books of political dissent and argument that challenged tyranny around the globe. He is also the founder and longtime chair of Human Rights Watch, one of the most respected human rights organizations in the world.

.   .   .

For fifty years, the banner of Public Affairs Press was carried by its owner Morris B. Schnapper, who published Gandhi, Nasser, Toynbee, Truman, and about 1,500 other authors. In 1983, Schnapper was described by *The Washington Post* as "a redoubtable gadfly." His legacy will endure in the books to come.

Peter Osnos, *Founder*